You Have Been Referred

My Life in Applied Anthropology

Michael Robinson

You Have Been Referred

My Life in Applied Anthropology

Michael Robinson

BAYEUX ARTS
DIGITAL-TRADITIONAL PUBLISHING

YOU HAVE BEEN REFERRED:
My Life in Applied Anthropology

Copyright © Michael Robinson, 2021

Publication: July 2021

Published in Canada by
Bayeux Arts Digital - Traditional Publishing
2403, 510 6th Avenue, S.E.
Calgary, Canada T2G 1L7

www.bayeux.com

Cover design by Lumina Datamatics
Book design by Lumina Datamatics
Cover photograph by Lynn Webster

Library and Archives Canada Cataloguing in Publication

Title: You have been referred : my life in applied anthropology / Michael Robinson.
Names: Robinson, Mike, 1951- author.
Identifiers: Canadiana (print) 2021019006X | Canadiana (ebook) 20210190078 |
ISBN 9781988440705
     (hardcover) | ISBN 9781988440712 (ebook)
Subjects: LCSH: Robinson, Mike, 1951- | LCSH: Anthropologists—Canada—
Biography. | LCSH:
     Anthropology—Canada. | LCGFT: Autobiographies.
Classification: LCC GN21.R63 A3 2021 | DDC 301.092—dc23

The ongoing publishing activities of Bayeux Arts Digital - Traditional Publishing under
its varied imprints are supported by the Canada Council for the Arts, the Government of
Alberta, Alberta Multimedia Development Fund, and the Government of Canada through
the Book Publishing Industry Development Program.

Printed in Canada

Table of Contents

Foreword

I began writing these stories in 2008 after I had run as a Liberal in the Alberta provincial election and, predictably, had lost. It wasn't a trouncing, but after knocking on 8,000 doors and giving it my all, in a constituency in which my wife and I had raised our family, I ended up about twelve-hundred votes short of victory. Prior to running I had resigned my position as CEO of Calgary's Glenbow Museum, in part, because I thought I would win and, in part, because I thought that if I lost, the reigning Conservative dynasty would take it out on my employer. In defeat, I thought it would be better to start again and to look at new opportunities.

It wasn't as if I hadn't done this before in my thirty years of working in Alberta with various oil-patch businesses, at the University of Calgary and occasionally as a self-employed consultant. It is important to understand the economic context of my mobility – between 1978 and 2008 Alberta was awash in oil-patch cash, experiencing the last great boom of the carbon economy. The public hadn't yet registered the climate crisis and, while economic diversification and the need for a healthy Heritage Fund were a growing part of political discussion, they were effectively marginal topics in a much grander scheme of affluence.

Before I hit the re-employment trail once again, I decided to take a few months off and to write a career memoir. I was exercising some significant privilege: my wife was now a partner in a national architectural practice; my children were at university; and I had a few paid board and consulting assignments to tide me over. As it turned out, when I began to write, my mind obsessed on dredging up stories, starting in the final years of high school and ending with my experiences at the Glenbow Museum some 40 years later. Looking back, it was as if these stories had lives of their own and insisted on being told. Try as I might, they refused to blend seamlessly into the theme of my career, but each one contributed to the preparation for it, or the conduct of some aspect of my work.

And then I was offered a challenging new position as CEO of Vancouver's fledgling Bill Reid Gallery of Northwest Coast Art. All of a sudden, pressing job realities intruded on my writing and I downed tools to focus on my new tasks. It wasn't until the COVID-19 pandemic of 2020, twelve years later, that I resumed writing, making the best use of social distancing and the new tranches of free time. Immediately I saw a need for two new chapters, one on my Alberta election experience and the other on my start-up labours at the Bill Reid Gallery. My wife, children and a nephew advised me to write a foreword that explained how the book was structured and why it might be of interest to Millennials and other non-Boomers. There was a uniform concern that a career memoir by a non-famous, ex-CEO would nose dive in any marketplace. They counselled that the book should offer readers more than anecdotes about me. I was also amusingly advised that a tome about my "excellence in the field of greatness" would not pass muster. So, I endeavoured to meet their challenges.

When I ask myself, what do all these stories have in common or what holds them together? I see that at a very basic level, they all involve people who know and love their place on earth. Most of the subjects of these stories are themselves good storytellers. All of the characters are, in fact, characters – they exhibit moral strength, commitment to sometimes impossible ideals, and they often manifest eccentricity. Many are charismatic. They all have a strong bond with the natural world, and most of them are skilled resource harvesters. Several of them dream about their connection to the land. While not all of them have met face to face, I know them all and think they would enjoy each other's company. Many are now dead. Strangely, their collective spirit is still very strong. Let me just say, that what they stood for in life continues in other ways and in other people

As the world pursues its fast-paced switch to urbanism and as climate change opens the Northwest Passage for the second decade in a row, these characters all ask us to think about our collective roots as land-based hunters and gatherers. As a species we did not evolve from a bricks-and-mortar environment, nor did we originate in agrarian societies. Those aspects of our collective journey on earth are like a skiff of fresh snow on a glacier of evolutionary ice. In our genes and our experience we still owe more to burial caves than to urban cemeteries, more to the trapline and the bush economy than to office towers and the stock market, and more to the coho and sockeye salmon than to muffins and chai lattes.

If the characters in this book leave us with anything, it is the need to venerate the land and the water by staying close and telling stories that tie us to where we came from. This earth truly is our home, and we celebrate its soul by narrating stories about its role in our lives. The best stories combine humour with spirituality, love with strength, and friendship with duty. Many will be told at bedtime to young hearts and minds just forming their connection to the land and all its creatures. Looking back at those people who influenced my career, there are a number of very strong women, like my wife Lynn Webster, Joan Ryan, Terry Williams, Dorthea Calverley, Nina Afanas'eva and really all the Sami leadership, but men dominate the corporate stories and many NGO stories as well. I think this reflects the corporate leadership of my era and the structure of many not-for-profit boards too. Nevertheless, the influence of the key women in my life has been profound.

At a very personal level, I can group these stories as short reveals about my career influences. With the exception of the first one, My Blackfoot Dream, to which I gave pride of place because of its singular power over me, all the rest are told basically in chronological order. But there is a deeper structure as well. A close reading indicates that my strongest career influences were not school teachers or university professors; rather they were my mother and father, family values, and friends who lived their values in their work. Many are Indigenous people who embody their cultural values implicitly in their lives. Paradoxically, my first decade of employment in Calgary was characterized by corporate values, often (although not always) at odds with my prior experience and my core beliefs. It wasn't until

I arrived at the University of Calgary's Arctic Institute of North America that my true instincts were allowed to guide my development – and that of others. Structurally, this book is the development of a career-values thesis; its deployment in a corporate-culture, or antithesis; and its synthesis and blossoming in non-governmental organizations (NGOs). Following this lead, the book is divided into three sections that correspond with my thesis, antithesis, and synthesis experiences at work.

What I take from this analysis is the understanding that I am best suited to those institutions of civil society, NGOs. At their best they combine environmental sensibilities, effectiveness in cross-cultural work settings, a participatory-action approach to problem solving, and a quality that I simply think of as human decency. NGOs also require endless fundraising to keep them afloat, a characteristic that can drain the most energetic of enthusiasts. Clearly NGOs lack the economic efficiency of corporations, but they can learn from them, and the ones I have run modelled aspects of their operations on corporate models. In this way they demonstrate another worthy aspect of NGOs – their ability to hybridize. My Métis pals call this quality *Metisism* – the combination of the best of two possible ways of knowing the world.

One cannot conclude a foreword written in May, 2020, without a link to COVID-19 and the pandemic's impact on our common future. I believe these stories contribute to our new reality by spot-lighting simpler, kinder ways of living and being in the world. Collectively they affirm the main theme of the Russian Sami reindeer herders' (see Chapter 22) origin myth, *Myandash*: "What is good for the reindeer, is good for the Sami." Their message for the rest of us is plain: it is time to move away from destructive carbon-combustion energy and brutal technologies and to embrace sustainable lifestyles that permit a healthy diversity of species. We humans need to learn to share the earth once again.

I hope this brief introduction to what follows has caught your interest! Giving these stories life has certainly caught mine. I am glad to see them on paper embarking on new lives of their own.

Dedication

This book is dedicated to my mother and father: Frances ('Frankie to family and friends) Robinson combined a lifelong interest in fine arts and entrepreneurship in a career spanning teaching at the University of British Columbia, (UBC) and starting and operating the Frankie Robinson Oriental Gallery (Frog). Dr. Geoffrey Robinson, who for forty years practised medicine as a pediatrician and was for thirty-five years a professor of medicine at UBC.

Mom was born in the Rocky Mountains, in Revelstoke, British Columbia, and grew up in small towns like Vernon and Williams Lake where her father worked as an engineer for the provincial department of highways. She combined an analytical and esthetic view of life and early on developed an appreciation for the work of Canada's Group of Seven, especially Lawren Harris, and for Emily Carr's evocative paintings of Indigenous villages and rainforest landscapes. Very much in this tradition, she took me as a young boy to paint in Vancouver's Stanley Park with her friend, Bess Harris (Lawren Harris' spouse). Mom also took me on summer painting trips to the Sechelt Indian Reserve on the Sunshine Coast and the surrounding beaches where she worked on portraits of children and sketches of waterfront architecture. I look back on those years now with a strong appreciation for her innovative maternal contributions to my developing cross-cultural awareness, and my own esthetic sensibilities.

Dad, born in Burnaby, B.C., was also an innovator. He was the father of diagnostic centres, care-by-parent and day-care surgery concepts and, above all, a writer in peer reviewed journals of pediatric practice. He dedicated his life to the welfare of sick children, and especially sick kids from far-away, small communities who had to travel to places like Vancouver for treatment. The diagnostic-centre concept was especially helpful for families from far-flung parts whose children had multiple handicaps because they provided 'one-stop shopping' with medical assessment, diagnosis and treatment all under one roof.

When I was an adolescent struggling with career decisions he took me on trips to remote communities like Yuquot (Friendly Cove) on Nootka Island off Vancouver Island's west coast; to Riske Creek, Anaham and Anahim, then Bella Coola on the crazy and unpredictable Chilcotin road; and Prince George, Vanderhoof, Terrace, Hazelton, and Prince Rupert in the mid-north of the province to promote his new children's hospital diagnostic centre concept with local doctors and nurses. I now suspect his ulterior motive was to interest me in medicine. I loved those trips, and admired Dad's vision for health care, but what really caught my eye was the diversity of Aboriginal cultures in B.C., and the way they were struggling with change. Sure there were sick children getting substandard care, but there were also whole communities of healthy folk who were living in a world characterized by the paternalism of church and government, subtle and overt racism, and a complex array of choices about their future. Sitting in the car next to Dad as he drove along the dusty gravel roads, I began to think about a career helping communities confront change on their own terms. I didn't know the words yet, but I was becoming an applied anthropologist.

Thirty-five years later as Dad was wrestling with Lewy body disease, a progressive form of dementia, which robbed him of rational thought and made his life with Mom very difficult, he sat next to me at a family Christmas party as I opened his gift. Somehow he had gone shopping and found and wrapped a present. He had scribbled three words on a little card: "Write more. Dad." I opened the parcel carefully. Inside were five, lined writing pads.

Section 1

Awakening to the Spirituality and the Possibility of a Cross-Cultural Career

Spirituality, the quality of being concerned with the human spirit as opposed to material or physical things, needs careful consideration in the process of choosing a career. The first group of stories in this book describe the people who influenced the development of my values and consequently my evolving career. While strictly speaking out of sequence, My Blackfoot Dream reveals the importance of spiritual connection in planning one's life. That is why it gets pride of place in my career memoirs and it reveals my career-values thesis.

1

My Blackfoot Dream

The power of Indigenous spirituality

The Glenbow Museum's *Nitsitapiisinni: Our Way of Life Gallery* opened to the public in November, 2001, at the end of my second year as CEO. Fifteen busloads of Blackfoot drove to the Glenbow from all parts of their confederacy, including Montana, to share in the opening celebrations. Frank Weasel Head, a sacred ceremony specialist, and Alberta Premier Ralph Klein spoke at the event, which drew about two-thousand people to the museum.

On the day it opened, *Nitsitapiisinni* became the first permanent First Nations gallery of any public museum in the world to be built around a co-managed design, a consensus reached by museum staff and traditional experts alike. For those involved in making the gallery a reality, it was the fulfillment of a dream that began in spirit in 1990 and culminated with the repatriation of Blackfoot sacred and ceremonial objects undertaken by the Glenbow in 1999 under the direction of then CEO Dr. Robert Janes. The return of more than three-hundred sacred and ceremonial objects, only a small part of the museum's Blackfoot collection, set the stage for the nation offering to tell their story in their own words in a museum that was prepared to take the risk.

I had become the CEO and president of Glenbow on January 1st, 2000, and encouraged the *Nitsitapiisinni* team to continue taking risks. As a result, the Glenbow was becoming the model for Canadian museums reconciling with Indigenous peoples. The success of our model was evident in both the number of public visits and the media coverage of the new exhibit.

Walking through the completed gallery was akin to walking through Blackfoot history, from myth-time to the present and the story was told without glossing over the well documented impacts of colonialism. The true spirit and intent of Treaty 7 with the Great White Mother, Queen Victoria, the subsequent move to reservations, the end of the Great Plains bison, the onset of introduced infectious diseases, residential schooling, and the loss of treaty lands to white settlers via allotments begun in the 1890s and then to veterans returning from the First World War, are all covered. The language of the text panels is direct and uses the first person. Harsh words accompany harsh reality. The last section, entitled Taking Control celebrates the new independence of thought and economic livelihood in Blackfoot communities.

In return for their friendship and professionalism, all of the Glenbow staff who worked on *Nitsitapiisinni's* planning and development were invited by the Blackfoot team members to attend a variety of sacred rites over the course of their ceremonial year. Traditionally, the year starts with the first thunder in May when the process of medicine-bundle openings begins.

In Blackfoot society, medicine bundle holders, who can be either couples or individuals, represent the "Blackfoot way to live." They are not voted into office, the position is not hereditary, it may not be purchased; rather it is earned by living well in accordance with the traditional ways of being a good person. Holding a bundle is a duty and an honour, and each bundle holder determines whom he, or she, will pass it to at the appropriate time. Becoming a bundle holder is a very important responsibility and carries with it costly and necessary responsibilities. The public opening of a bundle, quite literally to feed it, is one such responsibility. Being invited to a bundle opening is an honour and being present conveys reciprocal honour to the holder.

***

Frank Weasel Head and Jerry Potts Jr. invited me to a Thunder Medicine Pipe bundle opening in December of 2001, one month after the opening of the *Nitsitapiisinni* Gallery. Proud to be invited, I was eager to accept. Prior to the invitation, the Canadian Museum of Civilization had repatriated a medicine bundle to Mr. and Mrs. Potts, and this was to be their medicine-bundle ceremony. The event was to be held at the Peigan Reserve school, at Brocket in southern Alberta, and would take place on a Saturday. Frank informed me that all of the ceremony had to be completed before sundown. I was told that the entire day would be conducted in Blackfoot, but that I would be given the services of a ritual guide so that I would not miss any important instructions. I was also told that I could bring my family, but as it turned out, my wife, Lynn, felt strongly that it was my day and that I should go alone. I left Calgary at 8 a.m. and arrived at the school parking lot at about 10 on the appointed day.

A young man with shiny black braids and a big smile approached me as I entered the school. "Are you Mike Robinson?" he inquired. Upon confirming his guess, he took me into the foyer. The school's central meeting area was circular with large laminated beams mimicking the poles of a tipi. I was shown to my place on a Pendleton blanket to the left arc of the circle in between several older Blackfoot men who were already seated cross-legged; the women were seated opposite us. At the base of the circle were boxes of juice and water bottles along with closed white Styrofoam containers of what I assumed was food. Below the food sat a small audience in folding chairs that were facing the top of the circle where the medicine-bundle holders, Mr. and Mrs. Potts sat together as husband and wife. In the middle of the circle was a small fire whose smoke wafted out of the open skylight above us. Directly behind the bundle holders hung the bundle on a special rack made of poles.

"Would you like some water or tea?" asked my guide. He also told me that now was the time to go to the bathroom, as the ceremony was about to begin and would take about seven hours to complete. He also explained that it would be conducted entirely in Blackfoot. I quickly nipped off to the bathroom and returned to my seat. Frank Weasel Head gave me a big smile as I sat down again on the blanket. Allan Pard, conducting the ceremony, stood up and began to speak.

The bundle was taken down from its place of honour, and its elk-hide wrap opened to reveal many smaller parcels inside all individually wrapped in cotton squares of different sizes and colours. By now the entire vocal world was Blackfoot and the room was silent except for the speakers. Frank Weasel Head stood with an eagle's wing and held it aloft before taking it outside and raising it to the sun. Sweet-pine smudges and a pipe were lit and passed around the circle, stopping at the men's side. The women did not smoke. Alan uttered long passages of ritual Blackfoot.

After about an hour of bundle parcel openings, smudging and singing, two lines of people began to form in front of the bundle owners, women formed on the left and men on the right. Alan meanwhile had prepared a bowl of red ochre pigment and stepped forward to paint the first male face. My guide encouraged me to join the men's line. An elder woman I did not know began to paint women's faces. Everyone who came forward was daubed and all received buffalo-jaw outlines and sun motifs on their foreheads. After the adults had been completed, the children began to line up. Many people, but not all, were painted. At some point in the early afternoon a break was called for a small feast. Hot saskatoon-berry soup with potatoes and carrots was served along with tea, juice and water. There were granola bars, apples and cakes for dessert. We ate in our places, most quietly and alone. I was offered many extra packed lunches to take home.

The second half of the afternoon involved the opening of many more bundle objects. For the first time I saw money, mostly fifty-dollar bills, handed out to some of the older participants. A few people came forward with money tightly gripped to give to Jerry. The sun, meanwhile, was circling across the afternoon sky, lending a sense of urgency to the events, because everything had to be finished, and the bundle and its many components completely re-wrapped by sundown. Singing and drumming by those in the circle occupied much of the late afternoon and all the while, the fire was tended in the centre of the room.

I was overwhelmed by the complexity of the day, and the different roles in which I saw new friends. The power of spoken Blackfoot filled the room. Even the little children were taking cultural cues in their own language. I was entranced. This was a very different experience from exploring Blackfoot culture in the museum; it was a privileged entry to the sacred métier of Blackfoot life. And then, at about 6 p.m. the bundle was retied in its elk-hide blanket, and hung on its rack. The singing and drumming wound down. The room fell silent. Frank caught my eye, and said in English: "That's it, Mike. It is over now."

***

I had the strange sensation of falling awake. I walked over to Jerry and his wife and thanked them for inviting me. I did the same with Alan and Frank, and asked when I should wash off the face paint. Leave it on for one day until after sunset, said Frank. I said that I would. All of the participants then walked out into the parking lot to a waiting collection of dusty pick-ups and American sedans. I carried a few Styrofoam containers of uneaten lunches and a couple of bottles of juice to my car. I don't remember much of the drive home except the first traffic light when I approached the outskirts of Calgary. I stopped and looked at the car to the left of me. An elderly couple were staring at me very oddly. I peered in the rearview mirror and saw the red buffalo jaw and the sun on my forehead. "Twenty more hours to go before that comes off," I thought to myself.

At home, Lynn reminded me that we had a Christmas party invitation that evening. I dressed and looked again at my face in the mirror. "This will be interesting," I thought. The party guests mostly knew me as the CEO of Glenbow and would sort of understand why I had attended a sacred Blackfoot ritual. Nevertheless I had to tell my story many times before the topic changed to, "Where are you going for Christmas?" We drove home at midnight and went to bed.

The next evening, Sunday night, I stepped into the shower and washed off my Blackfoot persona. As I watched it trickle down the drain, I thought of the many others who had been painted also rinsing their faces in preparation for the world of work and school the next day. Given what a stark realization this was for me, I could only imagine how the Blackfoot participants must have felt as they returned to their everyday lives. The week began and while I told my story a few times to colleagues, it was back to normal on Monday. Monday night passed uneventfully. So did Tuesday. I was fully back into my world of budgets, deadlines, and board committees. Then came Tuesday night.

At 5 a.m. I awoke and immediately sat up in bed. My head was full of images from a dream unlike any I had experienced before. Lynn opened her eyes and asked me what was going on. I carefully told her the dream.

Moments before I had been standing alone on the outside beach at Friendly Cove on Vancouver Island's west coast. It was a magnificent starry night with no cloud cover and yet it was not cold. It felt like August. It was high slack – that time when the tidal currents take a rest before the great ebb begins once again. I could smell the salt air and the fir pitch from the forest. It was silent. Quite suddenly from the north and in single file, a parade of seven orcas were swimming towards me just offshore. The first one passed me. Then came the second. And the third. The fourth one paused right before me and rose up on its tail to 'spy watch' me. Its eyes looked right into mine. We both froze in that locked gaze. After a period of time the whale slid back into the water and headed on south in the wake of the first three. The fifth, sixth, and seventh orcas passed me by just as the first three had. I watched until they all swam out of sight in the direction of Escalante beach, a campsite well known to me in my early days as an outdoor educator at Strathcona Park Lodge. Remarkably, my senses were alive with the smell and texture of the beach, the salty odour of the waves, the echo of the breeze, and the sharp memory of what had just happened.

Lynn reacted to my first telling of the dream, saying, "You have been given that dream because of the bundle opening. It is a gift." She added that I should call Frank Weasel Head and tell him about it. "See what he can tell you." I said I would call him that very day.

I arrived at work still jingling from the dream. The piercing gaze of the fourth whale was particularly vivid in my memory distracting me from beckoning emails, spreadsheets, and business lunches. At 9 a.m. I called Frank at his home on the Kainai reserve.

His wife answered and soon Frank was on the line. "Hmmmm." he said when I described my dream. "Let me think about it. Can I come up and see you for tea on Friday? I have to be in town for some other business that day." We agreed to meet. I found it difficult to concentrate all day. I was sure my subconscious was still trying to process the dream.

Frank arrived at 11 on Friday morning. About sixty-five, tall and slim, he was dressed as always in black Wrangler jeans, a participant's nylon rodeo jacket, a dark blue pearl-buttoned cowboy shirt and a black baseball cap. He came into my office wearing a gentle smile. I noticed immediately that around his neck was a strange kind of onion-like bulb on a leather thong. He sat down at my office table to have a cup of tea.

"Mike, let me say right away, that was a good dream," he said. "You do not have to worry about anything bad. But it has special meaning. I want to ask you some questions about it." Frank took a cup of tea. He drank slowly and thoughtfully. "Let me say that seven and four are strong numbers to the Blackfoot. They are good numbers. The fact you saw seven killer whales is good. The fact the fourth one rose to greet you with his eyes is good. It is also good that the whales swam to you and not away from you. Do you originally come from the coast? Why is that place, Friendly Cove, special to you? Is anyone you know calling you back there?"

I explained that my family lived in Vancouver, and that Friendly Cove, or Yuquot, was where I had worked as an outdoor educator and staff anthropologist. I talked about my friendship with Ray and Terry Williams, with their family, the last residents of Yuquot. I also mentioned my father had just been diagnosed with dementia.

"These are all important things," said Frank. "You need to think more about them. I think that the central message of your dream is that the coast is calling you back home. I also wonder if those whales are all right. Could they be sick and asking you for help?"

I thanked Frank for his interpretation, and plunged back into self-reflection. Frank said that I could call him anytime to discuss it more, but now he had other work in town. I thanked him profusely for his time and help. As he prepared to leave, Frank told me that many Blackfoot dream like that almost every night. "In the old days people dreamed of their connections to the animal world, and they travelled widely in their dreams. You have just lifted the lid a little bit and look what you have seen! Imagine how much more there is for you to learn."

With that he was off down the hall to the elevator. I saw that he passed Gerry Conaty, the senior curator of ethnology, as he left. Gerry came into my office. "Did you see that medicine that Frank was wearing around his neck just now?" he inquired. "That is only worn when other people's dreams are being discussed or when you open your soul to spiritual guidance. Moments such as those require special care and protection. Frank was taking his visit with you very seriously." Once again I was disarmed by Frank's generosity of spirit.

That spirit drew on a field of life experience he had as a Blackfoot spiritual leader, and encapsulated the recent gifts of the *Nitsitapissinni* team to the Glenbow. Their efforts of reconciliation, fairness and cultural equity have provided me with great inspiration. In fact, when I think back on my career, they always provided me with the courage and energy to confront racism and cultural paternalism. Today I realize that my dream was also a reminder that sacred experiences are to be cherished and that the cultural practices that occasion them ought to be preserved without hesitation. Therein lies a special wisdom that the world needs to function properly.

To my conscious knowledge I have not dreamt like this again. In 2004, however, our family found a beautiful piece of property at Skelhp on the Upper Sunshine Coast in B.C., and bought it with a view to our return to the coast after thirty years of living and working in Alberta. This proved a timely purchase, as it coincided with my father being diagnosed with Lewy body disease and spiralling into advanced dementia that was at first incorrectly diagnosed as Alzheimer's disease. I was able to be with him in Vancouver for much of his last summer and fall in 2006. Frank was also prescient in his awareness of the difficult future facing orcas, and the growing desire of the Williams family to see their courageous life at Yuquot documented in story form. My desire to return to the coast enabled a decade's service on the David Suzuki Foundation's national board, and several stories of Ray and Terry's life follow in this book.

Further evidence of my dream's persistence was a phone discussion I had about my dream with James Ross, my Western Arctic Gwich'in friend and mentor, in early 2002. I described the dream to James in some detail, and asked him what he thought about it. "Several old Gwich'in already know that you have had this dream, Mike. You are one of only a very few people in your tribe to get those kind of dreams. Think about what that means." I still do.

2

A Trip on the Uchuck

First visit to Yuquot with my father

In the summer of 1968 I was seventeen and had just finished Grade 11. Lanky and academic, I was hungry to experience the world of work beyond mowing lawns and washing cars for small change. My father suggested that I might want to take on a few projects for him which seemed like a good idea. It was also the path of least resistance. The first project was ripping down an old garage on property that had just been purchased to create the Children's Hospital Diagnostic Centre. Dad was the creator and first director of this new facility and he needed a parking spot. We agreed that I could start on July 1st for the grand sum of three dollars per hour.

I sledge-hammered and crow-barred the old garage apart, towed the refuse to the city dump and gravelled the pad for him to park his old Rover by the construction-trailer office. "What's next, Dad?" I joked as he tried out the parking spot. "We're going to take the diagnostic centre idea on the road," he said, "And see if anyone else wants to buy into it. If the country doctors don't buy in, we won't have many patients. You will be my research assistant."

Over the next week I was paid to read up on the diagnostic centre concept and I proudly assembled notebooks, pens and office equipment like a stapler and a pencil sharpener for my new job. I didn't have an office, so I worked out of my bedroom. In the evenings Dad asked me questions about my reading and on Thursday night he said, "Next week we go to Gold River and Friendly Cove on our first field trip. We are going to visit some medical clinics and promote the one-stop-shopping, team-based assessment for

11

the multiply-handicapped child." Dad continued with considerable enthusiasm, but my mind had already drifted to the romance of the names – Gold River, Friendly Cove. Where were these places? What did people do for a living? How would we travel? I was ready to go.

Dad's secretary Ruby Kluckner had bought the tickets and organized the itinerary. We had a full week of travel ahead and would stay overnight in small motels. It all seemed very off the beaten track. We'd even have a rented car which I might be allowed to drive. We would travel to the west coast of Vancouver Island, far north of Victoria. To get to Friendly Cove we'd have to take a boat called the Uchuck III down a long inlet from Gold River to Nootka Island at the mouth of Nootka Sound. It almost seemed as though we'd be speaking a new language.

Dad sent me down to the Army & Navy store to purchase what he called "rain gear." I could tell from his approach to our trip that he was excited too. When he wasn't in his 'Dr. Robinson' mode, he was most at ease in his red Mackinaw jacket, wool pants and Romeo work boots. As a student he'd logged at Franklin River on the Alberni Canal like his father before him and he loved sawing and splitting wood, trolling for salmon in rowboats and exploring British Columbia's nooks and crannies. Having said that, he couldn't swim worth a damn, didn't understand anything about outboard motors, and was painfully shy around certain types of people, like affluent business types, socialites and anyone who belonged to a fancy club. Dad was at heart a struggling English-teacher's son who cared most for those who had least, and he was developing the diagnostic-centre concept for the children of just those kind of people. At seventeen I already knew him well enough to predict the kind of trip we were about to embark upon.

Dad was fun to travel with because he was more relaxed on the road. He made interesting observations about the communities we drove through, and the people we met. He was more like a pal and less like a Dad. He was funny, too, and didn't embarrass my adolescent sensitivities. We hit the trail early, went by ferry to Nanaimo and drove up Vancouver Island to Campbell River for lunch. In the afternoon we crossed over the spine of the island, and talked about Roderick Haig-Brown, one of Dad's favourite B.C. writers, who lived on the banks of the Campbell River. He was a strong conservationist, extremely knowledgeable about salmon, and wrote a book almost every year, all of which sold well, locally and internationally. Haig-Brown had recently written The Whale People about the Nootka Indians of Friendly Cove, which I had read in preparation for this trip. I talked to Dad about the Nootka people as we drove through Strathcona Park along a series of fake lakes that had been created by a dam on Haig-Brown's favourite river.

I think it was right there that I began to connect my growing sense of environmental concern with the situation of Aboriginal people who live in remote, isolated places, far from urban amenities and distant from a professional understanding of their needs. I felt that Dad was on the right track promoting the diagnostic centre a long way from Vancouver and the privilege it represented. I was glad to be on the trip.

We wound our way along and eventually across Upper Campbell Lake and, as dinnertime approached, we neared the instant town of Gold River. Dad had read that it was famous for its careful town planning designed to appeal to workers and their families. It was supposed to be the kind of place you moved to and never wanted to leave because all the amenities were already in place. Here we would have dinner with the resident general practitioner and prepare for tomorrow's trip down Muchalaht Inlet to the open Pacific Coast and Friendly Cove.

The little town was an eye opener for me. It owed its existence to a recently opened pulp mill, employing about two-hundred and fifty workers. Maybe a thousand people lived in the community composed predominantly of young families, judging by the residents we saw on the streets as we drove 'downtown.' I observed that the bosses lived in single-family homes on a hillside with expansive views of the surrounding forested mountains and the Gold River. The laboring ranks lived down below in townhouses, apartments and duplexes according to their means. All the housing had been built at the same time. A uniformity of stucco with wood trim and cedar-shake roofs predominated. The architects had also specified a rather boring mossy green for all the wood trim around windows and doors. A central mall provided the service and retail opportunities: a Chinese restaurant, a pizza outlet, a hardware shop, a food store, a clothing store featuring men's and women's apparel, a sporting goods shop, a real estate agent and the medical clinic. All the walkways around the mall and its little central park space were covered with rain screens. Across the street was the hotel with its large beer parlour. More properly it was a beer parlour with a small hotel attached. We checked into our room and headed over to the medical clinic for a 6 p.m. appointment.

The clinic's parking lot had assigned spaces for staff. I guessed the brand new silver Mercedes parked in spot No. 1 belonged to the doctor. Dad and I went in to sing the praises of diagnostic centres, but the meeting slid elsewhere. The doctor wanted to vent about the claustrophobic little town, the lack of mental stimulation, the excessive drinking, the depression he had to treat, the never-ending rain, and the long distance his patients had to travel for cancer treatment. He seemed to be treating a lot of cancer. "The last patient I saw will be dead by Christmas. She's a young mother, and understandably depressed. What can I do about it? She's terminal." Dad waited for his opportunity to make his pitch. And waited. Finally there was a lull in the complaining and he moved in. He got about four minutes of attention. "You know I have to go to a meeting, Dr. Robinson. Have you got some literature you can leave me?" interrupted the doctor. Dad got the picture. We left some pamphlets and excused ourselves. Outside it had started to pour. The sky was uniformly grey. We walked under the rain screens to the hotel restaurant.

Dad was philosophical about the meeting. "You really have to understand the pressure these general practitioners are under in small communities. They don't get many opportunities to talk about their work or their problems. It must be tough for them to be god all by themselves." We had hamburgers and pie and my first restaurant beer together. "Tomorrow will be different, however. Friendly Cove is in transition. The Department of Indian Affairs has convinced the community to move from their ancestral village to Gold River to find work in the mill. We'll be able to see what they'll be giving up in order to live here. How would you feel about that kind of move?" he asked. "I won't be able to answer that question until I've been to Friendly Cove," I replied.

We slept side by side in two single beds over the beer parlour. The music didn't stop until 2 a.m. Dad eventually took a sleeping pill. I lay there and thought about what a jerk the doctor was. I was angry that he hadn't paid more attention to us. The rain was still hammering on the roof as I fell asleep.

We woke early and had breakfast in the restaurant, packed our small bags, and went out to the car. Dad was wearing his wool pants and Mackinaw jacket. I put on my new rain gear. It was still raining and the narrow valleys seemed to be closing in on Gold River. Dad asked if I wanted to drive. Trying to hide my excitement, I took the wheel. The road led us out of town with the river on our left side. After about twenty minutes the pulp mill loomed ahead. Its huge concrete smokestack belched white clouds of chemical vapours into the low-hanging rain clouds. A chain-link fence topped with barbed wire ran around the mill property. Lots of shiny new pick-ups were stationed in the parking lot. Suddenly, just opposite the mill, between us and the river, a settlement still under construction appeared. "That's the new Indian reserve housing for the people of Friendly Cove," said Dad. A few families had already moved in. Their living rooms looked out across the rain-slicked road to the parking lot and the new mill with its enormous smokestack.

We drove on slowly as the end of the road was dead ahead. Muchalaht Inlet was opening up before us, and a government wharf emerged from the mist. Tied up at the wharf was an old coastal freighter, the MV Uchuck III. She was about one hundred and fifty-feet long, with a high wheelhouse, a low cabin near the stern, and a long, gently rising foredeck dominated by a tall mast and spar for loading and unloading cargo. I parked the car and we gathered our gear for the daylong cruise to Friendly Cove. We walked up a gangplank to the main deck. A crew member in a blue Greek fisherman's hat welcomed us and took our tickets. He told us that most people went astern to the little lounge and had a Nanaimo bar and a coffee in Darla's galley while they waited for the ship to sail. We took his advice.

Darla was a tough, old logging-camp cook with dyed red hair and a big smile. She greeted us as we entered what was essentially her kitchen. "Hello, boys! Come in and have something to eat." She placed two of the densest, richest, most chocolatey Nanaimo bars possible on china plates and poured two black coffees into MV Uchuck mugs. We introduced ourselves and explained a bit about our mission to this part of the coast.

"You are going to visit one of the most goddam beautiful coastal communities in British Columbia today. The Nootka Indians have lived there every summer for thousands of years. Captain Cook met their great chief Maquinna when he arrived at Friendly Cove in 1778. In fact he named it 'Friendly Cove' because it was. The folks who live there are still friendly today in spite of all the crap that's come their way. Go ashore and walk all about the village. You'll be welcome. But you won't be able to meet any Nootkas out there much longer, because everyone is moving here to this mill town over the next few months. That'd be the last thing I'd do if I was from there. I'd simply say no to the Indian-Affairs bureaucrats and stay. Their home is bloody paradise." She rolled a cigarette and passed us two stuffed brown bag lunches, saying, "They're part of the deal, boys." We got up from Darla's galley counter clutching our lunches, and thanked her for the hospitality.

In about half an hour the Uchuck cast off from the government wharf. Captain David Young introduced himself on the loud speaker and invited everyone up to the wheelhouse for a visit. There were only ten of us aboard that day, a Wednesday, the only day of the week that the Uchuck backed off her logging-camp itinerary and catered to tourists. Captain Young explained that the Uchuck's real work was hauling grub, cable, spare parts, oil and gas, vehicles, liquor and loggers to remote camps in places like Mooyah Bay,

Zeballos, Chamiss Bay, Kyuquot, and Fair Harbour. He explained that the Uchuck was originally a Second World War minesweeper and had been converted to a freighter in the early 1950s. At twenty-eight years of age she was still going strong. Her wooden hull, foremast, and graceful lines gave me the strange sensation that I was a young seaman aboard Captain Cook's HMS Resolution on the day we were about to make our first landfall since sailing from Hawaii on our quest to discover the Northwest Passage.

We left the wharf at 9 a.m. and started chugging down the inlet with the falling tide. Forested slopes on both sides of the channel cascaded down from green alpine heights to the water's edge. Dad and I were outside on deck, clutching the starboard rail and looking due west as we travelled at about twelve knots on a calm sea. Up ahead were two islands Captain Cook had named Gore and Bligh, after Captain John Gore, who was then first lieutenant of the Resolution, and Vice-Admiral William Bligh, who was then master of the Resolution, and would later be known as "Bread Fruit Bligh" owing to his notoriety and the mutiny on the Bounty. We learned these details by referring to Captain John Walbran's classic British Columbia Coast Names (1592-1906), first published in 1909, which Dad had brought along. As the voyage progressed, the clouds began to lift, and the landscape started to open up as the narrow inlet became wider and the forested slopes, more gentle. Soon we had blue sky and a freshening westerly wind creating white caps on the waves. The Uchuck's flags began to snap and crackle on her foremast and stern flagpole. She flew the Red Ensign at the bow, and the new Canadian Maple Leaf at the stern. As we approached the open coast Dad looked more relaxed than I had seen him in months.

Soon Captain Young was on the loudspeaker again pointing out that just ahead to starboard on the Clerke Peninsula of Bligh Island we would soon see Resolution Cove, where Captain Cook refitted both the Resolution and the Discovery from 31st March to 26th April, 1778. Dad had Walbran open in his hands, and we followed along in his text as Captain Young pointed out the sites. During their visit Cook's sailors made a survey of Nootka Sound, brewed spruce beer and took astronomical sightings. We were now travelling in Zuciarte Channel, "an old Indian name," according to Captain Young, "probably belonging to a clan of the Muchalahts, rivals in this area of Maquinna and his people." Maquinna, we knew by now, was the well-known chief of the Nootka, and a friend of captains Vancouver, Quadra, Martinez, Eliza, Meares and all the other Spanish and English seamen who were active here in the final years of the 18th Century. In 1803 Maquinna and his warriors captured the American ship Boston and massacred the entire crew with the exception of two men, John Jewitt, the young ship's armourer, and an old sailmaker named Thompson. They lived as Maquinna's personal servants until 1805 when they were rescued by the brig Eliza. Jewitt wrote a narrative of his time here and sold it door-to-door back home in New England to finance his retirement. "This area is full of stories like that," commented Captain Young. "I'll put 'em all in the book I write to finance my retirement! We'll be in Friendly Cove in half an hour. As we cross the mouth of Nootka Sound, dead ahead, the Uchuck will encounter some strong Pacific swells and start to roll a bit. Don't worry though, she is a seaworthy old girl, and well accustomed to these waters."

We decided to stay on deck. The open Pacific was right off the port bow. "Next stop is Japan," said Dad. The air was incredibly fresh and the waves were different from anything I had experienced before. They came in as massive rollers, easily twenty feet high, and without white caps. The distance from one wave to the next was more than a hundred feet, and the trough was so low that, when in it, all you could see was water in all directions except straight up. There the blue sky was holding strong. The sea air smelt clean and salty; there was an open ocean purity about it. Dead ahead we saw Nootka Island's southern coast, dominated by the volcanic Nootka Cone, and a panhandle lowland that stretched south to a pronounced low rocky headland that protectively cupped a human community. Just coming into focus was Nootka lighthouse, a curving row of houses fronting the beach, a beckoning totem pole in the centre of the village, and a background tuft of tall trees framing the scene. That's Friendly Cove, otherwise known as Yuquot, said Dad. I looked at it with a sense of wonder. It was at once exotic, historic, and friendly, just as it must have been to Cook and his crews in March of 1778. It was also a community clinging to the very edge of an immense, wild ocean. With the exception of some fresh logging scars on Bligh Island, the area was remarkably intact ecologically. It seemed strangely international and eclectic and somehow beyond Canada because of its history as the first point of culture contact on the Northwest Coast. I wanted to know more about Maquinna. "I wonder how Dad decided to come here?" I asked myself.

As the Uchuck approached Friendly Cove's inner harbour, it was impossible not to feel a sense of welcome. You could easily see why Captain Cook and all the rest who followed were drawn here by a safe anchorage just around the corner from the open Pacific with all her varied moods. The encircling beach was a perfect crescent clad in small pebbles that had been tumbled smooth over generations of tides. The internal waters were clear for several fathoms and calm without ripples. Above this natural splendour was a long line of houses, all built of milled timber, painted in varying shades of white, blue and red. A few people were walking along the path directly in front of their homes and beneath them you could see an eroding wall of shell midden extending down to the high-tide mark. A stark white Catholic-church steeple rose above it all on the left side of the picture. Here and there thickets of rose hips and Himalayan black-berries were ripe with fruit. The Uchuck tooted her whistle as she approached the government wharf to tie up alongside the local fleet of trollers. Dad and I could hardly wait to go ashore.

A few older children came down to the wharf to welcome the ship. As soon as the crew had rigged the gangplank, they headed right down to the galley clutching quarters for Darla's famous Nanaimo bars. I thought to myself that the tradition of this kind of shipboard visit probably went back almost two hundred years, most likely starting with galley visits on Cook's two vessels. We went down the gangplank to walk about the village. The wharf led us naturally to a meadow and a pathway that wound along the front of the houses. We could also see a further green space beside the church – the Friendly Cove soccer field. It was large and sculpted out of the space behind the houses. Above it rose another grassy berm. We crossed the soccer field and climbed the hill. Immediately before us was the open Pacific, with large waves breaking on a beach of smooth round pebbles that clacked together as they rose and fell with the waves. You could see that it would be impossible to anchor out front; Friendly Cove was only friendly to shipping on its eastern exposure. We continued walking down the open Pacific trail through a grove of first-growth Douglas firs swathed in trailing green moss. This was the kind of tree that Cook sought at Resolution Cove to replace the cracked and rotting masts on his ships.

A little further on we arrived at a freshwater lake that existed perilously close to the ocean. A little island floated in its midst. The wide, well-trodden trail continued into the forest, but we returned to the village. It was time to meet some of the local people who in this area are divided into two groups, the Mowachaht (People of the Deer) of Yuquot and the Muchalaht (People over the River) who live down the inlet by the mouth of the Gold River. We angled down from the Douglas firs past a well-tended cemetery with poured concrete grave covers and low, iron-railing surrounds. There were also little grave houses that mimicked the deceased's larger home in life. I peeked inside a few and saw first-generation chain saws, complete china tea sets, and one even had an old Singer sewing machine. We kept on walking past a freshly painted school with six classrooms overlooking the soccer pitch. It appeared to be closed for the summer. Or perhaps forever. It was hard to tell. The community was well groomed, painted, and trim in so many ways, but we knew it was being vacated for the plywood houses going up next to the pulp-mill parking lot in Gold River.

After we passed the school there was a monster patch of ripening blackberries, most of which were going unpicked. We walked through to the row of houses skirting the cove. The trail led us to the tall totem pole overlooking the harbour that we had spied aboard the Uchuck. We approached it from behind and noticed a small iron plaque fastened to its back. We read it before facing the pole with all of its bird, animal, and sea-creature crests. "The Chiefs of Yuquot Gave this Totem Pole to Governor General Lord Willingdon in 1929." Reading the pole and looking up we saw a bear, an orca, sea otters, a kind of sea snake with two heads, a raven and an eagle. I wondered why the Governor General left his gift at Yuquot. We kept on walking until we came to the first house beside the pole. An old man with a white crewcut was busily tying a rope around the door handle and the railing of his porch. "Hello," he said, glancing over to us. There was a beautiful cedar and spruce-root woven basket at his feet. It had a bald eagle design with spread blue wings, a golden head, an orange beak and talons. Noticing my interest he commented, "My wife made this basket, and I'm taking it to Gold River to sell. But first I have to lock my door with this rope."

We introduced ourselves as father and son and explained that this was our first visit to Nootka Island. "Welcome to Friendly Cove," he said extending his hand. We shook hands and told him how beautiful the village was, and asked if he too was leaving for a new life in Gold River. "It's hard not to go when most of your family is already there. My wife, children and grandchildren all moved last week. I stayed behind to fix a few things and to lock up. We'll come back in the summer like we always have, but the grandchildren need better educations than they can get here – only up to Grade 8 – and they need good jobs. In Gold River we'll have a doctor just up the road. The pilchard fishery has failed and the salmon harvests are getting smaller. Our cannery has closed, too. Most of the logging is based in Gold River now. It's hard to make ends meet here. I hate to leave, but what are my choices?" I asked about tourism, and the old fellow smiled. "Maybe it's a good idea, but there aren't that many tourists. We only see them in the summer on the Uchuck. And I don't think tourism can support all six-hundred Mowachaht. That's how many of us there are now." I asked him what Mowachaht meant. "That's us – we're the people of the deer."

Dad looked at the basket at our new friend's feet. "Can I offer to buy that remarkable basket?" he asked. "It is for sale. Fifty dollars."

was the response. Dad replied, "Cash or cheque?" The answer was immediate: "Cash is better kindling; you can use it right away to start a fire!" Dad pulled the bills from his wallet and I picked up the basket. Our friend said, "My wife is the best basket maker I know. Every time you look at that basket, think of this place." We both said we would. Just then the Uchuck's whistle blew, signalling it was time to return to the ship. The three of us walked together past the other locked houses and the Governor General's totem pole. I looked over my shoulder as we reached the wharf; there were three deer watching us from the meadow at the start of the trail.

Strangely, I don't recall anything of the trip back to Vancouver. I suppose it was uneventful, normal perhaps. We just retraced our steps. However, the detail of my first visit to Friendly Cove is as fresh in my mind today as if it had just happened. You cannot visit Yuquot without being touched by its staggering beauty, its resilient human culture, and its life-affirming spirit. Over fifty years later I realize that on this trip I made the emotional and intellectual connections to what I wanted to do with my life. I think Dad had sort of planned this all along – except he thought it would lead to medicine.

3

West Coast Survival

Working with Jim Boulding at Strathcona Park Lodge

It's about 9 a.m., July 1, 1975, at the entrance to Nootka Sound, about twenty-five nautical miles due west of Gold River. The morning wind is picking up, and some big swells are starting to break over Escalante Reef. A blow from the southeast is in the air. The gang of Saturday morning fishermen from the fishing camps around the sound are scattered about in big, top-heavy fibreglass boats with names like Coho Chaser, Pair-A-Dice and Jail Bait. Open bottles of beer are sliding back and forth on Formica chart tables, and Mickey Mouse radios are relaying all kinds of fisherman chatter about hot spots, weather conditions, and killer lures.

One of the guided boats has a fish on its line and the skipper is racing back and forth across the stern to keep the propeller of the big Mercruiser from slicing through the taut line which is headed straight down. Two of the fishermen clients are urging the rod holder to "Keep the head up; keep the tension on; move to this side of the boat; keep the fish away from the motor . . ." Now the skipper is picking up a huge scoop net on a five-foot handle to land the big spring salmon. Someone yells, "It looks like a 'smiley' from here!" A 'smiley' being the word for a spring salmon that is so large it brings a grin to the happy fisherman's face.

Meanwhile the wind is picking up and big white caps are forming over by Nootka Lighthouse. The tops of the Douglas firs are starting to sway at Friendly Cove. With a blue, smoke-producing roar, one of the guides signals that he's had enough and is returning to camp to wait out the weather. Another deep V-hull vessel rears up and starts pounding its way home down Muchalaht Inlet. Lots of the other boats are winding in their lines on Scotty downriggers. Brand new Tom Mack dodgers and green and white hootchies come clattering into the boats. It's definitely roughening up and the lighter aluminum runabouts are taking a banging. A loud cry of "Buggernuts!" comes from the Coho Chaser as the prop finally and decisively slices through the fishing line. A big chinook salmon known as a tyee, a coastal word meaning chief, sounds with ten yards of thirty-pound-test monofilament, dodger and lure to drag about. Awful news not just for the fisherman, but also for the fish. Within ten minutes, all the remaining boats have cranked up and are heading into shelter at Friendly Cove.

Just as the last guide boat heads in, a rakish twenty-five-foot, clinker-built cedar launch rounds Anderson Point. You can just make out the name Fairisle on her white bow. Thirty feet behind the Fairisle neatly surfing in her wake is a sixteen-foot grey Zodiac loaded down with nine people in life jackets and wet-weather gear. The two boats are riding up and over the approaching swells with grace. The mothership is churning through the sea leaving a calm wake for the Zodiac to fly on.

In the cabin and at the wheel of the Fairisle is an interesting man. He is in his early forties, well over six feet tall and has the physique of an aging but still trim football player. He has a big-jawed, weather-beaten face and an engaging, crooked smile under a pair of aviator glasses. A somewhat out-of-place broad-brimmed Stetson rides on his bald head and he clenches a briar pipe between his gold-filled front teeth. He has one large workingman's hand on the wheel, and the other on the throttle in preparation for the great sea swells ahead. As the Fairisle's bow climbs each wave he throttles up momentarily to sink the stern a little deeper. The boat performs this drill like an extension of its operator. His radio is tuned to the Nootka Lighthouse frequency, but the nonsense chatter of the Saturday fishermen is jamming out the station. To no one in particular Jim Boulding growls, "I just wish those plastic arseholes would go home and leave this coast to us!" It is a typical Boulding line, a bit vulgar, part threat, part humour and delivered too loud because he is a good part deaf. The young man beside him grins and continues unrolling the nautical charts from a waterproof tube.

Behind them on the open rear deck, six rain-suited people are clustered around an enormous mound of gear. Backpacks, duffle bags, tool boxes, fishing rods, blue plastic tarps, axes, shovels, coils of yellow, polypropylene rope, a plastic toilet seat, sealed white plastic pails full of dry food, a barbecue grill and a kayak are all visible under an orange plastic tarp. Behind the pile is a huge, rectangular, welded-aluminum fuel tank that spans the stern from gunwale to gunwale, a distance of eight feet. And behind the fuel tank hums the largest production outboard ever made, the legendary Black Max. The Fairisle's thirty-year-old transom quivers with the motor's vibrations, probably more than it should. There is a definite air of organization here. By their easy smiles and knowing banter, you'd think the crew and captain had made careers of sailing around the real West Coast. And yet, with the exception of Jim and his two loyal assistants, me and David, everyone is here for the first time.

By now the Fairisle and the Zodiac are approaching the last of the retreating fishermen. Jim slides back his cabin window and flashes a wicked smile at the sick-looking greenhorns. "Having fun?" he talk-bellows in a voice that travels far out over the water above the machine whine of the Black Max. Spray from a cresting roller breaks over the Fairisle's bow and fans out to either side as the charging cruiser begins to climb the face of another oncoming wave.

Jim looks at me and says, "I think we need to talk to the Department of Highways about this road!" He picks up his radiophone and clicks it to the Nootka Lighthouse frequency, "Fairisle here, anyone home? Hey Ed, can you give us a weather report?" Ed Kidder, the longtime senior keeper, comes on: "Hello Fairisle, as you can see its blowing southeast with gusts to 40 knots. Why not come into the cove for coffee?" "Roger on that, Ed. Tell Pat we all want some whale steaks for lunch, especially the Greenpeacers." At this comment a couple in the stern look incredulously at each other. "He must be kidding?" Of course he is, but part of the Boulding persona manifests itself in amusing hyperbole and it keeps everyone on their feet.

We tie up at the Friendly Cove government wharf where the coastal freighter Uchuck III moors on Wednesdays and Fridays to drop off tourists and supplies for the ten residents of this isolated Indigenous reserve and lighthouse. Boulding takes his time to introduce me and my mission to the paying guests. "Mike's our twenty-four-year-old Sherpa-anthropologist. He's studied Maquinna, the grand chief of the Mowachaht-Muchalaht and written a book called Sea Otter Chiefs about his influence on this coast back when Captain Cook arrived in 1778. Mike's also spent the past few years at Oxford trying to figure out what he wants to be when he grows up – a lawyer or an anthropologist. He's still confused. Listen to him and tell him what you think!" Jim next explains that besides the two lighthouse keepers' families, Friendly Cove is the home of Mowachaht First Nation members Ray and Terry Williams and their family.

In 1968 when the Department of Indian Affairs announced that everyone had to move to the instant town of Gold River to take advantage of new housing and potential jobs at the pulp mill, Ray and Terry stayed put with their children Daryl, Sanford, and Sharon. Yuquot ("the place where the wind blows in all directions,") the proper Mowachaht name for the village, did not lose all its residents after all. Home schooling worked for a while, and friends in Victoria lent a hand boarding the youngsters when it was time for high school. Meanwhile Ray and Terry became good friends with Jim and Myrna Boulding, just beginning new careers as the proprietors of Strathcona Park Lodge and Outdoor Education Centre based inland on Upper Campbell Lake in Strathcona Provincial Park. Ray and Terry helped with the West Coast Survival courses like this one, which were then held two or three times every summer.

After Mike's wharf-side lecture, everyone had time to explore the village with the Williams' permission, as long as the only things taken were photographs. Everyone is back at the boats by 1 p.m. for the final leg of today's trip. Ray, meanwhile, has walked down to the wharf and is introducing himself as "the Mayor of Friendly Cove." Fortyish and still sporting a 1950s Brylcreemed duck-cut, he is the consummate Mowachaht ambassador, quietly humorous, knowledgeable of his culture, fluent in its language, and patiently respectful even to the most inquisitive visitor. When questioned about tourists' most frequently asked questions, he replies," There are several that are repeated all the time: Do you speak English? What do you eat? Do you carve totem poles? Why is this place called Friendly Cove?" He then explains that in 1778 Captain James Cook and his crew from the HMS Resolution landed at Yuquot, and probably began by asking almost the same questions.

Ray makes an important observation about the word 'Nootka,' much in evidence on today's charts as an island, a sound and mountain cone. "That word means nothing really. It sort of sounds like a Mowachaht verb for 'go around'," says Ray. "Probably Captain Cook was trying to find a safe anchorage on the exposed side of the village, and the people went out in their canoes to guide him around that headland and into the safety of the cove. Because the people were friendly to the British expedition, Captain Cook called this place 'Friendly Cove' in his logbook. They were the first Europeans to arrive here. In Mowachaht, we call you guys '*Mumuk'ne*' – it means people who live on floating islands. To our old people that is what those sail boats looked like. And we thought it was funny that you had no women on your floating islands. You looked like a society of men." Then Ray invites the guests to walk about his village with him. I walk down the wharf with the crowd and then angle up the shingle beach to Ray and Terry's house by myself.

Terry greets me at the door with a cry of "Aaahhh, good to see you, Mike!" and gives me a hug. She invites me in to have coffee and speak with her now teenage daughter, Sharon. "Mike, talk with Sharon about how to go to law school like you." I enter and give Sharon a high five and sit down with my coffee. I look around the room and see several new masks carved by Sanford who is now a student at the K'san School of Northwest Coast Art in Hazelton. His work is really coming along. Sharon explains that her brother Daryl is working as a guide for a locally-owned outfit and that he is their 'highliner,' or top fisherman. I am not at all surprised. Every time I visit Yuquot, I marvel at Ray and Terry's moral toughness in 1968, rejecting all the modern conveniences of Gold River – free housing, easy access to everything from bingo to buses, and pulp mill employment. Boy, did they ever make the right decision!

Before I can get too far into law-school admission procedures, Jim appears at the door and receives the same welcome I did. He explains that he has been up at the lighthouse with Pat and Ed having a beer. Terry gives him a coffee, and Jim goes briefly outside, returning with a large box of oranges. "You guys need more vitamin C," he says as he puts the box on the kitchen table. Terry counters with a hot plate of her famous sockeye sticks—salmon in bread dough. "And you need more of these!" I look at my watch and it is nearly 1 p.m. Time to go. We drink up our coffees and Terry wraps the sockeye for the Fairisle. "It's for snacks," she says.

We both promise to stop by next week on our way back from our Escalante Beach camp, and I ask Terry to book Ray for a Mowachaht history and First Nations' politics lesson for this crop of Strathcona students. Back down on the wharf I talk with David, the Zodiac operator and No. 3 man on this trip. Jim refers to us by number just like they do in coastal logging camps. David, Jim and I had all worked in the forest and knew the ranks from first-hand experience. No. 1 was camp boss, No. 2, woods foreman, and No. 3, shop foreman. As No. 3, David looks after the engines and runs the Zodiac. In camp he and I follow Jim's directions, but as No. 2, I understudied the boss and threw my weight around a bit more. I also lectured the guests (we never really called them tourists or students) on anthropology and got to be a big wheel intellectually. This used to bug Jim because he loved to be looked up to as the lead hand. When I overdid my role, or gave an exceptionally good lecture, he would mutter that all he was apparently good for was "bell-hopping and portering; perhaps you'd like me to get some ice cubes for your drinks." However, when we were travelling, setting up camp, or dealing with a weather crisis (and there were many), we all deferred to Jim. He also elevated the mood in camp, deploying a direct and gregarious sense of humour, particularly aimed at the women. Jim's ability to form a team in the rain was legendary, and he used that skill creating difficult and complex tasks for us all when the rain began to bucket down and the fog rolled in from offshore. But now it was time to get on the water again.

After we counted everyone (eight guests for the Zodiac and six for the Fairisle), and ensured that the wet gear and life jackets were back on, Jim fired up the Fairisle, and David began untying the Zodiac. "No. 2, why don't you run the Zodiac over to Escalante so I can talk to David?" We were breaking a major rule by doing this at nearly 2 p.m. in a moderate southeaster that was possibly still building, but Jim wanted to set up camp before nightfall on Escalante beach. In the back of my head Ray's famous rule of coastal travel loomed large. "The most important thing my Dad taught me about travelling on the water was, GO EARLY." We clearly weren't doing that this afternoon. I told Boulding I'd be glad to run the Zodiac. The Fairisle slowly led the way out of Friendly Cove under Jim's command and we all waved to Ray, Terry and Sharon, who were standing on their front porch. I could see that Ray was wearing his disapproving face.

As we turned south out beyond the lighthouse headland we beheld a very different Nootka Sound from the one we had crossed that morning. It was bloody rough, with big ocean swells easily twenty-feet high, and one-hundred feet or more from wave crest to wave crest. I had only once before crossed this body of water in conditions like these and that time I was safely on the Uchuck.

Boulding speeded up and I had to gun the Zodiac to stay in his wake. He was taking the waves at an angle to keep from running in the trough, and this meant his true bearing was more south-southwest. The southeast wind was hitting him square abeam and I am sure it had the effect of pushing him further and further out to sea. Escalante beach was due south, and to make this landing eventually we would have to steer straight back into the gale for a long stretch. I looked at my crew. Everyone was looking at me. The happiness of ten minutes previously had been replaced by fear. Of the eight, two were men, and they were doing their best, I guessed, to be stoic. They were probably hoping I knew what I was doing. The women, all school teachers taking this

West Coast Survival Course for credit, were hoping they'd live to earn their credits. They were all quiet and one was close to tears.

Up ahead Boulding went over a wave crest and then dropped from sight. I gunned the fifty-horsepower Merc' again to catch up, just as the approaching crest formed a breaking cap that tumbled right over us and filled the boat with cold green water. The Zodiac was designed to perform in conditions like these and it sped on with a much lower centre of gravity. Inside the boat everyone clung to the lifeline that ran along the sides of the sponsons and was looking at me with fear that was quickly turning into terror. Boulding was now completely out of sight, probably two wave generations ahead of us. "Why don't you bloody steer this boat properly!" shouted the older of the two men. I nearly lost it and shouted back, "Please sit down and shut up." I don't know where that came from, but it had the effect of causing the entire crew to look dolefully into the bilge and away from the storm.

I gave the order to bail. We had one large plastic bleach jug, cut away to form a kind of water shovel, tied to the painter in the bow. The older fellow retrieved it and began bailing as if he had done this sort of thing before. I was impressed with his skill and soon the water level started to go down. Meanwhile I glimpsed Fairisle's stern in the next trough, and it looked as though Boulding was slowing down for me. He was. He came out from the cabin and bracing himself against the rolling boat bellowed in classic form, "What did Oxford University teach you about this kind of work?" He was using humour to settle me down and he succeeded. He added, "We're changing course and running into shore now; I want you to travel in my lee so old Fairisle here can dampen out the weather for you. Just don't come too close!" In this fashion we came about and began a messy retreat with the waves to Escalante. Jim's plan worked and the weather co-operated as the southeaster began to wind down. I looked at my watch: it was 4 p.m.; we'd been messing about out here for two hours.

Escalante reef was soon off our bows, and Jim took the lead position to guide us through the only opening in the offshore reef to the anchorage. We flew through into miraculously calm water, and even the sun came out with a scorching end-of-day heat. Boulding had David pitch the anchor off the bow, and quickly began rigging a circular pull-away rope so that the Fairisle could drift ashore onto a sand bar for unloading. Soon his crew were happily ferrying the gear to a spot specified by Jim above the high-tide line. I nudged the Zodiac up onto the sand and everyone hopped out. Boulding gave my passengers the task of gathering firewood and making a fire. The two men were also asked to dig a deep and secure latrine. I was told to anchor my boat and report back for other duties. I did this and swam ashore in a stupid act of bravado.

Jim was up at the fire pit making coffee in a huge blackened, camp coffee pot when I stopped by dripping wet. "Nice work No. 2, you nearly drowned the paying guests and now you've probably got hypothermia." I thought of saying something in rebuttal but didn't. Jim cracked a smile: "What rule did we break out there?" "Go early," I replied. "Yup, and also the rule about discussing how we'll make the crossing together. But, you know what, it all adds up to a quality experience and I can feel a kind of psychic energy in this camp already. I don't know what it is, but I know when it's there." Classic Boulding, I thought to myself.

Soon all of the guests had put up their tents and were settled around a raging driftwood fire. Everyone had a coffee and the big pot had lots left for seconds and thirds. Terry's sockeye sticks were passed around, along with a "one-each" ration of Nanaimo bars from the lodge kitchen. Caffeine, chocolate and sockeye worked their collective magic. Boulding sat on the biggest log and began to deliver one of his trademark talks about why he does what he does:

"You know, Myrna and I could make more money running Zodiac trips for tourists from the Campbell River wharf. Or, I could have got a Keg and Cleaver franchise from my old rugger pal, George Tidball, and just flipped steaks for a living. But I chose not to. This, to me, is the most beautiful country in the world. And no matter how hard the challenges from loggers or miners or whatever else type of fly-by-nighters, I'm trying to keep some of it this way.

I'm one of the biggest supporters the tourist industry has in this province because it is the only industry that benefits from leaving all this beauty the way it is. Tourism doesn't rip all the hillsides apart or cut all the trees down. Just by taking people out here and exposing them to all this beauty they'll hopefully learn to love it. And then, hopefully, they'll go home and do something about keeping it this way. I think that this is the only way we are going to save some of this for the next generations. As for Myrna and I, we'll be here to the end of our lives because we are stewards. That's an old English word for someone who looks after an estate. In England they make sure the rabbits and squirrels and pheasants get a fair shake, because all of the real wildlife is long gone. We're here stewarding Roosevelt elk, Trumpeter swans, killer whales and five species of Pacific salmon. That's just for starters. And I'm trying to show people something I call 'generosity of spirit' in the process. It don't pay well, but you sure feel good at the end of the day. I won't lecture you anymore because I'm starting to sound like No 2. Next you'll expect me to write a book! Now let's have some more coffee!"

The guests had by now broken up into small groups, and were looking variously hungry and ready for an early night. Boulding slammed down his huge mug and asked, "Who wants to eat before we sleep?" Just like when we landed, he snapped into organizational mode and delegated the cooking tasks. "We're short of hostesses, cooks and waiters tonight, so we'll all have to pitch in." One group was given the salad pail and told to get inventive for seventeen; another was assigned potato and onion peeling; and the luckiest group got to learn how to cook four coho salmon that Jim secretly bought at Friendly Cove from Terry. When they were taken out of a burlap sack, Jim asked everyone to gather round and learn the "Indian way to barbecue salmon."

First four, five-foot cedar tongs were cut from a drift-wood shake block. They were next half-split lengthwise and wired tightly half-way down to stop further splitting. Next, several dozen cedar-kindling cross pieces were cut from the same block. At this point Jim instructed No. 3 to start organizing the fire for hot-coal production.

One of the already cleaned cohos (about an eight pounder) was taken to a flat log and split completely open dorsally and ventrally, both exposing the backbone on one side and leaving just enough dorsal flesh to hold the fish together when flattened out. A double lattice of cedar kindling was constructed to hold the fish together on both flesh and skin sides. Thus contained, the coho was slid into the opened five-foot cedar tong, friction fitted into place, and wired shut at the top end. The procedure was then passed on to three groups of novices to try while Jim carefully angled the first salmon over the built-up coals. "The trick is to get the tong anchored in the sand so that the salmon and the cedar don't burn. If the cedar catches fire, you're too close. You have to watch it continuously, but who wouldn't want to watch such a beautiful fish cook? You'll see a white fatty paste start to ooze out of the red flesh; that is the sign that the technique is working. Now, why are you guys going so slow with that lattice work? And let's not forget to thank Terry for these fish when we go back to Friendly Cove."

The dinner was a great success with one barbecued coho left-over for breakfast. The group began losing members fast as individuals and the odd couple said their goodnights. Jim said it was "Time to hit the sack." No. 3 went down to check the boats as they rode at anchor in the gathering dark. After helping wash the dishes at the surf line, I bumbled off into the woods to climb into my tent, dead tired. Suddenly I heard a coarse whisper from Jim who was camped somewhere up behind me. I struggled through the low cedars in the direction of his voice, and found him dimly lit by a candle under an ingenious clear-plastic rain fly. He had a plastic sheet on the ground and his gear and sleeping bag spread out on top. The fly was tethered at four corners and, via a small stone, gathered and tied dead centre in the plastic fly, a line led up to a cedar bough where it was knotted. The net effect was a perfectly sheltered camp, and the great man was already snug in his sleeping bag. He said, "Mike, have a slug of this," and passed over an open mickey of over-proof Hudson's Bay rum. I gulped back a slug. "Now get out of here and get some sleep! It's been a good day because we all learned something!

And by the way, in case you are really stupid – that young teacher, Susan, has her eye on you."

Immediately I could visualize the young teacher he was referring to in such a typically Boulding manner. Jim had a special wavelength reserved for his discussions with women, and another one for discussing women with men. This was the first time he had indicated any interest in my love life, so I paid some attention. Susan was indeed attractive. She was blonde and very fit, and had been part of the Fairisle crew on the way up Muchalaht Inlet. She had also been the subject of the considerable Boulding wit around the campfire, but everyone knew that Jim was well married and the father of three teenage daughters and a young son. So why was Jim charming women my way? That was just his style. He wanted everyone to eventually end up as part of a couple. He thought it was the natural order of things. Predictably, he also thought that he knew who was best for whom.

The morning broke clear and quiet, and the open Pacific stretched west, calm as far as the eye could travel. I rose and walked down to the high tide line looking for signs of life. No one else was up. Suddenly a tall, black, upright shape caught my field of vision just at the reef's edge, maybe a hundred yards in front of me. As I watched, it moved slowly from right to left. Running down to the water I wondered if it were a transient orca scouting the reef edge for sleeping seals or sea lions. I jumped through the shallows and climbed up onto the dulse-strewn reef, stupidly falling and cutting my knee. I kept going right to the edge of the reef and looked down maybe three feet right into the eye of the biggest orca I had ever seen. I was right. It promptly occurred to me that, failing a seal or sea lion, a 24-year-old human might do the trick. But for some reason I stood my ground. We actually looked into each other's eyes. Neither of us blinked. And then the great whale started slowly out to sea.

Without a hell of a lot of thought I raced over to the circle-pull line for the Zodiac and hauled her quickly into shore. I untied the painter and cranked the motor over two or three times until it sparked. Before I knew it I was chasing the killer whale. I caught up quickly, cut the motor and drifted forwards silently almost to the point of touching. The glistening black and white body rolled over to get a good look at me through one unlidded eye. The dorsal fin was completely erect and easily six feet tall. Again we stared at each other for what seemed a long time. Then the whale sounded. I raced ahead and looked about. No whale. I shut off the motor and sat awhile. Suddenly he rose about ten boat lengths in front of me and you could see that he was starting to pick up speed. God, what a being. So powerful; so in control; so much of this place. And that was all. The whale sounded by the reef opening and took off. I motored out beyond the reef and cut the motor once again. The last I saw of him was a spy jump way out to sea, maybe a mile or more. The sun was shining over the coast range on Vancouver Island. Conuma peak (Mowachaht for unripe salmon berry – just what it looked like) was clear and stark on the eastern horizon. I started up the motor and went back in.

Jim and several of the crew were standing about the fire in jeans shorts and T-shirts. "So Big Mike (Jim was constantly inventing new nicknames and terms of endearment, or were they derision?), did you catch us a salmon for breakfast?"

"Actually Jim, I just missed netting you a whale."

"Better luck next time, No. 2." We organized left–over barbecued coho, porridge and toasted Logan bread for breakfast and brewed another monster pot of coffee. At the meal's end Jim laid out his plans for our day: "You guys have several choices; I'll be taking six of you in the Fairisle down south to 'Mexico' (Ray's William's term for Hesquiaht, Ahousaht and Tofino, all villages to the south of us by ten to thirty nautical miles); Mike will be giving one of his fascinating lectures on Chief Maquinna and Captain Cook – you'll need to take notes for the test; and No 3 is taking the rest of you fishing. And there's another option: just sitting here and sun bathing, which also involves doing most of the dinner prep for the real workers, umm, with the exception of those of you who hang around to listen to Mike." There was a sudden burst of consulting and talking and sizing up of options. Exactly six guests, interestingly all women, elected the Fairisle cruise; four chose my lecture and beach walk; and four chose David's fishing trip. I was amused to see my group included the older fellow who was such a good bailer and Susan.

Jim's crew was off first after a big speech by his lordship about the importance of "GOING EARLY," the subtleties of which were lost to none. David's bunch were all eager to catch 'smileys' (because you smile when you catch one), and my guys were motivated to learn about the history of this place and hike about for a few hours, given that for the past day they had mainly sat in boats.

The sun continued to beat down and the sea stayed calm. I amused myself by thinking of the course description for what we were doing: 'West Coast Survival.' This was more like Club Med Escalante. We gathered our note books, pens, cameras, water bottles, sandwiches and the last Nanaimo bars for lunch, plus shade hats, and headed down the coast to the point overlooking the mouth of Nootka Sound. Here I began to talk about the anthropology thesis I had written at the University of British Columbia for Professor Wilson Duff about the three great 'Sea Otter Chiefs' Maquinna of Nootka Sound, Cuneah of Kiusta village in Haida Gwaii, and Legaik of Lax'Kwallams near the mouth of the Skeena River. I was so enthusiastic about my still relatively new knowledge, and could talk endlessly about the dynamics of chiefdom expansion; the local economic impact of the fur trade unwittingly begun by Captain Cook in 1778 when Maquinna gave him a lustrous sea-otter pelt cloak; and the Nootka Convention conference between Captains Vancouver and Bodega y Quadra in 1792. On and on I went under the hot sun, oblivious to the world, until the older fellow started to snore. Susan smiled. The other two women stood up. "Can we go for a walk?" "Yes, yes of course. Now would be a good time," I replied.

We started off down the trail to Burwood Bay, a south-east protected enclosure for ducking into if a trip to, or from, Escalante, had to be curtailed because of bad weather. It had a classic canoe beach composed of smoothly-rounded, small pebbles that made a characteristic clattering sound as the waves washed up and down.

Atlantic Ocean

United States

Pacific Ocean

Canada

Washington, D.C.

Ottawa

Chip-Ali

Fort Mcleay

Magrath/ Medicine Wheel

Brocket

Calgary

Kelly Lake

Yupot

Vancouver

Hazel Grove

Whitehorse

West Moberly

Dawson Creek

Siusteau

Lutsel

Fort Good Hope

Fort McPherson

Inuvik

Kugluktuk

Fairbanks

Anchorage

Alaska

Barrow

Queen Elizabeth Islands

Canada Basin

Beaufort Sea

Chukchi Plateau

Chukchi Sea

Bering Sea

Aleutian Islands

Gulf of Alaska

Bristol Bay

Pevek

East Siberian Sea

ARCTIC OCEAN

North Pole

Laptev Sea

Tiksi

Greenland (DENMARK)

Greenland Sea

Baffin Bay

Nuuk

Davis Strait

Hudson Bay

Hudson Strait

Foxe Basin

Labrador Sea

Halifax

Kara Sea

Barents Sea

Novy Port

Dikson

Novosibirsk

Irkutsk

Kamchatka Peninsula

Petropavlovsk-Kamchatskiy

Asia

Russia

Europe

ICELAND

Reykjavik

Denmark Strait

UK

NORWAY

Oslo

SWEDEN

FINLAND

DENMARK

Copenhagen

Stockholm

Helsinki

Moscow

St. Petersburg

Arkhangelsk

Murmansk

Kola Peninsula

Lovozero

Yona

EUROPE

THE COMMUNITIES VISITED
IN THE STORIES

Names and boundary representation are not necessarily authoritative. August 7, 2016. U308 (8/16)

MV Uchuck III at Yuquot wharf

Tourists follow the path through Yuquot village in 1968

Photo credits: all are by Mike Robinson, Lynn Webster, and Allan Beaver (no. 5).

aven and Killerwhale totem pole at Yuquot

Cedar strip woven basket made by Mrs. Dick

Photo credits: all are by Mike Robinson, Lynn Webster, and Allan Beaver (no. 5).

m Boulding and Mike Robinson at Escalante Beach,
'ootka Sound, 1975

unga House, in Gwaii Haanas, Haida Gwaii, in 1978

oto credits: all are by Mike Robinson, Lynn Webster, and Allan Beaver (no. 5).

En route to Tanu by kayak

Photo credits: all are by Mike Robinson, Lynn Webster, and Allan Beaver (no. 5).

Gathering mussels for dinner at low tide in Tanu

Photo credits: all are by Mike Robinson, Lynn Webster, and Allan Beaver (no. 5).

Grey Whale vertebrae on Kunga Island in Gwaii Haanas

Ray and Terry Williams and the Robinson family (Lance, Mike, Lynn and Caitlin) at Yuquot in 1988

Sarah Jerome, elder Peter Vittrekwa, and Dr. Joan Ryan in Teetl'it Zheh office of Gwich'in Language and Culture Project, 1989

Graduation Day, Gwich'in Language and Culture Project: Hon. Ethel Blondin-Andrew awards Rosie Firth her diploma

Photo credits: all are by Mike Robinson, Lynn Webster, and Allan Beaver (no. 5).

Gwich'in trapper at Rock River, NWT

Photo credits: all are by Mike Robinson, Lynn Webster, and Allan Beaver (no. 5).

Fort McKay Metis elder Fred MacDonald (left), Game Warden Gordon Armitage, and trapper Willie Grandjambe in Fort McKay, 1994

Sami elder Maria Sergina validates the first Yona map with project leader Tat'yana Tsmykailo

Photo credits: all are by Mike Robinson, Lynn Webster, and Allan Beaver (no. 5).

Mike Robinson and Leif Rantala fill gas cans for the trip from Ivalo, Finland to Lovozero, Kola Peninsula, Russia, in 1995

Photo credits: all are by Mike Robinson, Lynn Webster, and Allan Beaver (no. 5).

Right to Left: Leif Rantala, Mike Robinson, Lloyd Binder, and Nina Afanas'eva present plans for traditional land use and occupancy mapping in Lovozero

Sami women singing at Sami Cultural Days festival in Lovozero, 1996

Photo credits: all are by Mike Robinson, Lynn Webster, and Allan Beaver (no. 5).

Pavel Fefelov points out Russian Army tank tracks on the fragile tundra near Lovozero

Photo credits: all are by Mike Robinson, Lynn Webster, and Allan Beaver (no. 5).

Karim-Aly Kassam, Mikhail Gorbachev, and Mike Robinson, at University of Calgary in 1998

President/CEO Mike Robinson (left) and President/CEO Colin Jackson (right) promote the Glenbow Museum and the Epcor Centre at their the Calgary Stampede 'Offices in the Mall,' 2003

The beach was crescent shaped and darkly overhung by first-growth cedars and spruces because it faced north. Probably it had been a small village site for the Mowachaht, although there was no characteristic traces of midden anywhere. They probably had used it, just like us, as a weathering spot en route to where they really wanted to go. The trail broke out onto the beach at the mid-point of its arc. Our little group moved onto the pebbles and Susan cried, "Look, a whale skeleton!" Sure enough, just above the high-tide mark there was a baby grey-whale skeleton, picked clean by the eagles and ravens and bleached white by the sun. Two whales in one day, I thought. It must be a record. We gathered around the disarticulated ribs, pelvic girdle and magnificent skull. Bits of flipper bone and vertebrae were littered all around us. Instinctively we started to gather them up. I thought the better of us lugging them back to camp and said, "Let's leave it here and come back in the Zodiac tonight. Escalante beach is two miles behind us and it's a hot day." Everyone agreed. The older fellow said, "Who gets to keep it?" Everyone thought Susan should decide because she saw it first. Looking at me and smiling, she said, "I'd like to give it to Strathcona Park Lodge as a memento of this wonderful day." And so the Whale Room back at the lodge received its identity and a whale to hang on its western wall.

Back to camp we went, laughing about 'West Coast Survival' and in high spirits. The older fellow walked alongside me, eager to talk. I asked him about his work. He was a school principal in Nanaimo, nearing retirement and eager to develop new interests for his leisure time. He looked about sixty, and I asked him what he did before taking up teaching. "Oh," he said, "I was a frigate captain in the Royal Navy." That explained his anguish yesterday, I thought to myself. "And I never would have begun that crossing you made in that south-easter. You took a big risk." I didn't know what to say, but ventured, "I know, and please excuse the way I spoke to you in the moment." We kept on walking. Camp was in sight, and so were the 'Mexican' adventurers, now back and drinking coffee around the newly kindled fire.

Boulding was in high form, laughing uproariously at his own jokes and smiling at all the women. They'd obviously had a good time too. Jim saw me and said, "Too bad you didn't come with us. We all went skinny dipping at Hot Springs Cove. And you know, there were six very pretty women in that pool, and only one fine specimen of manhood. And that wasn't you, No. 2." I smiled secretly very glad that my skinny physique hadn't had to compete with Jim's that afternoon. Sometimes his humour at my expense cut pretty close to the bone. In socially vulnerable situations like skinny dipping, he was capable of saying anything to another guy, very much in the spirit of competition. Right now I didn't have much ammunition to throw back, and I was still recovering from the frigate captain's comments. I noticed that Susan was watching this exchange with some enjoyment.

The roar of the Zodiac's motor cut through this temporary tension as the four fishermen and No. 3 hove into view. David was also in high spirits, smiling and yelling, "Who's the high liner in this camp?" The answer appeared to be obvious. The boat ran up on the sandy beach, and the fishers jumped out, turned and reached into the boat to lift out about a forty-pound halibut, what Ray Williams confusingly called "a 'doormat' because it was bigger than a little 'chicken' halibut. They also had two thirty-pound smileys, and a three-foot-long red snapper. Jim looked pissed: "Okay, Einstein, who's gonna eat all that fish? We have no ice and only seventeen stomachs here." David whipped back, "Don't worry, boss, I'm taking the 'doormat' and the snapper over to Ray and Terry right now, we'll keep the springs."

Jim grunted his approval. It was coming on 5 p.m., and David backed off the beach, cranked up the motor and quickly got the Zodiac up to plane. With the sea still calm as glass he would cover the five nautical miles to Friendly Cove in twenty minutes. The rest of us started to prepare dinner; fresh salmon for the second night in a row. This time we did spring steaks – about two pounds each – in the frying pan with lemon butter. As we were finishing up I remembered the whale skeleton and our plan to retrieve it that night. With no David in sight we'd have to leave the bones for another day. At about 7 p.m. David was spotted humming over the flat waters of the sound, about half-way home. We all imagined that Ray and Terry would be pretty happy right now. They were.

At 8 p.m. Jim built up the fire and asked the guests what they wanted to do tomorrow. Everyone opted to cycle round the three activities of today. This was fine with me, and we'd try to include a whale carry back before the fishers went out to try their luck with green 'hootchies' and 'buzz bombs'. At 9 p.m., various bottles of scotch, wine and even liqueurs began to appear from the guests' tents. A full moon rose behind us over Nootka Cone. Our beach was awash in its pale light. The inevitable sing song began shortly after the drinks were poured, and after a few rounds of the Strathcona standards (When the Coho Flash Silver All Over the Bay and The Name of that Place is the Grand Hotel), I took the opportunity to return to my tent and grab my sleeping bag and pillow for a night out under the stars. I chose a secluded spot well down the beach, out of sight of the fire, and safely above the high-tide line to bed down. What a day of whales and unrelenting sun!

I lay down and looked up. The evening sky was aglow with constellations, shooting stars, red and yellow planets, the Milky Way, and the stark pale moonlight. Just then I heard soft footfalls approaching. I looked behind me and saw Susan bringing her sleeping bag down to join me. "Do you mind if I sleep outside beside you?" she asked. "No. Pull up a sand dune," I joked. She placed her sleeping bag beside mine, and lay down. She was wearing jean shorts and a white T shirt, her blonde hair was tied in a ponytail, and she was smiling the same way as when she found the baby-whale skeleton this afternoon. We lay side-by-side and stared up at the stars for a long time. Then she rolled towards me and asked if I was surprised that she had come to sleep with me on the beach. Before I could answer, I heard unmistakably heavy steps approaching. There was a coarse whisper: "You better not screw up now, No 2."

4

"He Won You; You Have to Go and Sit on His Knee!"

I bet my young wife in a slahal game – and lose!

Lynn and I were married in June 1977 to some degree because my Dad and Jim Boulding saw a certain chemistry between us and both of them pointed it out to me. Let me explain. Lynn was a fellow anthropology student at the University of British Columbia. When she graduated she found employment as a research assistant to my father with a great reference from my mother who had been her fine arts professor. Together they reworked the design of pediatric hospital facilities advocating for a new child-centred model that was described in a ground-breaking video that playfully used a young patient's words for the title, The Electric Happy Hospital,. When Lynn and my father worked together, I would occasionally meet her at Christmas parties and other social occasions linked to Dad's work. It was always fun to reconnect and to share stories about our evolving careers.

When I returned to Vancouver after my grad school experience in Oxford, I found employment at Strathcona Lodge. One day Dad took me aside, and casually said that I should invite Lynn to the lodge for a weekend. I was a bit surprised, but acted on the suggestion all the same. And so Lynn spontaneously turned up one day during the latter part of the summer of 1975. It was an immediate delight to spend time with her and it was wonderful to have my love for Strathcona with all its obvious idiosyncrasies confirmed by her. After carefully observing the chemistry, Boulding said to me in private, "That one is a keeper. If you don't marry that young gal, I'm becoming a Mormon so I can take a second wife. You'll never find a better life partner than her. So get on with it. Don't be so tentative!"

I had already formed my own opinion and I was pretty sure Lynn had made up her mind too, but Jim's sense of urgency pushed me over the brink. Asking Lynn to marry me was the best decision I've ever made, and it set the stage for a new approach to life in which I would "paddle my own canoe," to borrow a phrase much used by my paternal grandfather, Captain Basil Robinson, the junior school headmaster at St. George's School for Boys, when advising young men about their careers. But first we had to reconcile our individual career paths. UBC had accepted me into the law school's freshman class starting in the fall of 1975. This was complicated by Lynn's parallel acceptance into the University of Calgary's architecture program in the faculty of environmental design. We reviewed our options and decided to get married after we had both completed a year of our courses, even if it meant spending time apart. And so began a marriage of loving partners initially separated by the need to complete professional grad-school courses in different cities.

Engaged to be married, but living singly in Vancouver, I found law to be increasingly boring and then extremely boring, consumed with business-like detail that had no intrinsic intellectual appeal to me and unrelenting in its deepening levels of arcana. Most students in my year were volunteering in legal-aid clinics or working in law offices during the summer, a prospect I simply couldn't stomach. I went back to Strathcona with Lynn after we returned from our honeymoon. In a burst of welcoming bonhomie Jim said we could work together "on my famous West Coast Survival course," breaking the long-time Boulding edict that "couples are lousy working together, and therefore can't work together at my place." It didn't seem to matter that he and Myrna owned the place and ran it as a couple, because Jim could always tolerate exceptions to the rules when he was involved. It was nice he gave us the same grace. We were both happy to be back at Strathcona doing something we enjoyed with old friends. Boulding upped the ante at dinner the first evening by announcing to a room full of guests that "Mike and

Lynn will be running West Coast Survival this August and you'd better sign up right now tonight if you want a place on our signature course!" This was interesting. Boulding, apparently, was leaving it all up to us.

The next day I said that Lynn and I were very happy with our new assignment, but felt that we had better go out to Friendly Cove immediately to do some grass-roots organizing with Ray and Terry. Jim agreed and said he'd give us the Fairisle for the trip, but she was in dry dock in Campbell River finally getting her transom strengthened and he'd give us the Zodiac, but she was laid up on the floats with an, as yet, undiagnosed leak. So, we could take a tin boat. This meant an old Strathcona aluminum fifteen-footer with a twenty-horse outboard and gas tanks bouncing around in the bilge. But we jumped at the chance to go out to the real West Coast, mindful of all the old rules, especially "Go early."

We planned for a five-day trip, with enough gas for one hundred miles of small-boat travel in an area known intimately to us for its sudden storms, hidden reefs, howling southeasters, and twenty-foot high waves with crumbling crests. We packed a box each of Florida oranges and Okanagan apples for Ray and Terry. The traditional Strathcona gear pile included our Polar Guard sleeping bags and foamies, Mustang floater jackets, a weather radio, rain tarps and yards of yellow plastic rope to tie them down, a long handled and newly sharpened axe with a blade guard, a serious first-aid kit, white plastic sealer pails of Nanaimo bars, Logan bread, pancake mix, raisins, bannock mix, peanut butter, jam, brown rice, and a bottle of rum for Ray. Clothing for the trip, to be undertaken in mid-July, included full rain suits, gum boots, extra pairs of wool socks, woollen Stanfield's loggers' itchy underwear and our Cowichan sweaters and toques. All of the above was checked and double checked with a captain's checklist vetted by Jim and packed in two waterproof duffle bags.

The day before our departure we drove the old Strathcona Chevy Suburban to Gold River and the government wharf where the tin boat was moored. We purchased fresh boat gas and packed the boat that night. We slept in the wharf shed to get an early start – 6 a.m. to be precise. I was pleased that the five-year-old outboard started with one pull of the cord. The boat was a little dented and dinged, but soon we were whining down Mowachaht Inlet under a grey morning sky. We passed the familiar land and seascape of old-cut block scars, logging camps, raging creeks, forested islands, and within half an hour the pulp-mill smoke of Gold River was far astern. The crew-cut peaks of Bligh Island loomed ahead, a particularly sorry piece of coastal rainforest devastation. At the eastern tip of the island we had to make a weather call: going for broke down its south flank exposed us to the full swell of Nootka Sound's fury if a storm was damping down or rising up; taking the northern route was longer and required some careful map reading to avoid hidden reefs and many small islands, but it was more protected. We stopped as we reached Breadfruit Bligh's island and looked long and hard down the south passage. Sure enough, we could see white foam and breakers around and over Anderson Point, the indicator that the north route was safer. Overhead, the ceiling was low and a light rain had started to fall. With several nautical miles yet to run, we revved up and headed north. A light chop had formed in the channel.

By the second hour of any small-boat trip, the outboard's roar starts to annoy the operator. Sitting on the port side of the stern seat next to the motor, and gripping the steering arm with a white-knuckled right hand, I was looking west for the familiar outline of Friendly Cove. Gradually it became visible on the horizon as we passed little gull islets and reefs in the greying spray. It was surprisingly cold for July. Lynn opened the lunch bag, and we began to chew away at fried-egg sandwiches from the lodge. Black coffee flowed from the Thermos and she found two Nanaimo bars. We continued to whine on through the weather. Soon the Douglas firs on the Friendly Cove rocky promontory became more distinct. I checked the Nootka Sound chart and calculated that we were about six nautical miles from Ray and Terry's house and its dry, warm interior. The rain was becoming more steady and falling harder by the minute. We put on our sou'wester foul-weather hats and our Helly Hansen rain pants. Still the rain picked up its intensity. The waves were growing lumpier too. The bow of the tin boat began to bash down on the lines of waves that came directly at us from the southwest. A quick look around from my vantage point showed no other boats in sight. Lynn got on the radio, found Ray standing by on channel 8 and told him where we were.

"Hi you guys. Good thing you came up the north channel. I can see the big waves really smashing on Anderson Point from our window. Terry has fresh bread in the oven and her dad, Harry Dick, is here. Molly Andrews and her husband David are also here, and Maurus McLean is coming over tonight to play slahal with us. You guys can play too. See you soon. Oh yes, Father Frank Salmon is with us." We were warmed and calmed by Ray's voice. Neither of us could remember Father Frank, but the rest of the gang were old friends.

Friendly Cove was pulling at us with her magnetic force. The last mile of the crossing from Bligh Island was completely exposed to the prevailing winds. The tin boat was rearing up against the incoming swell. I could remember Boulding telling me something about the power of wind and tide combined out here; this was surely a textbook case. I asked Lynn to move up to the bow seat to hold the boat down. I slowed the motor to give her a chance to climb over the gear pile without being tossed against the gunwale. She made it, but when she tried to sit down she was pitched up by the boat's bucking motion. She simply could not sit still against the power of the oncoming swells. She did her best to hold on, and I did my best to steer a workable course. Just as we were about to enter the protection of the cove, a huge wave caught us by surprise and tossed Lynn up about four feet in the air. Luckily she landed in the boat on the gear. "That will be noticed," I said to myself as I looked up at Ray and Terry's house on the level terrace above the beach. I knew we were being watched through the binoculars. Lynn lay splayed on the blue tarp looking at me with a huge smile on her face. Luckily no bones were broken, but my boat operator's pride was sure bruised.

Ray opened the front door of the house and started down the path to his log float to greet us. I managed a very good approach to the tie-up spot and shut down the engine. "Boy, we all thought you had flipped Lynn into the chuck," laughed Ray. "Welcome home Michael and Lynn." It felt like we were home, too.

We immediately moved all the gear up to Ray's porch and put the tarp over it. I carried the two fruit boxes inside and Lynn gave Terry a big hug. "Aaah … I'm so happy to see you!" she said. I went out to rummage about for the rum bottle for Ray, found it and brought it in, closing the door behind me. A hot, Douglas-fir stoked fire was burning in the cast-iron stove. Wet clothing was hanging from a rack suspended from the ceiling. Immediately opposite me on the couch were Harry Dick and a stranger. Harry we had met once before, and he was even more formidable now. He was one of the last of his generation, about seventy-five, and still powerful of build and face. He was about five and a half-feet tall, perhaps two hundred pounds, with a paddler's long torso, well muscled arms, and short, squat legs. His Mowachaht name was Klasnik. He wore an old pair of brown wool pants, red logger's suspenders and a grey-wool, open-necked Stanfield's pull-over. His hair was still jet black. One of the very last Mowachaht to have gone whaling as a boy, Harry spoke his language more often than English. His eyes sized us up against all the other *Mumuk'ne* he had met in his long life as a fisherman, logger, and trapper. "Hello," he said. Gesturing to the younger man sitting on the sofa beside him, he added, "This is Father Frank."

Father Frank Salmon was a thirtyish Catholic priest famous on the west coast of Vancouver Island for kayaking about his parish of Nuu Chah Nulth First Nation villages. For some reason I was suddenly conscious of the bottle of Hudson's Bay over-proof rum I held by the neck in my right hand. I gave it to Ray who immediately disappeared with it into Terry's kitchen. He seemed quietly embarrassed about the gift. I wondered why.

Father Frank broke the silence: "Do you often come to Yuquot?" Right away he went up a notch by using the proper name of Friendly Cove. Lynn explained that we were teaching the West Coast Survival Course this August, and were here to do some planning with Ray and Terry. "Do you speak Mowachaht?" he enquired. I explained that we were trying to learn, but were slow. Just then Terry came into the room with a tall, aluminum, logger's thermos and offered everyone coffee. She asked me to come into the kitchen to help out with something. "Father Frank is here to see if we are still on the wagon after last year's AA meeting in Ahousaht. You embarrassed Ray with that bottle." "Just another Strathcona fuck-up," I thought to myself. I told Terry I was sorry. She gave me a conspirator's wink and a shy smile.

I returned to the living room to find Father Frank engrossed in a long animated Mowachaht discussion with Harry Dick. Ray was watching approvingly from his easy chair by the window. "He speaks Mowachaht better than me, I think," he said to Lynn and me. "He speaks it the old way, like our elders, the people who taught him. Come on upstairs; I'll show you your room." Up we went with our clothing bags to find that we were bedding down in Sharon's old room at the front of the house overlooking the cove. We thanked Ray and explained that we would like to go for a walk down past Jewitt Lake to the lagoon. He said that was a good idea, and asked if we'd like to play slahal tonight. "That would be fun," said Lynn. "Be back here at dinner time," said Terry as we went out the front door. "When is that?" I asked. "Boy, I can tell you guys are still in the city! It is when Terry puts the food on the table," said Ray. Off we went, glad to be in a place of no watches.

About 6 p.m., hungry, re-soaked and looking forward to playing the hide-the-bone hand game, we arrived back at Ray and Terry's. The kitchen table was set for dinner, and we were offered time to go and wash up. When we returned with dry clothes and combed hair, Terry told us to sit where we wanted. I sat between Ray and Father Frank; Lynn sat with Terry and her Dad. On the table were two loaves of fresh, white bread just out of the oven, a baked sockeye, some salted herring and cod, homemade blackberry jam, Terry's garden potatoes and more black coffee.

"Father Frank, will you say grace?" asked Ray. And so he did, in Mowachaht. Somehow the conversation moved to people who had recently died. Ray explained that the Nuu Chah Nulth custom was to hold memorial potlatch feasts every year to commemorate those who had passed on. The surviving family members always arranged for someone to dance in the hall with a picture of the deceased. Small gifts like glasses and tea towels are given to the guests who bear personal and silent witness to the names and achievements of the dead.

Ray said that Father Frank attended these memorials with a framed picture of Jesus Christ and danced Him about the room. "It is one of the high points of my year," said Father Frank as he sliced the end off one of Terry's loaves. Soon all the salmon, cod and herring were eaten and Terry cleared away the plates in anticipation of dessert. She went over to the window ledge above her stove and fetched two home-baked pies: "There's rhubarb and blackberry." "Bless you," said Father Frank. Harry Dick got to make the first choice and asked for blackberry. Terry cut him a big slice. "Ever since I was a little girl, Dad always liked that kind," she said.

Ray said that he had obtained some new Mowachaht music tapes from the Alberni Valley Museum that he would play for us during the hand games. He also explained how the game of slahal was played in response to a question from Lynn. Basically two teams are chosen, and they sit opposite each other on the floor. Then each team takes turns singing and one member, the slahal player, moves two bone pieces from one hand to the other until the music stops. Then the guessing team has to choose which of the slahal player's hands the longest bone is in. And there's betting involved. At this point in the explanation he looked sheepishly at Father Frank who smiled in reply. Ray kept on going: "The game can go all night until one team has lost too much and has nothing of value left to bet. And, oh yah, I forgot to tell you, I don't know what slahal means. Harry Dick says it isn't a Mowachaht word. Some other Indians made it up I guess."

The front door opened and Maurus McLean, Molly Dick, and David Andrew entered. The rain was still bucketing down outside. "Hello this place! I am Nuukni," called Maurus, their oldest neighbour who had returned to his ancestral village of Yuquot for the summer with his daughter Molly and her husband David. "Is there a slahal game here?" he asked. A crack of thunder echoed around the darkening curve of the cove in reply. Everyone laughed. Ray said he was going outside to top up the gas in the generator so there would be "plenty of juice for the tape player." Terry set everyone to re-arranging the furniture so that there would be enough room for two teams to face each other sitting on the floor. She also picked the teams. Lynn and I, David and Maurus would square off against Ray and Terry, Harry and Molly. Father Frank could gamble if he wished. He asked to play and was told to play with us.

Ray turned off the living-room lights and turned on his stereo tape player. A low drumming began to flow from the speakers and Harry began to sing along in Mowachaht, as did Maurus. Ray stoked up the stove and gave Maurus two slahal bones, one half the size of the other. He took them in his hands and spoke to them. He blew on them and wished us great luck. The drumming began to get louder and Maurus started to rock from side to side. The rest of us, shoulder to shoulder, began to imitate his motion. Then Maurus began to sing his good-luck gambling song. We struggled along in broken Mowachaht, and Maurus smiled at our opponents who were watching his every move. Outside the wind howled in the rigging holding up Ray's radio mast, and the rain sluiced off the gutterless eaves of the house.

Terry, meanwhile, had put a five-dollar bill on the floor between us. David bent over and picked it up; he held it in his hands and smiled at it. He kissed it and pretended to hide it behind his back. Maurus spoke to it in his Mowachaht song. Suddenly the music stopped. Ray had turned it down. After a suitable period of thought, Terry reached over and pointed to Maurus' right hand. He waited awhile and cajoled the opposite four before opening his hand palm up. In it was the shorter bone. Maurus laughed and claimed the five-dollar bill for us. Father Frank looked a bit worried. Molly let out a mock cry of anguish. Terry stared at Maurus' hand in disbelief. Maurus handed Harry the two slahal bones.

Now it Harry's team took its turn. Ray cranked up the drumming. Molly and Terry began to sing a woman's gambling song, swaying rhythmically. Harry placed one bone in each palm, and moved his hands back and forth in the dull glow of the stove light. He blew on his fists and moved them slowly up and down, back and forth. Maurus' team watched like attentive wolves as the bones rose and fell. Lynn reached over and placed five dollars on the floor between us. Molly and Terry began to taunt me as I watched them. Their movements became flirtatious and they blew kisses at the men opposite.

Harry's voice deepened and became more serious. His arms were flying and the slahal bones were god-knows-where. The music lulled and stopped. Lynn immediately pointed to Harry's left hand. He scowled back at her and at us. He slowly unclenched his fingers. There it was, the long bone. Lynn reclaimed her five dollars and Terry wailed as she passed another five dollars to Lynn. Father Frank looked more serious than ever.

And so it went for several more hours. By my calculation there was over two-hundred and fifty dollars in play and the betting pace crept steadily up, each team eager and ready to wager twenty-five and then thirty dollars a round. Then the luck changed. Harry's team had four consecutive wins and Terry held over two hundred dollars. Maurus received the bones and began his best good-luck song. Lynn placed our last forty dollars between the groups. Maurus abruptly stopped singing, and said something in Mowachaht that astonished the opposing team. Roughly translated later, he had said, "We are betting Lynn, our only woman, in this round." I didn't know what he said; neither did Lynn. The singing resumed, the drums pounded, and Maurus gave it his best shot. Terry laid two-hundred dollars opposite our forty, indicating Lynn's dollar value that night – one hundred and sixty dollars. The music stopped. Terry pointed at Maurus' left hand. He unclenched his fist revealing the long bone. Terry looked at Lynn and said: "He won you; you have to go sit on his knee." And so Lynn realizing her fate, looked at me, stood up and crossed over to sit on Harry's lap to be his woman. I had lost my young bride in a bet. Father Frank began an engaged discussion in Mowachaht with Maurus and Harry pointing frequently at me.

Our team had neither money nor women left to gamble, and Maurus thought we might as well call it a night. A tough night, but a night. Father Frank's proposal, whatever it was, was not accepted. I had no idea where all this was heading. Finally Harry spoke. In English. "I am an old man now and have outlived my own wife. I don't have the energy that I used to have, and I know that it takes a lot of energy to keep up with a young woman. Especially a beautiful one like this. She belongs with a young man. One who can look after her and protect her. So I am giving her back to Mike – after tonight. Just kidding, I give her back now." And so Lynn and I were re-united. Father Frank smiled his broadest Catholic smile, Ray turned the house lights back on and Terry made us all coffee.

5

Burial Cave

*"Terry and I want you to make sure we are put here
when we die."*

Following a night of friendly competition, and potential matrimo-
nial ruin, Ray asked me if I wanted to go for a short boat trip with
him to check out a burial cave. I said, "Of course!" and we set off
right after a breakfast prepared by Terry and Lynn for all of the previous evening's players. We untied Ray's aluminum 'tin boat' and
pushed off under blue skies on a falling morning tide. "Whereabouts
is it?" I asked as Ray started turning north at the cove's entrance.
"Just a few nautical miles up Tahsis Inlet, beyond Bligh Island, on
beyond Boca del Infierno Bay and the old pilchard cannery." So
here we were travelling with a mental map filled with Mowachaht,
English and Spanish names. Ray thought nothing of it; he had been
born into a trilingual Yuquot world.

Ray steered us along the rocky coast he knew so well. "I always
find it funny that visitors to Yuquot mostly come because of Captain
Cook or Vancouver or those Spanish guys. What about coming here
just because it is beautiful or for its Mowachaht-Muchalaht history?
After all, we've lived here for thousands of years. The archaeologists
think Yuquot may have been a village for 8,000 years!" I said that in
my opinion things will gradually change. "Don't forget that people
have been writing about Yuquot since 1778, and the written record
is what creates the history in the first place for most people. There
needs to be more written about our history" Ray said, "You should
start that process by writing a book." I replied that I was thinking
about it.

Up ahead of us was a rocky headland with a few tall Douglas firs on its crown. "We are going ashore there, Michael." It looked like a tough landing. There was no beach to speak of, just a tiny notch in the rocks below one of the big firs. "The tide's still falling, and there's just enough space to pull the bow in over a few rocks," said Ray. I clambered up to the bow and prepared to jump out. The boat crunched softly ashore on some barnacle covered rocks. I jumped out with the painter in hand and climbed up the cliff face about ten feet to the first big fir. "Just tie the line around that fir," shouted Ray. Then Ray and I scampered up the rocks a few more feet to the top of the headland. "Do you see it, Michael?" asked Ray. "What am I looking for?" I replied. "That secret entrance," said Ray pointing at my feet and laughing.

Sure enough, I was standing by a crevice in the rock. It wasn't very big, about one and a half feet square and quite open to the elements. I got down on my hands and knees and looked in. There was a kind of incline plane leading down into a darker chamber. Ray stepped in up to his arms and suddenly disappeared like a seal slipping quietly under the waves. He called up, "Come on down, Michael." I followed him just as he had entered, legs first.

Considerably less gracefully, I found myself groping down a gentle earth slope to a rocky floor. When I had enough room to stand up, I slowly lifted my head. Just then Ray lit a match. We had company. We were standing in a large subterranean cavern, maybe twenty-feet long by ten- feet high. All around us were bent-wood boxes with carved, heavy lids. There were also old chainsaws, sewing machines and kitchen utensils piled up by some of the more recent box burials.

Ray called me over to the one nearest him and opened the lid. Inside was the desiccated, mummified body of an old woman. She was sitting up, with her hands clasping updrawn knees. Her hair was elaborately braided on top of her head. "I don't know this lady, Michael, but part of what Terry and I are doing out here is protecting places like this. We are doing it because these old people have asked us to do it. That is why we cannot leave." All at once, I felt like an intruder, yet strangely okay because Ray was with me. "No one else knows about this burial cave anymore, Michael. Just us." Ray carefully closed the box lid.

After we had climbed out of the cave, Ray asked me why I thought he had brought me there. "To learn more of Mowachaht-Muchalaht history and culture?" I guessed. "That is only part of it, Michael. Terry and I want you to make sure that we are put here when we die." I promised I would do my best.

6

Ray's Cousin Elmer

"You people are here without proper permission."

As it turned out, the August 1977 West Coast Survival course was booked entirely by the University of Berkeley extension department. Somehow they discovered Strathcona Park Lodge and decided to offer this course in their summer-program guide. It sold out. As a result, Lynn and I were required to liaise with Berkeley extension staff about the special needs of elderly, wealthy Californians, most of whom had never been to the true northwest coast. We developed a captain's checklist to ensure that no one forgot to bring essentials like gumboots and rain gear. We modified the stress level, too, situating the course on the reserve at Yuquot instead of Escalante beach. This meant we could work more intensely with Ray and Terry. Everything was acceptable to the Berkeley folk and we were eager to take the guests out on the Uchuck to start proceedings.

Everything went according to plan on day one. The Berkeley group landed at Yuquot and was welcomed by Ray at the wharf. We wheelbarrowed the gear up to the Nootka Island trail, and moved everyone down to the *Ah-Puk-Si* (Jewitt Lake) meadow where we pitched tents and set up a camp kitchen under a canvas rain fly. Lynn was surprised to see one of the guests walk by in oddly, pebble-textured, knee-high boots. She asked the woman where the boots came from. "Well, you asked us to buy gumboots, and these are made of Argentinian chicle gum. It was absolutely hell finding a pair!" Lynn countered that they appeared to be extremely waterproof.

Several of the guests were dealing with major health issues that prohibited any strenuous activity, ruling out day hikes, long Zodiac trips to 'Mexico,' offshore fishing for smileys with Ray, and even portaging canoes into *Ah-Puk-Si*. Consequently the survival element of the course took a big hit. In fact many of the participants said they were happy just to stroll about Yuquot, sketch the totem pole, and lie in the sun. We both hoped the weather would hold so that this option would be successful.

Meals became the big attraction. The first night featured a salmon barbecue cooked by Lynn and Terry. Afterwards Ray took everyone who wanted to go on a short walk to *Mow'enass* spring for a talk about the Whaling Shrine on the island in *Ah-Puk-Si,* where the old Mowachaht whalers went to prepare for the rigours of the whaling season. He also told the story about how his father left his sealing harpoons in a big surf cave by Maquinna Point and how he had been looking for them without luck for several years. After the walk, the group gathered at the camp fire for a talk by me about Maquinna, and the great Mowachaht-Muchalaht chiefdom during the days of Captains George Vancouver and Francisco de la Bodega y Quadra. As darkness fell everyone was able to find their tents, and Lynn and I made one last flashlight round to ensure that the guests were well and secure for the night.

The next morning broke clear and blue with a modest off-shore westerly blowing. We served blackberry pancakes, salal berry bannock, and rosehip tea for breakfast. The day was organized into sketching sessions, archaeology walks, bird watching strolls, Mowachaht-language-for-beginners class and a visit to the Nootka Lighthouse and its proprietors, Ed and Pat Kidder. There was also a do-nothing option for those content to sit and talk or read by the fire. I was actually thankful that Jim wasn't with us because he would go nuts with such a cerebral and quiet group. His natural instincts would probably push him into some provocative activity that would be over the top for this gathering of retired doctors, lawyers and professors. He might also deliver an outburst about his growing irrelevance to the course he had invented and dive into a sulk. All in all, this was a perfect group for Lynn and me to work with alongside Ray and Terry.

The second evening Terry and Lynn again prepared a feast with local foods. They featured Mowachaht steam-pit cookery with beach delicacies like giant blue mussels, butter clams and Japanese oysters. Troll-caught lingcod and red snapper were steamed between layers of kelp on top of red-hot beach cobbles. They also cooked frying-pan bannock over the fire; Terry's blackberry jam was an incredible hit with the diners. Oddly, Ray was missing at dinnertime. Terry said he was busy with something, but that his cousin Elmer had just arrived from Gold River by tin boat and would join us for an after-dinner chat.

Just as Terry's famous blackberry pies were being carefully cut and democratically allocated to plates, Elmer loped into camp. He had on sneakers, black jeans, a white armless T-shirt under a jean jacket and a red bandana around an unruly mop of long, black hair. Wearing dark aviator glasses, he carried a guitar case under one arm. I had never met him before and in fact had never heard him mentioned by either Ray or Terry. He came over to me and said, "I'm Elmer. Who are you?" I introduced Lynn and the group from California. Elmer nodded in everyone's direction during the introductions and then sat down to my right at the fire. He exuded a strange air of menace. As the group ate their pie in silence, he began to talk.

"You people are here without proper permission. Chief and council don't know you are on our reserve and you haven't paid our fees. You're also eating beach foods from our chiefdom without our permission. I'm surprised at your rudeness. Your attitude is just like all those of your tribe who come here to the place you must call Yuquot. I don't want to hear any more "Friendly Coves" from any of you. That name was given to us by our colonizers. We never use it. So stop right now. Also, you must leave tomorrow. I know the Uchuck won't be here for you, so you will have to go in tin boats back to Gold River. I want you packed up and gone right after breakfast. Is what I say clear to you all?"

I sat there stunned. Terry looked down at her lap. The guests were downcast. No one spoke a word. I tried to respond by explaining how Strathcona had worked for years with Ray and Terry. Before I could get any words out, Elmer spoke over me.

"All of you, bow your heads in shame for your actions. I want you to sing along with me to an old Muchalaht tune: your part is the chorus, it goes 'heh, heh, heh, heh; heh, heh, heh, heh.' Now start that chant and I'll sing along." Without hesitation, we all started the chorus as directed. Elmer took his guitar out of its case and started to strum and sing, "Heh, good lookin', what ya got cookin'? How about cookin' something up with me?"

All of a sudden the bandana and long hair came off; it was a wig. Underneath the aviators was Ray. Terry broke out laughing. Ray smiled his broadest grin. Stony faces melted into laughter as the group's discomfort at being labelled neo-colonialists faded. The group's mood made a tectonic shift. "I sure got you guys! Especially Mike! You looked really guilty!" Ray was being the trickster. His hereditary role in the Yuquot-Tahsis Muchalaht chiefdom is speaker for his chief, and he was a consummate speaker, capable of eloquence, humour, ridicule, diplomacy and thunder at the drop of a hat. I had never seen his skills so masterfully deployed. "You got me good, Ray, I was completely convinced that we would have to head back up the inlet tomorrow morning towards Strathcona." "Well, you don't, Mike! Let's have some of Terry's blackberry pie, and I'll sing you guys some songs from the good old days when Elvis was the King of rock 'n' roll."

7

Cook the Captain!

"Getting to know you has been very hard for us"

It was a typical soggy Vancouver afternoon in February 1978 when Ray phoned from the bus station. "Hi Michael. Do you recognize my voice?" I could tell it was Ray, and asked where he was. "Terry and I are here in Vancouver. Ambrose Maquinna, our chief, asked me to speak at the Museum of Anthropology tomorrow. Is it okay if we stay with you tonight?" "Of course it is, Ray. I'll come and get you."

I drove off to the downtown bus depot in my little red Datsun 510, wondering about how this visit would impact my law studies over the weekend. Third year mid-terms were approaching and I was planning on revising tax law all day Saturday at least. I had no idea about any event at the University of British Columbia Museum of Anthropology. Ray and Terry were waiting at the curb as I approached. They had a big suitcase and were dressed differently from anything I had ever seen them wearing at Yuquot. Terry had on a fashionable purple dress with a cloth coat on top; Ray was wearing a grey suit, white shirt and tie with his dark aviator glasses. They were excited to see me and to be in town.

"Where's Lynn?" Terry asked. "She's in architecture school in Calgary," I explained. "That must be tough for you guys to be married and be apart," she replied. I said that it was, but soon we would be together when I graduated in June. As we drove back to my basement suite in Dunbar, Ray explained more about their trip. "It is my job to speak for our chief on special occasions like this, Michael. The guys at the museum sent him a fancy invitation to the Captain

James Cook Bicentenary exhibit they had curated. Is that how you say it?" "Yup," I replied. "Anyways, we aren't too happy about the whole thing."

I could imagine why. There was always a big deal made about Captain Cook's landfall at 'Friendly Cove,' and his 'discovery' of the Pacific Northwest in 1778. We used to joke about it in the West Coast Survival course at Strathcona. Jim Boulding enjoyed pretending to be Cook during my beach talks, and to exclaim in a mock British accent: "Hello Maquinna, do you have a nice flag? No? Why, then let me give you this one!" as he rammed a Union Jack into the sand, and claimed everything for King George III. This was, of course, very funny but it also set the stage for one of Ray's talks about how lost, hungry and thirsty the sailors were on that fateful day. "Our people took them in, gave them fresh fish and water and explained about the best places to anchor while the crews rested up. Chief Maquinna came aboard Cook's big ship, the Resolution, and called him a *Mumuk'ne,* the term we still use for you guys today. It means 'people who live on floating islands.' We thought it was very strange there were no women on board. And we were scared by some of the crewmen. One guy had a very red big nose and a hunchback. We thought he was the ghost spirit of Dog Salmon. Another guy had a very shiny plate and was eating blood and bones off it. We thought he must be a spirit too because he had a star for a plate and was eating human flesh. I guess he was just eating jam and hard tack off a tin pie plate. It was also funny that all of Cook's minor chiefs wore white powdered wigs on their heads. We wondered why they all had white hair so young."

We finally arrived at my place, a modest basement suite. As we walked in I thought about how little food was in the house. I offered to make them boiled eggs, toast and tea. It was a far cry from what they always offered me at Yuquot. But it would have to do. I made dinner and we talked about the event tomorrow. Terry said, "Ray has worked on a real good speech that will explain how our chief feels." Ray continued, "The last two-hundred years haven't been good for us. You know this. Other people need to hear our story. After Captain Cook many very bad sailors came who abused our women and took our wealth away from us. We started with kindness, but soon we realized that we had to fight them. That is why we captured John Jewitt and his friend (John) Thompson after putting to death all the rest of Captain (John) Salter's crew. And the troubles continued. You know, the residential schools, diseases, racism, kicking us out of Yuquot." I was familiar with this story, and was already imagining what tomorrow held in store. After dinner and much laughter at the retelling of the story about me nearly losing Lynn to Harry Dick in the slahal game last summer, I gave Ray and Terry my bed and went to sleep on a foamy on the living room floor.

The next morning the rain was coming down in drenching sheets as I rose to make tea. Toast and peanut butter was all I had for breakfast. Ray and Terry came into the kitchen already dressed for the museum. Ray had slicked down his hair, and wore his aviator glasses as he drank his tea. Terry was very quiet, thinking of what was about to happen. I tried to be helpful, explaining the way museum openings worked and speculating who would be on the podium as special guests. Ray got out the chief's invitation. It said the ribbon cutting would take place at 1:30 p.m. We had a few hours to kill, so I offered to take them around Stanley Park.

We all climbed into my little Datsun and started off through Dunbar to the Burrard Bridge. It was only then I realized that this was their first time in Vancouver. They were both concerned about crossing the bridge and surprised at how tall the apartment buildings were in English Bay. Ray thought all the little balconies were like the nests of cliff swallows. "What do all these people do?" he asked. Terry was still very quiet. At one point as we stopped for a red light she turned to me and said, "Look at all the people staring at me because I am an Indian." I didn't know how to reply.

Stanley Park was a big hit because of the presence of so much nature in the heart of the city. The hollow tree was remarkable because there was one like it near the lagoon back home. The totem poles were strange because they were lavishly painted odd colours and placed well back from the beach in a parking lot. "Who owns those poles?" asked Ray. I said I thought they belonged to the parks board. "What tribe are they, Mike?" he joked. "My tribe," I said. On we went past the swimming pool at Third Beach, and Ray asked why people don't swim in the ocean. Another good question.

Finally we circled the park and headed back to UBC and the museum. Both Ray and Terry closed their eyes for a little nap. I was acutely embarrassed that we hadn't had lunch after so meagre a breakfast. I promised myself we would go to a restaurant after the opening was over. It would blow the week's food budget, but what the hell. How often were Ray and Terry my guests? I pulled into the museum parking lot where there were very few spots left. I ended up next to a CBC-TV satellite truck with all sorts of electrical cords and wires running into the building. We got out of the Datsun and straightened out our clothes for the grand entrance. Ray went first, followed by Terry. I went last, my head now full of potential outcomes for what was about to happen. They ranged across a spectrum covering everything from official upset to arrests for disturbing the peace. I looked at my watch. It was 1:30.

We pressed on to the big front doors which Ray was already holding open. He then marched up to the ticket counter and said that we were here for the Captain Cook opening. The young woman minding the entry asked: "Are you members?" Ray said he was "a member of the Mowachaht-Muchalaht Tribe, and speaker for Chief Ambrose Maquinna." The young woman looked puzzled. "If you are not members, it will cost eight dollars each to go into the museum, but you can't go into the great hall right now because we are having a members-and-guests-only opening." That did it. Ray fumbled for his invitation, but it was back in the car. "My grandmother's baskets are in this museum, and so are Terry's mother's. And lots of our peoples' artifacts. We are not paying to see our stuff. We are just going in. Please do not try and stop us." In he marched with Terry at his side. I followed with a sheepish look and a vague awareness that none of my family's stuff was in the museum. There was no turning back now.

Ray sat in the last row of chairs in the great hall. There were only three seats left. A few heads turned to look at us. I quickly scanned the audience. There were no other First Nations people present, but all of the city's elite were there. The minister of tourism was on the podium resplendent in a canary yellow suit and a mountain of back-swept, dyed-red hair. Beside her was the university president, and flanking them both were the mayor, the director of the museum, the chief curator of the exhibit, and the British consul general for Vancouver. The audience was packed with philanthropists, bureaucrats, assorted well-to-do professors and what I guessed to be a few history and anthropology graduate students. The chief curator was at the microphone extolling "the help of the British Museum in loaning a wonderful collection of artifacts from Friendly Cove collected by Captain James Cook during his re-provisioning sojourn in the spring of 1778." On and on he went. Ray muttered to me under his breath, "He makes me mad using the term our colonizers use for Yuquot." All of a sudden Ray was becoming Elmer again. Terry went very still, looking intently at the stage, the podium, the suits and the pomp. I was tingling with anticipation of what was about to happen.

After the curatorial speech, the president rose with a pair of shiny silver scissors, and the mayor and the museum director spooled out a gold ribbon for the consul general and the minister to cut. In anticipation, there was a general clearing of throats and shuffling of feet. Just then Ray stood up, squared his shoulders and walked down the aisle to the stage. I have never seen him more in control of a situation. He rose up the steps and walked to the podium. He clasped both sides of the lectern to brace himself and looked out upon a sea of curious faces. The mayor and the museum director let the gold ribbon billow to the floor. The minister and the consul general backed away from the centre of the stage. Ray began to speak in a clear and resonant tone he reserved for ceremonies and other serious occasions.

"Honoured guests, all the people on the podium, people in the audience who travelled a long time to get here, I am Raymond

Williams, speaker for Chief Ambrose Maquinna of the Mowa-chaht-Muchalaht people of Yuquot. As I look from this lectern I can only see one other person here from Yuquot, my wife Terry Williams. Listen carefully to what I have to say. I hope it will make you think about your ways and about your history with my people. We do not praise Captain Cook as a hero like you do. We see him as a colonizer who was blown to our village in 1778, two-hundred years ago. His men were on their last legs, hungry for fresh meat, thirsty for good water, and with many repairs to make to their two ships. Our Chief Maquinna Ambrose, the present day chief's long ago family relative, gave those people everything they asked for. We saved them from starvation and the pain of thirst. Chief Maquinna even gave Captain Cook his best six-pelt sea-otter robe as a gift. They were welcome in our homes and received kindnesses even from our slaves. And what did we get in return? The sea-otter trade brought many boats to our chiefdom and your people became meaner and meaner. They took and took until the sea otter was nearly extinct, and they gave us your horrible diseases. I even forget all the names for these terrible dis-eases. We went from being strong people in our own land, to a weak people in your land. How did this happen? We showed you gener-osity of spirit. You gave us residential schools and took our children from their mothers and fathers. You washed out our mouths with soap for speaking our language. The nuns and priests did unkind things to our younger brothers and sisters. Getting to know you has been very hard for us.

"So, pardon me if I am angry and not happy today when you come together in this nice building to celebrate the captain. The Mowachaht today say, "Cook the captain!" If he was to come again to the village of Yuquot where I live, I would not invite him ashore knowing what I know now. I would tell him to go somewhere else. When Terry and Mike came in here with me today, the young woman at the front door – I don't exactly know what you call her – asked us for eight dollars to come in. I told her that Terry and my relatives have made artifacts that are on display in this museum. I don't think we should have to pay to see these things our mothers and grandmothers made. And if we want to bring our friend in here, we should be able to get him in for free. And another thing, I want to know how the British Museum got all these artifacts that the curator guy was talking about. Those things are all from my village of Yuquot. Why were they taken away? Who said you could have them? Why can't they all be sent home where they belong? I can feel the spirits of these objects crying out for help.

"I also want to say that when you have a big party like this with all of our peoples' artifacts on display you should invite more than just our Chief Ambrose Maquinna. I thought we taught you how to be generous of spirit back in 1778. It seems you have forgotten the lessons we gave you. Terry and I had to pay our own money to come here. Where are our children in these seats in front of me? Not one student from our village is here to see these things. I hope you will think about what I have said. I am not going to stay for the tours. I may come back another day. Okay, Mike, it is time for us to go."

Ray walked to the back of the hall with all eyes upon him. Terry and I got up and followed him out through the lobby chased by radio, television and print reporters intent on a story. I looked back at the podium one last time and it was chaos. The poor chief curator was a wreck. The minister of tourism looked as though she wanted to be on a tour out of there. The president looked mortified. The museum director was furious. The British consul looked confused. The mayor had disappeared. We headed out into blossoming sunshine in the parking lot. The rain had finally stopped. I helped Ray and Terry into the car. For some reason they both got into the back seat. A radio guy stuck a microphone in my face. "Did you organize this?" he asked. "Nope. I'm just the driver," I replied. Ray said, "Michael, let's go back to your place for lunch." I looked at my watch: it was 2:30. We had accomplished quite a lot in an hour.

On the way back to my basement suite I suggested Italian food. Ray said, "Terry and I have never had it. But if you think we would like it, we'll have it." So we went to a little Italian place in Kitsilano Beach and had lasagna. I was so happy to be able to provide a decent dinner after my pathetic failure the previous night.

Today when Ray and Terry jointly tell this story, it usually starts with the opening: "This is a story about when Michael was poor and he gave us his last food to eat." When Lynn hears the story, she wonders why I didn't go shopping before my guests arrived. I blame my situation on the stress of studying for my tax exam. And, irony of ironies, I aced the damn thing. Strangely, when I now think back on law school, tax looms in my memory as my favourite course. How did that ever happen?

8

Crossing Cumshewa Inlet to Skedans

Lynn was already one hundred yards into her crossing

After I finally graduated from law school in June, 1978, I asked Lynn if she wanted to kayak into the Moresby archipelago in Haida Gwaii (then known as the south end of the Queen Charlotte Islands). I had gone logging in the Charlottes after high school in 1969 and had always wanted to kayak to the old Haida villages of Cumshewa, Skedans, Tanu, and S'kung Gwaii. Somehow, of all the Northwest Coast cultures I had studied, these villages possessed an uncanny lure, perhaps because of their abandonment after the epidemics caused by contact with Europeans and their still vibrant collections of standing totem poles and massive house pits. Luckily, an old school friend, Dave Ellis, had moved to Queen Charlotte City to work on preserving the Haida language and he was now making a living as a commercial fisherman. He had recently returned from kayaking "down south" with his wife Eileen, and had annotated charts and kayak gear to loan us. Before thinking about finding jobs, Lynn and I flew north for an adventure.

Dave and Eileen met us at the Sandspit Airport. They were happy to see us and pleasantly unconcerned about our plans compared to parents and friends in Vancouver who thought we were risking our skins by travelling somewhere no one had gone in kayaks. Technically they were wrong. By 1978 at least a hundred kayakers had "gone south," the very vanguard of the northwest-coast kayaking culture just starting on Vancouver Island and the Gulf Islands. Dave was one of the first and his advice and counsel were just what we needed. The only real problem was that Lynn had never been in a

kayak before. We fixed that by heading down to the Queen Charlotte City government wharf on our second morning with the Ellis
family. Dave and I slipped a kayak in the water, helped Lynn climb
aboard, passed her a paddle and gently pushed her out to sea. "It's
sort of like cross country skiing, Lynn. It's all in the rhythm of the
stroke," I called from the wharf. If Lynn heard, she didn't acknowledge me. She was already lost in a kayak reverie.

Using our Strathcona Park Lodge planning skills, we pored over
'captain's check lists,' double-bagged our dry clothes, organized
meals down to the day, packed quick-drying Polar Guard sleeping
bags, our classic Jones Tent and Awning pup tent and its waterproof
fly, stored charts in a plastic map tube, first aid in waterproof containers for both boats, and a fibreglass repair kit just in case we hit
a rock. Dave warned us to carry lots of water as paradoxically it was
often hard to find in the high summer rain forest. We filled four
large plastic pop bottles with tap water in the Ellis kitchen. The final
gift Dave gave us was a detailed review of his annotated trip charts.
On our hands and knees in his living room, we rolled out three
charts, cluttered with penned comments and observations. "Rip tide
here … watch out!" "Big black bear in the creek fishing." "Kunga
Island has Norwegian rats." "Good place to jig for cod." "Check
out the fluting on the house posts here." "Emily Carr sat here and
painted." When we had finished asking questions it was time for
bed. We could hardly wait to get going.

Just before noon the next day, David, Lynn and I unloaded the
kayaks and gear from the Ellis family's old Toyota pickup just south
of the Sandspit Airport on the golf-course road. The beach was in
front of us, the South Moresby wilderness area stretched away to the
south. David said: "Goodbye, please return and have a good trip."
That was it. So we packed and launched our kayaks determined to
survive and return. It was calm and hot out on the water. We took a
couple of hours to settle into a rhythmic cadence in which we managed to keep together and to travel at a reasonable pace. Strangely,
I don't remember much of the first day's paddling. I think we were
both keeping our eyes in the boats and trying to hone our very basic

skills. The first chart we had reviewed with David showed a good campsite at Gray Bay. We pulled up onto its mixed sand and shingle beach in the late afternoon. I carried the gear from the kayaks to make camp while Lynn set about gathering wood for a cooking fire – a routine we followed at every camp on this trip.

Once the little canvas tent was up and covered with its tight rain fly, I headed back to the beach to find Lynn. She was a long way down the curve of the bay combing for wood. As I watched her walking away from me, a good-sized black bear ambled out of the forest onto the beach between us. For some reason I had expected this to happen. I pulled my bear whistle out of my shorts pocket and gave it a long tweet. Both Lynn and the bear turned immediately to look at me. Lynn began to talk in a loud voice. "Hello, Mr. Bear. Hello." I blew another couple of ear-splitting blasts. The bear looked at me again, turned and strolled back to the forest, showing us that he was in no hurry. Lynn walked back to our campsite and we heaped wood on the fire to make a human statement. She cooked the least smelly meal possible: rice, turnips and noodles. We each had a shot of over-proof Hudson's Bay rum and checked out the chart for tomorrow's paddle. "Let's try for Skedans," suggested Lynn. According to the chart it was a run of about ten nautical miles. The biggest challenge would be crossing Cumshewa Inlet's mouth, about a four-mile pull. I agreed, secretly hoping I'd be up to it. There were no other boats or people in sight and we'd be totally reliant on our own abilities and resources. I thought to myself, "It can't be any worse than three bloody years of law school."

We broke camp early and settled into our boats for the morning's paddle. We both had full water bottles in our laps because it was another scorcher of a day. The wind was blowing low out of the west and the tide was falling as we began our trip to Cumshewa Head, the rocky northern headland that defines the entrance to Cumshewa Inlet. A little in front of me and to my right Lynn was paddling through the growing clumps of inshore kelp. To the east the sky was blue most of the way across Hecate Strait. Patches of high-blown cumulus clouds rose on the horizon. The important thing was that they did not seem to be moving towards us. It was that rare commodity, a perfect Queen Charlotte's day. Terns and gulls wheeled overhead and every so often a seal appeared amidst the kelp bulbs in our path.

I paused and looked shoreward into the forest. The loggers hadn't cut this old-growth Sitka spruce yet and the understory was uncluttered with brush to block the view. Beneath the branches the forest floor was green and open, punctuated with rare shafts of sun and overhung with drapes of moss. Every dark space we passed suggested an abandoned village or fortification site. Big Haida ravens glided through these openings calling back and forth in hoarse croaks. The audible swishing of their black wings was becoming a familiar sound. High above the spruce tops the bald eagles soared, riding the thermals that took them far offshore and back again. If you focused on one eagle, your eyes would soon find several more hang-gliding nearby on outstretched wings.

I looked down into the clean waters. You could easily see to a depth of about twenty feet. The ocean floor was even more richly populated than the forest. Schools of anchovies and shiner perch passed slowly beneath the kayaks. Sea cucumbers lay fastened to undersea cliffs amidst hundreds of invading sea urchins. Gooseneck barnacles and mytilus californianus mussels crowded each other for a perch near the low tide line. Red, orange, and yellow starfish and green sea anemones radiated colour from the seabed. Small horned grebes were diving from the surface and swam open-billed into the passing schools of silver fish. We were paddling through a visual feast.

By 10 a.m. the sun was so hot that we had to take off our floater jackets. We doubled them up to use as back rests. Out from their top-most place in the packs came our baseball caps to ward off sunstroke and to shade our eyes from the glare. We were now becoming aware of the surge of tide and backwash off Cumshewa Head, just two hundred yards in front of our bows. This was the first spot David had warned us about when we were consulting the charts in Queen Charlotte City. "Make sure you cross the inlet with wind and tide behind you flowing south. The rising flood tide can easily move at two knots, and a strong southeaster will blow you backwards," he said. "Crossing Cumshewa against wind and tide might kill you. Crossing Cumshewa with wind and tide opposed has killed people. So pick your crossing time carefully. Read the weather first." I noted that our chart had little rectangles of zig-zag lines right off the head. The definition of this symbol wasn't included in the chart's key. I had asked David what it meant: "Oh yes – rip tides. In a really good one, the waves will stand on end. Prime conditions for a rip are a falling ebb tide and strong southeast wind. Stay off the water in those conditions."

With David's words ringing in my ears, we cautiously approached the long profile of Cumshewa Head that signalled we had reached the mouth of the inlet. We paddled around the head into a monster bull-kelp patch that served to smooth the surface of the water. Lynn laughed as the bulbs banged against the hull of the Queen of Tsawwassen, her new kayak's name. Looking due south we could see the Skedans panhandle reaching east from the steep bulk of Mount Carl on Louise Island. We could also see a good fifteen miles west up the inlet, right to Newcombe Peak. It was calm and flat. The southeaster was nowhere to be seen. For the first time since launching at Sandspit we could also see old and new logging scars. I quickly glanced at my plastic chart case and suggested a stop at Kunhalas for lunch. David had marked it in pen on our chart as "an interesting place to stop for a break at half-tide or better." Given the tide was clearly falling, we'd have to move quickly to take advantage of his advice. David further noted that Kunhalas is the Haida word for 'hole in the nose' or nostril, and it appeared to be the nostril to Cumshewa Head's nose.

Finding Kunhalas proved a bit tricky. We paddled along a rocky headland until suddenly a ten-foot-wide gap appeared in the steep shoreline. We turned into the gap and paddled hard to negotiate the rollicking tidal surge in the passage. After about thirty feet, the passage opened out into a much larger enclosed bay. The tide was falling fast and I knew lunch would have to be quick. The beach was angled very sharply up to a line of spruce and fir. We came ashore, got out and stretched our backs because we were already discovering the only major drawback to kayak travel: sore lower backs. Because our water was running low, we searched the area for a water source. If it exists, we could not find it. We'd have to fill up at Skedans. Temporarily forgetting our thirst, we walked into the forest. Almost immediately a large house pit opened up in front of us. Stretched down the middle of the forty-foot-square house was the fallen, rotting remnant of a house pole. In the complex society of the Haida, the pole signalled a village belonging to the Eagle moiety. All Haida identify as either an Eagle or a Raven and within those halves, or moieties, there are numerous clans. And, my Haida friends tell me, that an Eagle may not marry another Eagle, and the same for Ravens, ensuring that no one sets up house with someone from their immediate bloodline. Back to the pole, we could just barely make out the vague face of a bear cub on the pole. As I walked its length, I noticed a sawn stump at the base. Many years ago it had been cut down like a tree in a logger's forest. We thought of the first missionaries and totem-pole-collecting museum curators and wondered who had lifted it from its home.

Up behind the house was a sunlit clearing. Hundreds of slim, light-green nettles jostled for space here on what once must have been a garden plot. Its edges were piled with stones culled from the rich, black midden soil. This was probably one of the potato patches where Haida women grew crops that were often traded with the visiting Europeans. All around us edible plants pressed in on the small village site. Bushes of ripening rose hips and vines of salmon berries interwove with blackberries, thimbleberries and crabapple trees. Further up the slope enormous huckleberries hung from ten-foot thickets and at their feet salal-berry bushes fought for a share of the sunlight. At the top of the slope where the forest enclosed and darkened the ground, the food plants came to an abrupt stop. There were so many clustered around Kunhalas, it seemed they had been cultivated like potatoes, at least through selective weeding and removal of the forest cover. What a rich place!

After eating hardtack and peanut butter and many handfuls of berries, it was time to push off. The tide was way down the beach and the sun was high in the sky. We hauled the kayaks to the water's edge and slipped away. It was time to cross the inlet. This meant it was also time to deal with my growing fears. Lynn paddled strongly out of the Kunhalas nostril and waited a few yards off shore for my exit. I stroked out into a still calm inlet. Skedans was now a shimmering blue hump on the southern horizon about four miles away. We had never crossed so much open water before. I thought about chickening out and paddling up Cumshewa Inlet and around to Skedans by the 'back door' via Carmichael Passage and Selwyn Inlet.

Just then I looked up and saw that Lynn was already a hundred yards into the crossing. That was it. I had to go; she'd made her mind up for me. As we moved offshore, a slight swell developed, but the sun continued burning a hole in the blue sky. The tidal current ran smoothly out of the inlet and David's conditions for a safe crossing were all met. As we reached mid-inlet, Lynn rested her paddle on the gunwales and stretched her back. She trailed her hands in the water and stared skyward. She almost looked as though she was sleeping. I caught up and demanded that we continue before riptides, southeasters and flood tides asserted themselves. She told me to relax. I too stopped and feigned relaxation. Underneath my façade I was as stressed as ever.

Slowly Lynn began to paddle on. I slapped the water with my paddle and scanned the Skedans shoreline for a big Douglas fir that I could set my course by. I chose one and began to paddle in a straight line towards it. I called to Lynn to do the same. I hoped the tree would act like a magnet and pull us into Skedans by magic. We paddled and paddled for several minutes, but for some reason I was sure we were making no headway. Could we be locked in some form of Skedans doldrums where progress was impossible?

New varieties of fears and disasters loomed in my mind. I wondered if the two of us could ever upright an overturned kayak in mid-inlet. Water began trickling down the paddle shaft and into my lap. It seemed to be getting colder. But over to my left Lynn was paddling calmly along with a contented smile on her face. I looked up at my fir and I realized it was getting closer. Suddenly my fears melted away. We were now more than half-way to Skedans. With each paddle thrust, my magic Douglas fir came more sharply into focus.

We knew we were almost there when another massive kelp raft loomed dead ahead attached to Skedans reef. The kelp bulbs began their familiar bob-banging against the quarter-inch of plastic that kept us dry as we moved across the water's surface. Once again terns, gulls, loons and black sea ducks flocked in large numbers. I estimated we were about one nautical mile west of Skedans Point and one hundred yards from shore. We could paddle the rest of the way inside the lee of the kelp line, and even if the wind did pick up, we'd be guaranteed a safe arrival. We had made our first big, open-ocean crossing in just over two hours. Without hesitation I agreed to push on to Skedans without a rest stop.

The shoreline we were travelling alongside was shaded by Mount Carl, named after a deceased director of the British Columbia Provincial Museum in Victoria. I had done archaeological-site surveys with his son, Alan, a few years before and I thought of their family as we moved along the rocky headlands. Somehow the sense of isolation lifted as we paddled – the landscape now had human connections. The temperature was falling and we glided to a stop to put on sweaters. While we were doing this, the kayaks mysteriously drew together and gently collided. We would experience this several times and grew to think of it as a rule of nature – kayaks attract kayaks. Stronger forces were also at play now. An urgent feeling of discovery was pulling us through the water.

The village of Skedans was located just around the point and in my mind's eye it was still as it appeared in George Mercer Dawson's photograph of 1878. I visualized twenty-seven big plank houses ringing the protected canoe beach. Somehow I conjured up sprays of yellow-orange sparks rising from the smoke holes and halibut strips drying on racks by the beach. It was not ruins we envisaged as we approached the final kayak turn into Skedans Bay. Before we rounded Skedans point we saw the watchmen – two mature bald eagles hunched on black-rock outcrops. Their wary eyes turned on us silently as we stroked past their perch.

As I turned to face Skedans, I saw a small cluster of crabapple trees on the point. When the bluff above the village came into view we could see it had recently been logged. There was a small island off the mouth of the bay with common murres scrambling up its rocky face to the safety of their nesting caves. And then – there it was. Our first view of Skedans covered only the far western part of the crescent beach. Two weather-bleached mortuary columns leaned forward in greeting. A half dozen more paddle strokes and we were in the centre of the bay. Skedans, or Grizzly-Bear Town, as the Haida call it, even though now there are only black bears in Haida Gwaii, was all around us. We could glimpse poles through the spruce trees. The plank houses had collapsed and were rotting in their excavated and now enveloping interiors. But so many beautiful silver poles still stood watch in the encroaching forest. Only a few were upright; most had yielded to the southeasters that whistle up from Lyell Island and over Laskeek Bay. The struggle to remain aloft continued, however, and it was wonderful that so many poles remained to bear witness to Chief Skedans and his people.

We paddled quietly to the beach and ran the kayak bows up onto finely rolled gravel. We got out, stood up and stretched for the first time in nearly three hours. Conscious of our responsibility as guests we walked up the beach and climbed over piles of driftwood at the high-tide line. As soon as we entered the forest we saw deep house pits fronting onto a green-grass street. House followed house in ranked order, declining from the centre in both directions around the sweep of the beach. Hand adzed corner posts and massive six-sided roof beams were jumbled in and over the house pit excavations. We bent on hands and knees and looked under a twenty-foot, by three-foot, by eight-inch thick cedar house plank. The underside was bone dry and traces of red ochre remained to reveal the secondary formline of a painted design. Rows of carefully placed adze strokes marched down its length. At the front of many house pits, huge cedar mortuary columns rose up to hold the dead aloft. Most of their ornately carved front plates had broken off, exposing hollowed out interiors where the highly ranked had been placed in death. One of these columns was fluted along its entire length, completely altering the perception that it had once been a cedar tree. Now it looked like a Greek column standing alone after the rest of the temple had fallen.

We decided to walk along the front trail to the base of the bluffs to look for water. We also had to think about making camp, as it was getting on for 5 p.m. Before long, we were at the side of a recently fallen pole. The major crest at its base was Grizzly Bear of the Sea. Two rows of bared teeth smiled upwards from a broad lipped mouth. Two ovoid Haida eyes stared up at the clouded sky. Rows of small adze marks were visible throughout the design. They were the tiny, measured signatures of a great carver. Even when fallen, his work had the dignity of a masterpiece.

It was puzzling that so much beauty was rotting in Skedans. But as we continued walking beside the poles, we began to understand that this is where they belong. In every sense they were born of Skedans and had lived long lives there. Now the tall poles and square depressions were all that remained of the human history of this place. If they were carefully salvaged and hermetically sealed in some museum they would lose their real meaning. Just as they were the heart of the living place, they remain its heart in death.

In the very middle of the village we stood before an incredible house pit. Lynn recognized it as the remains of The House So Big The Clouds Sound Against It As They Pass Over, described by anthropologist J.R. Swanton of the Jessup North Pacific Expedition some ninety years before our arrival in Skedans. We thanked him out loud for his scholarly diligence and climbed down four banked tiers to the firepit floor. Along the external walls the house was forty paces square and it was easily fifteen-feet deep at its centre point, the firepit. The remains of six-inch thick cedar planks still sheathed the tier walls. Some of them were four-feet wide and twenty-feet long. They had been split like roof shakes from a single cedar tree. We sat down on the mossy floor and imagined a howling southeaster driving rain clouds against the walls and roof so that we heard them bumping on the planks and echoing out over Cumshewa Inlet to Kunhalas.

After a few minutes silence, we climbed out of the great house and paused by the remains of an adjacent mortuary pole. Two white skulls lay at our feet. Both had tumbled from their burial boxes when the front plate had rotted away and fallen to the ground. A gentle fringe of moss was creeping over their scalps like a new growth of hair. Their hollow eyes stared upwards towards the sky. Our minds went back to Dawson in 1878. In that year he reported that sixteen houses were still occupied in Skedans. By 1888 a few survivors were packing their belongings to move north to the village of Skidegate, where the Haida diaspora of the smallpox holocaust was gathering. Ninety years later the village had fallen silent.

We finally found a little well at the base of the bluffs on the very edge of the village and refilled our water bottles. How odd that the rainforest should have so little water. We walked out of the village just in time to find gentle waves lapping at the kayaks. We'd have to be more careful in the future. Looking south we could see lots more interesting country: Limestone and Reef Islands, Vertical Point, Kunga Island, and in the distance Lyell Island, the last stand of the clear-cut loggers. It felt as if we should leave and camp somewhere down there. David, our reliable source of local knowledge, said there was a provincial government fisheries cabin at the mouth of Skedans Creek, so we climbed into the kayaks, pushed off with our hands and said goodbye to Skedans.

As we slowly paddled our way out of the bay we heard twigs snapping in the forest as a black bear walked along his street trail to the crabapple trees on the point. All around him the grizzly bear crests looked down in approval.

9

Kunga-House Logbook

"Glad to see Terry Jacks was constipated this year"

We camped that second night at the Skedans Creek fisheries cabin. It was a good thing too because it poured all night. Lynn and I slept soundly on a spring mattress in our Polarguard sleeping bags. In the morning we awakened to the grandmother of all low tides. We'd have to carry the boats a good three-hundred yards to put them in the chuck. I kindled a fire and we made tea and porridge. Afterwards Lynn had a sponge bath with hot water. It was a cooler than yesterday and by the time we launched the kayaks it was halfway through the morning. We decided to push on to Vertical Point where David reported there was another tiny cabin belonging to the local artist Bonita Saunders. Given that yesterday we had travelled ten nautical miles, today we would only paddle about three.

Limestone Island was our first port of call, or rather passing call. It was surrounded by formidable cliffs and reefs and was also posted off limits as it is a nesting colony for ancient murrelets. Our bird book said these small alcids have floppy white tufts that extend back from their eyes like the bushy eyebrows of an old man. They apparently nest in burrows at the base of old-growth spruce and firs. I say apparently because we didn't see any. They probably didn't see us either, because the adults exchange incubation duties at night and the chicks race into the ocean to feed two days after hatching. Then there was the fact that when we paddled by it was no longer nesting season. After nesting, the ancient murrelets spend their lives at sea which is where they are in August.

We paddled on to Vertical Point, another limestone outcrop, this time on the southeast corner of Louise Island. We followed David's instructions to round the point and tuck in behind the little forested island. As we cleared the island the rain began to fall. Directly in front of us we spied a little cedar-shake cabin in a clearing exactly where David said it would be. We left the kayaks on a perfect canoe beach, and in front of us was another old Haida potato patch surrounded, predictably, by every kind of edible plant. Behind the old garden was the cabin. Bonita Saunders had crafted a simple retreat in a south-facing location on the mouth of Selwyn Inlet. It was an esthetic gem. I went up to the screen door of the small porch. Inside was a homemade driftwood table and chair. The cabin proper was one room with a sleeping bench that doubled as the table. There was one window facing the sun and the water and one more chair. A little airtight stove completed the furnishings. All-told the interior space was about eight feet by six feet, some forty-eight square feet of living space. Candles supplied the light and a few paperbacks abandoned by other kayakers lined a single shelf; notable were Ayn Rand's Atlas Shrugged and The Fountainhead. We couldn't have asked for more because the rain started pounding down in earnest. I carried up the gear and Lynn started the fire in the stove. The adjacent wood box was full of dry cedar kindling and split blocks of pitchy fir were neatly stacked on the porch. After a last check of the beach I overturned the kayaks and ran up the path to the house just in time for hot tea. We both came out and sat on the porch. It was 4 p.m.

The evening came on sooner than expected as the storm grew in intensity. Sure enough, it was our friend the southeaster. "Let it howl and blow," I said as the heat built in the little firebox and I began Atlas Shrugged. Lynn had the rice on and was mixing tinned tuna with tomato soup. We had our rum early and thought about a Mars bar for dessert. It was bliss at Vertical Point cabin. Outside the rain sheeted down. Our tent would have been bloody miserable. How would we ever have kept dry outside in conditions like these with our clammy rain gear and open kayaks? It was worth some thought because we would run out of cabins as we headed south. As far as we knew, only Kunga House remained for our use as we moved on down the archipelago.

Once again my fertile mind began to wander. On the plane coming up I had sat next to a Canadian Coast Guard member about to return to duty at Sandspit. He chatted away about his last two-week shift when his team had seen what they were sure was a great white shark in Selwyn Inlet. "You know, it's the deepest inlet in the Charlottes, and lots of big critters go in there," he said. Delightful news. We would cross the inlet tomorrow as we headed south to Tanu and Kunga House. Right now in my mind's eye I could see the crescent shape of the great white's dorsal fin cutting through the waters. I imagined what a kayak would look like from below as it moved over the surface. Very like a big, slow sea turtle muddling its way to somewhere. And don't great whites eat sea turtles? Of course they do. They are probably the staple of their diet. Ye gods. I tried to focus on Ayn Rand, but I was having a hard time with her extremely selfish agenda.

We ate dinner on the porch and watched the grey clouds swirl over the entrance to Selwyn Inlet. The rain was approaching tropical-deluge proportions and we mentally thanked David over and over again for recommending this retreat. It was pointless to go for a walk, so after dinner we got out the drawing materials and sketched each other, the little island offshore and the candle-lit room. Tired and lulled to sleepy thoughts by the storm, we zipped up the sleeping bags at 9 p.m., and blew out the candles.

I awoke at 6 a.m. and found it was raining harder than ever. I reflected on how lucky we were that the second day of this trip had been warm and calm as we crossed over Cumshewa. It didn't look like we'd be able to travel today. There was a bay full of white caps in front of me, and I could no longer see the landfall of Heming Head on Talunkwan Island four miles to the south. I dressed and went outside to get some split fir for the stove. Whoever was here last had left several days' supply, and I thanked them out loud as I bent over the wood pile. I also thought that before we left I'd have to find some way of replenishing this gift. Inside the cabin Lynn was stirring. "I love this little Hobbit house!" she said. "Is the tea ready?" I kindled a little fire in the charred remains of last night's and set about making a kayaker's breakfast of porridge and brown sugar with a hard tack biscuit and jam. The tea was ready first and served at the bedside with a flourish. I explained that we would likely be reading and sketching all day because of the weather. "That's okay, I like this place," Lynn responded. Soon the cabin was toasty warm and snug. We rolled up the sleeping gear, ate porridge and read. The rain continued its muted pounding on the roof shakes.

And that was the day. And the next day. On the third day the rain began to slacken, and we bundled up our gear to stow in the kayaks. As wonderful as Vertical Point was, it was a small house on a small peninsula with only one view. Cabin fever drove us back into the boats. By 9 a.m. we were on the water stroking our way to Heming Head. We went via Haswell Island to narrow our crossing somewhat, as it was another four miler. The day was shaping up to be an exhausting exercise.

Once again, remembering our Cumshewa Inlet crossing, I seized on another big fir to guide me across Selwyn Inlet. For a while I thought about great white sharks, but as the sun came out and the land all about us began to steam, I thought only about Tanu and Kunga House. We came abeam of Heming quicker than I expected. There was no obvious beach so we decided to press on to Helmet Island and the Tangil Peninsula.

Helmet Island looked sort of helmetty, but to be honest it was a stretch of the imagination. Maybe it looked like a European helmet to an 18th- or 19th-Century sailor thinking of European armies. Porter Head, at the tip of Tangil, gave us just enough room to land at half tide and have lunch. We kindled a little beach fire, made tea and looked south to Flower Pot Island and Tanu Island. Tanu's location is quite hidden, unlike Skedans which was intriguingly visible from Cumshewa Head. Meanwhile, somewhat predictably, an afternoon southeaster was building in Laskeek Bay. We doused the fire and jumped into the boats. The wind built all the way to Flower Pot, a distance of about one nautical mile, with two more miles remaining to paddle from there to Tanu. By the time we entered the island's wind shadow it was really blowing hard. We tucked in close to the rocky shore and kept the kayaks head to wind in a tiny bit of lee space. There was no beach to land.

Two hours later the wind started to abate and we broke out of our confined space and headed over to Klue Passage and Tanu village. By the time we could make out Tanu's canoe beach it was late afternoon. We pulled up on the soft gravel and got out to walk about. This was a very different place from Skedans. We could see no standing poles and the house pits were hidden behind a thick growth of cedar and spruce. There was a path to the north-end of the village where there was a graveyard and a lookout. Along the way a reef divided the town in two segments. We doubled back on a higher bench and came to a huge house pit with three major tiers. One of its corner posts was still standing. Remarkably, it was fluted like the mortuary pole we had seen in Skedans. It looked as if it had been patterned on one of the Parthenon's marble pillars. Its vertical channels were perfectly formed in cedar. But it was time to go.

We returned to the beach and pulled the kayaks to the water's edge. Kunga Island and David's little Kunga House were just a few hundred yards across the passage in front of us. It was a calm journey motivated by growing hunger and the continuing sense of discovery. Once again the kayaks' bows crunched gently over a shingle beach. We pulled the boats up and carried our gear to the door of the little cabin. It was perhaps one third bigger than Bonita's at Vertical Point and much less frequented. David had characteristically pinned a plastic-covered typewritten note to the door: "You are welcome to use this cabin. Please observe the time-honoured custom of leaving more wood in the wood box than you burn, and close the door firmly when you depart. David W. Ellis" The cabin was dimly lit by one window and a large candle preserved from little teeth by a tobacco tin with a screw top lid. Everything smelt strongly of rat feces and urine. On the table in the centre of the room was a hardcover, black notebook wrapped in a plastic bag. I carefully removed the book, and saw the David W. Ellis inscription: "Kunga House Guest Book: Please Sign." Over the past seven years many people had done just that. It was an ethnography of the first generation of kayakers to travel in South Moresby and it displayed incredible thought and art on just about every page. The writers wrote in neatly scripted black ink. Their words were chosen with care, written with cramped kayaker hands, and often took the form of a haiku. The accompanying sketches interspersed in small spaces in the text were inspired by the ocean, the winds and the land. The overall effect was one of sustaining paper, condensing thought and emotion, and some pages were the essence of northwest-coast sensibility.

Then I turned a page about halfway through the book and saw: "July 24/'78: Dropped in on a hot afternoon for a few minutes, had an enjoyable shit on the beach while Maggie picked some mint leaves, and then headed south. Thanks! Terry Jacks MV (Motor vessel). Seasons in the Sun." The words were scrawled across the bottom and top of two pages. The net effect was extraordinary. The sacred and the profane, the core angst of the world all in one book, juxtaposed for only a very few to read. It was incredibly funny and incredibly sad all at once. It certainly cast Terry Jacks, then one of Canada's most famous popular artists (his most recent hit was Seasons in the Sun in 1974), in a different light from the South Moresby kayak brigade.

Flash forward one year: Lynn and I returned to South Moresby in August of 1978 to make a second and longer trip down the archipelago. Once again we pulled into Kunga House for a dry night in the cabin. The wrapped logbook was still on the table. I picked it up and leafed through its contents. Halfway through, there was Terry Jacks' piece, but the poetry soon recommenced and the gentle thoughts flowed for another ten pages. Then the familiar handwriting reappeared: "3 July/ '79. Just dropped in to say Hi to everyone! Thanks again!! Terry Jacks. MV. Seasons in the Sun. This was followed by a full page describing Terry's new suspense film, also called Seasons In The Sun, and featuring Kunga House as the temporary home of a CIA agent before his pick-up by a Soviet trawler. Clearly, Kunga House's magic had worked its way into Terry's creative mind. I turned the next page carefully to find a kayaker's fond reminiscence of a 1972 visit to Kunga House, and an amusing postscript: "Glad to see Terry Jacks was constipated this year."

Section 2

Reconciling the Spiritual and the Materialistic

The second part of my career arc documents the conflict between my career-values thesis outlined in Section 1 and my struggles applying those values in the corporate world. In many respects key corporate values were antithetical to my spiritual ones. Reconciling the two took a special kind of effort. And on top of this struggle, the four major Canadian energy projects I worked on (the Alaska Highway and PolarGas pipelines, a Kitimat LNG plant, and the Monkman Coal Project) were all cancelled or went into a decades-long hiatus.

10

On Being Idealistic in the Oil Patch

Northern Frontier; Northern Homeland

After our first long paddle in Haida Gwaii it was time to find work in Calgary where Lynn was in her last year of architecture school. My arrival there was in every sense a grand adventure, underscored by the culture of the city that was so un-Vancouver. Our standard explanation of how different, went like this: "In Vancouver when you meet new acquaintances, the first conversation generally zones in on what part of Vancouver you grew up in and where you went to school. As in my case, 'Kerrisdale and St. George's School.' The reason for this is patently obvious – to peg your socio-economic position on the civic ladder. In Calgary, the first conversation is all about finding out what you do and for whom you work. Because almost everyone is from away, the focus is on who you are in professional and work terms, not where you grew up and who your parents are." This reason alone made Calgary more worldly; we found it way less provincial than Vancouver. And so was its dominant industry – oil and gas. From Royal Dutch Shell to Texaco to Elf Aquitaine, Calgary's major employers were all global players.

I faced up to the fact that law school was a wrong turn on life's road and threw myself into short-story writing for three months. That meant I was a writer when people asked me what I did. However, when a package of my work was rejected by the New Yorker, it seemed logical to head downtown for job interviews. The federal Northern Pipeline Agency (NPA) was hiring staff to regulate construction of the Alaska Highway Gas Pipeline. Part of this was the creation of an environmental and socio-economic affairs group to set out terms and conditions to build a pipeline that mirrored Canadian expectations of fairness for northerners, especially Indigenous ones, and to set a new standard of environmental-impact mitigation. This approach immediately caught my attention, and I applied to the NPA's human resources office for an interview. Within a week the chief operating officer, Harold Millican, indicated an interest in my credentials (I was fast learning that in government circles being a Rhodes Scholar was akin to having Willy Wonka's Golden Ticket.) At the end of the interview he offered me a job! My love of anthropology and my practical bent combined to make me the advisor to the manager, socio-economics. For one year I wrote draft socio-economic regulations, attended meetings with the proponent, Foothills Pipelines, and, as hearings' secretary, prepared for and administered a major public-hearing process to review the draft environmental and socio-economic terms and conditions in northern B.C. and the Yukon. The Alaska Highway Gas pipeline inquiry was led by a distinguished public servant, Bill Mair, from Victoria.

For a first real full-time job it was stimulating, but required a high degree of personal circumspection around ambitious pipeline engineers, many of whom, to be critical, did not have an abiding interest in involving local people in their project. They wanted it to be built safely to exacting engineering standards and on-budget by professional union crews from the south. This was an important lesson for me, schooled as I was by Judge Thomas Berger's monumental Northern Frontier; Northern Homeland (1977), the final report of the Northern Pipeline Inquiry, also known as the Mackenzie Valley Pipeline Inquiry. It had just been published to broad national acclaim – except in Calgary where the engineering ethos trumped anthropological and environmental concerns. The NPA staff were professional and argued their best case(s) for new approaches to northern pipeline construction, but for the most part I felt that they were unwilling to risk direct confrontations with the corporate party line.

And then rather suddenly in early 1980, the era of the northern-energy mega project waned as southern natural gas markets began to weaken and construction costs started to inflate. A rumour started circulating that the Alaska Highway Gas Pipeline Project would go into a hiatus or be cancelled altogether. The dedicated NPA bureaucrats hunkered down, many apparently quite happy to do nothing if there was nothing to do. I couldn't stand the slowing pace and days went by without me creating any stories worth telling or writing. When compared to kayaking in Gwaii Haanas, or being No. 2 to Jim, or helping Ray and Terry challenge the world, the oil and gas milieu seemed so banal. I was young and wanted more adventure than this bureaucracy provided. I decided to quit.

As luck would have it, some wonderful new Calgary friends to whom I had been introduced by an old Strathcona Park Lodge alumna, Reva Robinson, asked me to interview at Petro-Canada. It was the brand-new, state oil company with a mandate to do things differently in the oil patch. Again I was fortunate to be hired after one interview, this time to join the Petro-Canada corporate office of environmental and social affairs. With a mandate to lead and enforce social and environmental standards throughout the company, the corporate office reported through a vice-president to the president of Petro-Canada. The work promised to build on many of my responsibilities at the NPA. I hoped that it would also allow me to continue my quest to live out my values in the workplace.

Petro-Canada was my first corporate job. It required a significant investment in new clothes, a regular appointment with Chelsea at the unisex hair salon and a willingness to travel at the drop of my vice-president's hat. My position had the grand title of special advisor, socio-economics. Lynn was also now in the corporate sector, completing her architectural apprenticeship, and at least, for a while, we were child free. My work was broadly defined as helping Petro-Canada meet and exceed environmental and social regulatory requirements imposed by Canada's provinces, territories and the federal government. Petro-Canada at its inception was a quasi-federal agency mandated to set high standards in the oil patch and to give Canadians a window on the industry. I do not think any Canadian company had ever before created a position quite like mine, and I was eager to give the work my best efforts.

I remember going into the vice-president's office to learn my duties. Everything was new. The furnishings in his office radiated new wealth and exemplified life near the top of the oil patch: leather, granite, wool, glass, and Canadian landscape art portraying untouched frontiers. I was made to feel welcome, and even a little powerful, "I want you to advise me on how you think we are meeting the test in the small communities where we operate. I especially want to hear about how we are doing with Aboriginal people, the Indians, Métis and Inuit in the regions where we operate. You are going to be part of the ethical conscience of Petro-Canada in your work here, Mike." Wow. I bounced home to our little suburban tract house on the prairie to tell Lynn about my new calling. She was pleased my values were engaged.

Soon I was called in to be briefed on a special assignment. The company was about to place a liquefied natural gas (LNG to the engineers) plant on the British Columbia coast and I was to help choose the location. Quite a large group of biological, geotechnical, engineering and shipping consultants was to fly from Calgary in a company plane to check out potential port sites from the air. I was to tag along as the "social affairs guy." I went to an organizational meeting and took copious notes. The trip was a "locational survey," and the ideal outcome was "the best site location." On the flight my job was to look out of the window and record the best potential sites along with the scientists. Once we found a few, we would narrow down the selection by making "community presentations." I would be part of the "sales team." I didn't hear much talk about ethics and local involvement.

In fact, right from the start I wondered just how Jim and Ray and Terry would feel about the process and LNG which I had begun to read about. It turned out to be a potentially volatile, explosive and highly combustible commodity that required very sophisticated care and attention, especially at LNG facilities where it flowed as a super-cooled liquid into pressure vessels on what were euphemistically called "LNG carriers." For some reason they were not referred to as ships and a member of the locational-survey team told me that the carriers were potentially so dangerous, that their crews were unable to purchase travel and general work insurance. Our task was to find a suitable place near a willing host community to fill ships with the highly explosive liquid. The way I read it, my job was to talk with people and to put them at ease.

This didn't sound very ethical to me so I went home to talk it over with Lynn. I decided to speak with the vice-president as soon as possible, get his okay on a line of action, and act. The next day I spilled the beans as I saw them. The vice-president looked very concerned and agreed with me that gazing out of an airplane window to assess social impacts was bizarre. He told me to go to the next meeting of the LNG team and to speak my mind. So I did.

From the start of this assignment I felt the science boys (there were pointedly no women) were uptight about my presence. I was tolerated, but not much more. It didn't help that I came from the corporate office of environmental and social affairs, where the dominant philosophy was 'top-down' application of standards (and strangely this irony was lost on the 'window viewers' on the location-spotting airplane trip.) The individual project groups in the company increasingly resented being told how to do the social and environmental aspects of their work, and many technical experts assumed that our input was a significant and largely unnecessary extra cost. Bearing all this in mind I attended the next meeting of the LNG planning group with grim determination. Trying not to be strident and as diplomatic as possible, I made my point that I was not just a member of a sales team. There had to be true involvement of community representatives and fully informed decision-making at the local level. When I came to the end of my presentation there was stunned silence. There were no questions. The donuts were eaten and everyone returned to their granite-veneered offices. I reported back to the vice-president who thanked me at the end of the day for "holding the corporate-office banner high."

Things were very different the next morning. Summoned to the vice-president's office, I was told to wait in the anteroom while the boss finished a phone call. In I went as soon as he hung up the phone. "Your behaviour yesterday embarrassed me a great deal," he almost whimpered. "That is not what I want for our office. We have to get along with everyone in the company. We won't be asked to advise anymore if we go in there as if we have all the answers." Then the coup de grace: "I'm taking you off the LNG project and putting you on research and writing assignments." So much for my activism, but at least the value of the experience couldn't be denied. I had been demoted. Given my toned-down approach at yesterday's meeting, I wondered, what would have happened if I'd gone in with both guns blazing.

Shortly after that meeting and the start of my new research career, Jim Boulding phoned me at the office. "How's the oil patch treating you, No. 2? Myrna and I would like to talk with you about returning to BC, living at the lodge with your bride, and helping build the business. I'll even call you VP of Westcoast Survival and Story-Telling, if it would help your bruised ego. What do you think, Mike?" I told Jim that Lynn was hard at work on her architectural registration and that I was enjoying my work at Petro-Canada.

What a lie! I'd certainly learned that the human connection of Strathcona days didn't easily factor into the profit motive of my big-time corporate employer. However, in declining Jim and Myrna's offer, I felt I had to start making my own way in the world. Besides, being paid to write and to think all day had some advantages. And who knows, there might be other, more receptive projects to work on, because the economy was heating up again along with the price of oil.

11

"Back Then You Didn't Need a Job, Just a Trapline"

Creating a compensation policy "just like jam"

About three months into my rather solitary corporate research-and-writing career, I was asked by my vice-president if I would like to assist Petro-Canada's new coal division with the regulatory approval process for their Monkman Project in the Northeast Coal Block in British Columbia. I was pointedly being given a second chance at working with an operational group, and I was appreciative of the invite. I remember being counselled to take on the task mindful of the lessons learned from the LNG-project debacle. Northeast B.C. was just opening up to wide-scale mineral exploration. John Steward, the coal division vice-president responsible for the project, needed help with archaeological and social impact assessment. We went for a long lunch and the deal was done. I'd be seconded to the coal division for a few years. From the start it was appealing that many of the division's staff had lived in small mining communities earlier in their careers and knew the value of a stable, happy work force and strong community support. Some of them who had also worked with Indigenous peoples on coal-mine development in other countries, already understood the importance of learning about the land from other cultures. I felt that John Steward also understood the need to give young professionals some responsibility as they learned the business. Finally, I had a project that promised to be an engaging challenge and that could, possibly, fit my values.

My first step was a trip to the Monkman property in northeast B.C. to meet with the very small coal division staff there to see what work needed to be done. There were a few consultants already working on impact-assessment studies, and John thought it best that I meet them "in the field." Off I jetted to Fort St. John and then by rental car to Dawson Creek. Here I met the coal division's archaeology consultants at a local hotel and I listened to their stories. They had found a deserted community of six abandoned log cabins near Kelly Lake and were preparing an ambitious excavation plan for the coal division to consider as part of its responsibility to mitigate archaeological impacts. Under B.C. regulations the company had a duty to locate, survey and report on archaeological sites that would be destroyed by its mining. Over a beer I asked them how much the excavation would cost. They casually replied, "About $200,000." I noted to myself that John Steward would think this a lot of money for excavating six log cabins and finished my beer.

The next day I drove south and west of Dawson Creek to Kelly Lake, and found a small community of about two hundred Métis trappers, guides and outfitters hidden away in the bushland. Many families still lived in log cabins with bush-economy gear stored in their yards. Snow machines, well-used fibreglass canoes and corralled horses were juxtaposed with old pick-ups and trailers parked in log barns and sheds.

My first contact was Jarvis Gray, an engaging young man in his late twenties and one half of a father-and-son team whose trapline was overlain by Petro-Canada's coal lease. Jarvis had already written to Petro-Canada outlining his family's long history of trapping in the Monkman Pass and Trail region, making a case for compensating his father, David, still trapping in his seventies. Jarvis said that his father was out on the trapline that day, but he drove me to Mrs. Annie Gladu's cabin. Annie (as most Kelly Lakers called her) was the matriarch of the community, a woman in her eighties whose opinion was sought by the Métis leadership on all major decisions.

Annie, predeceased by her husband, now spent her days tanning hides and sewing in a one-room log cabin by the side of the dusty main road. She was dressed in a blue floral-print blouse, and what I guessed to be a pair of her husband's pants. About five-feet tall with close-cropped white hair, she was quick and sure in her movements, mentally sharp, with a ready smile and full of stories about a life well-lived in the bush. She had trapped and hunted with her family from the 1920s to the late 1960s, based out of Monkman Cabins, a now deserted community close by. In fact, she said it was "near where you want to put the coal mine." Immediately I realized it was the log cabin community that had been the topic of last night's beer with the archaeologists. They wanted to spend two-hundred thousand dollars digging it up to discover what it was and maybe who had lived there. Within an hour Mrs. Gladu had drawn me a basic map of the houses indicating which cabin belonged to which family. She also said, "You should meet Mrs. Calverley in Dawson Creek, because she has made a study of the Métis history of Kelly Lake. And you should also meet Gerry Andrews. He was our first teacher in Kelly Lake in the 1920s. He's about my age. I think he lives in Victoria now." With that Mrs. Gladu said she wanted to take her afternoon nap. I thanked her for being so helpful, aware that I had interesting local information to share with John Steward. As I was preparing to leave, Jarvis pulled me aside and said, "You should create a trappers' compensation policy with my Dad. He wants to retire and your mine will wipe him out. Now is the time to do the decent thing." I told Jarvis I would try as soon as I had permission from my boss. Finally, I had a delightful sense that all my training was bearing fruit.

Back in Calgary, I told John Steward that we could accomplish a great deal if he would let me negotiate with the B.C. coal guidelines bureaucrats; I thought we could replace a big archaeological excavation with an oral history of Kelly Lake for local schools; a trappers' compensation policy, first for the coal division and later for all of Petro-Canada; and a social-impact assessment written by local historians and residents instead of consultants. John said he would support me, but I had to keep him fully informed every step of the way. Agreeing, I flew to Victoria to see if the B.C. officials would permit me to do some creative regulatory work. To my surprise they agreed completely with the proposals, principally because local people wanted to do things differently from usual and because there would be real benefits for those closest to the mine – the Métis of Kelly Lake. After a weekend at home I returned to Kelly Lake to start work in earnest.

The first step was forming a local committee to oversee all aspects of the oral-history project. From the start, I thought that I would be the writer, but all content would be determined and edited locally. Everyone in Kelly Lake wanted Mrs. Calverley involved, so I went to Dawson Creek to invite her to participate. Recently widowed, she lived in her life-long home, a small brown, shingled, frame house in the centre of town. It was surrounded by her summer flower garden and boasted a serious vegetable patch. I went up the crushed stone path and knocked on her front door. It soon opened and there she stood: seventy-ish, strongly built, about five foot five, with white permed hair, rouged cheeks, sparkly eyes and wearing a simple print dress with an apron over the top. "Come in; I've been expecting you, Michael. Jarvis Gray said you wanted to meet with me about a history project at Kelly Lake. Let's have some tea." I walked into her living room which was really more of a work area. "Since my husband passed away, I've become much more studious. As you can see I have several projects on the go. The main one is on the orchids of the Peace Country. I think we have twenty-two distinct species of orchid hereabouts. But enough of flowers. Why does a coal company care about Métis history? Tell me a bit about who you are." I launched into my corporate-ethics speech and watched Mrs. Calverley coolly assess what she was hearing. "You should know, Michael, that I regularly attend Rotary and the Chamber of Commerce. I have heard quite a bit of corporate bumf in my time. And I've never heard someone like you." I told her she could report me to the chamber if my actions didn't match my words. "So you think they give heed to little old ladies, do you?" I told her that her reputation preceded her and that I hoped she would chair the project's steering committee. She replied, "I will on three conditions: Kelly Lake agrees with the choice; Jarvis and Clifford Calliou, a fine young Métis leader, work with me here locally; and Gerry Andrews is recruited to the committee." It was a deal.

Then we set about the planning. There would have to be a meeting with the Kelly Lake elders very soon; we needed to get a consensus on the table of contents; interviewees would have to be contacted; and tape recorders, tapes, cameras, and honoraria would have to be provided. I concurred with her sense of direction. "And one more thing, Michael, stop calling me Mrs. Calverley. I'm not your teacher; I'm your colleague. Call me Dorthea (sic) from now on."

The next step was to call Gerry Andrews, but not before a garden tour. "Come outside and see my marvellous cannabis plant. It's nearly as tall as me now!" We found it hidden amongst some rising corn stalks. It was about five-feet tall and was definitely marijuana. "I was given the seed by a young friend, and planted it this spring. If the Mounties come to haul me away I'll just flutter my eyes and do my dear little old lady act. It works every time."

I returned to the hotel to phone Gerry Andrews, recalling Dorthea's briefing. "You'll get him via directory assistance in Victoria. Remember that he was surveyor general of B.C. A real provincial big-wig. He pioneered photogrammetry after studying its wartime applications at Oxford University. He had what we used to call "a good war." I'm telling you this to give you some idea of how to approach him. I think he will say yes because he is also working on a book about Kelly Lake genealogy and would like one last trip up this way. Good luck."

Gerry was true to form: "Andrews here; with whom am I speaking?" I introduced myself and made my pitch. We were soon on familiar ground. "I'm too old to drive my van up to Kelly Lake, Mr. Robinson. I'm seventy-eight and barely able to ride my bike to the Union Club for lunch anymore. I suppose you're still based in a tent camp?" I assured him that the company could provide airfare and accommodation – not tents. "Just goes to show how much money the private sector is used to flinging around. In my day at the front end of a project it was camp grub, tents and horses." I negotiated a trip in two weeks' time, aware that Gerry was increasingly nervous about the cost of our long-distance phone call. "How will I recognize you at the Dawson Creek airport, Mr. Andrews?" "I'll be the distinguished looking chap in the white beard and the moose-hide jacket." We arranged our airport rendezvous and then we would head off for dinner with Dorthea. "Good show," he said.

In the midst of crafting – at long last – a meaningful project, our son Lance was born on July 6th, 1982. It was definitely a time of great happiness on both the home and work fronts. After spending ten days getting to know each other and helping Lynn as best as I could, I was winging north again to Dawson Creek, conscious of my new responsibilities as a dad. Clearly I'd have to do a better job of balancing my responsibilities to Lynn and, now, Lance, but given my new-found confidence at work, it seemed to be a possibility.

I arrived one hour before Gerry and began imagining him in my mind's eye. His plane landed on time, and scores of oil-patch hands filed off. Then Gerry made his entrance. With a freshly lit pipe, he strode into the small waiting area clad in his moose-hide beaded jacket, woollen work pants, red suspenders, white rolled socks, and in his words "well Dubbined" (a water-proofing grease) leather, high-top boots. He was wiry, surprisingly short, and sported a fine, trimmed white beard. It struck me that he was dressed for bush work as surveyor general circa 1960. No one stood out more in the entire town of Dawson Creek. We checked in at the Alaska Highway Hotel, where we made reservations for dinner. Gerry insisted we economize by sharing a room, and we lugged our gear up two flights of stairs. Once settled, Gerry said it was time to bring out "the old red sock." He pulled it from his duffle. The sock contained a bottle of scotch. We each had two fingers "to brace ourselves for Dorthea" at dinner.

We picked up Dorthea in our rented pickup. The three of us sat in the front seat as we drove to dinner. First introductions were quite formal: "How do you do, surveyor general?" "How do you do, Mrs. Calverley, celebrated archivist of the Peace District?" Much laughter ensued. From that point on it was Mike, Gerry and Dorthea. We had a fine meal, drank some British Columba wine, and sketched out a plan for the oral history project. Both Gerry and Dorthea offered to pay for their meals and were surprised that the company had an entertainment budget for volunteers. Tomorrow we would drive to Kelly Lake at 8 a.m. We returned Dorthea to her house at 10 p.m., and headed up to bed. Gerry donned red-flannel pyjamas for his night in the hotel.

The morning trip was great fun. Gerry reprised his coureur-de-bois attire, supplemented by a moose-hide rifle-shell bandoleer. Dorthea wore a floral-print dress under a canvas bush jacket that had once belonged to her late husband, "Just in case we need to go walkabout." I drove the truck and listened to the two elders yarn us with tales of the early history of this part of B.C. By 10 a.m. we were pulling into the Kelly Lake School parking lot. Gerry got out and straightened his various pieces of clothing. Just then a door opened in the side of the gym and an elderly Métis woman appeared to shake out a broom. "Is that you Eva?" called Gerry. "Yes it is," she replied, and then she let out a soft scream of recognition. "I have missed you teacher! I thought we would only meet again in Heaven!" Gerry walked slowly over to give Eva Calliou a big hug. Then in the middle of the parking lot he embarked on a story. I was all ears.

Between 1923 and 1925, starting when Gerry was nineteen, he was the first school teacher at Kelly Lake. His father was a pharmacist in Elgin, Manitoba, and had sent his son off to work with a well provisioned first-aid kit. Gerry was a good teacher and one of his favourite students was trapper Milton Campbell's daughter, Eva. She was almost Gerry's age and worked hard to impress her teacher. One night in late February 1925 she came to the log cabin teacherage with desperately sad news. Her father had been brought in sick on a toboggan from the traplines. He couldn't get out of bed and was having great trouble breathing. The family had gathered round fearing the worst. Eva remembered Gerry's classroom stories of his father's first-aid kit. Perhaps he could help? Gerry grabbed his kit and paid his first house call. He asked Milton to open his mouth wide. Inside Gerry spied a quinsy – a kind of abscess – that had erupted from the skin of his throat. It was blocking Milton's airway and preventing him from eating or talking. Gerry took out a throat atomizer and asked Milton to keep his mouth wide open. He sprayed a liberal dose of undiluted peroxide down as far as possible. He then massaged Milton's throat and neck vigorously with camphorated oil, and wrapped a wool sock round it, fastening it with a safety pin. "I told them this was all I could do, and hoped it would help."

"The next morning good old Celestin, Milton's father-in-law came to see me," said Gerry. "By God!" he said. "One hour after you leave last night, Milton, he's alright, by God." Gerry's diagnosis had been correct and his reputation as a *muskeekee weyinu* (Cree for doctor), rose to an all-time high. Several days later Eva, Milton's eldest daughter, came to his door with a neat package sewn up in a clean, cotton flour sack. "That's for you," she said shyly. Inside was a beautifully beaded moose-hide cartridge belt for Gerry's 30-30 Winchester rifle shells. "I made it for you for saving my father's life, Mr. Andrews." And here he was today, fifty-seven years later, wearing the Metis bandoleer in the Kelly Lake School parking lot. Arm in arm he and Eva strolled into the school for our meeting.

Everyone else was already assembled in the classroom set aside for us. Annie Gladu, David Gray and Eva had brought many other elders to the table. Jarvis Gray and Clifford Calliou each rose and spoke about the value of the work and volunteered to act as community interviewers. A basic table of contents and an interview schedule was reached by consensus, and everyone concurred that Dorthea would be the perfect chair. Gerry offered his genealogical research on the westernmost Canadian Métis settlement to the project along with his collection of historical photographs. All agreed with my offer to be the writer. The company's role as paymaster, equipment supplier, and ultimate publisher was approved unanimously. The Kelly Lakers at the meeting thought that this was a better way for the coal mine project to be regulated than relying on archaeological consultants to excavate an abandoned site that everyone already knew about. As Annie Gladu said at the close of the meeting, "The old ones have lots of good stories to tell. We need to put them in the machine, whatever you call that thing, so that they will not be forgotten. We also want those stories in a book for the school, for our children and grandchildren to read and learn from. This is a good idea."

As we were packing up to return to Dawson Creek, David Gray handed me a bag of dried moose meat and asked if we could discuss trapper's compensation issues. I asked when he would like to meet, and he replied, "Can you come out and live on my trapline with Jarvis and me for a few days?" I said I could do it in two weeks' time. "Then it's a deal," he said. So saying, the three town's folk headed back to Dawson Creek.

That evening as we were finishing the dessert at our celebratory dinner, a rather self-important fellow came up to our table and said hello to Dorthea. "Why, hello, mayor. Let me introduce you to Mike Robinson of the Petro-Canada coal division and Surveyor General Andrews." After hand shaking all around, the mayor asked me why I was in town. I briefly explained. The mayor looked befuddled. Do you mean to say Dorthea is acting as a consultant to the regulatory review process for your Monkman coal project along with elders in Kelly Lake?" I had no choice but to say, "Yes." "I think you and I should have a chat, son." We agreed to meet in his office the next morning.

Gerry and Dorthea had no interest in meeting the mayor so I went on my own. I wondered what John Steward and the senior managers in the coal division had said to him over the past year. I strode into his office at 9 a.m. He greeted me with a firm hand-shake and a civic-booster lapel pin. "Mr. Robinson, I think the council and the Chamber of Commerce should know more about your project than Dorthea. Why haven't you given us a briefing?" I promised to do so in two weeks when I would return for more local research. "What have you got planned then?" I said I was going to spend a week on David Gray's trapline. The mayor looked perplexed. "Whatever for?" "To research how the company will deal with trappers' compensation issues." "Those people don't trap anymore. You should be training them to run front-end loaders and D8s (a piece of heavy equipment.)" I declined a coffee, and set dates for my civic presentations two weeks hence. The mayor escorted me to the door of city hall, and I walked out into the sunshine to take Gerry to the airport. His leaving was uneventful except for an unexpected bear hug in the departure lounge. I then went over to Dorthea's to say good-bye.

"Don't worry about the mayor, Michael. I've lived here for over fifty years, and it just gets his goat that I know more than the council. Give them a nice talk when you come back with lots of coloured slides of tips and crushers and big pieces of equipment. You'll get your picture in the paper and all will be well with the world. You'll see. Just keep doing what you said you'll do in Kelly Lake. Don't forget that those people are the real stewards of this land and they'll get the least monetary benefit from your project." With that I said good-bye and drove back to the airport.

John Steward was happy with my progress, but somewhat worried about the mayor. His instinct was for the two of us to present to council and the chamber. He also wanted to go to Kelly Lake to meet our "consultants" face to face. Together we developed a colourful slide show, just as Dorthea had advised. I prepared for the rest of my week on the trapline by buying some new boots and gloves. Baby Lance was now a chubby, round-faced delight. I was surprised at his rapid growth over his first three weeks of life. It was hard to contemplate leaving again so soon for Dawson Creek. Lynn was sad too. I went out of the door with mixed feelings about all this travel, but not about the value of the work.

John and I flew up on a corporate King Air aircraft that was more convenient for his schedule. We drove in from the airport to the same hotel. It was a different place without Gerry in his buckskin and red suspenders. We had a quiet meal and made one last dry run of our talk for the next day. John opened and covered the market and technology; I closed with employment and local business benefits. We steered clear of trapper's compensation, oral history and locally written social impact assessments. The speeches went well. We wore suits and ties dressing, as all corporate consultants try to do, just a bit above the clients. The question-and-answer session was low key. Afterwards the local print and radio folk scrummed us in the lobby. Again, Dorthea was right. Our pictures were in the paper.

The next day John and I dressed for Kelly Lake, leaving our suits behind. I was always more comfortable in my old jeans anyway; John's were brand new, but he was making an effort to fit in. We headed out at 8 a.m., and made good time on the dry, dusty road. I had arranged for Jarvis to take us to Annie's for tea. We arrived at 9:45 and she was already outside her cabin scraping the fatty tissue off the underside of a stretched moose hide on a pole rack. John was observant and kind. Jarvis was unfailingly hospitable, and Annie, eager to talk about the old days in Kelly Lake. She gave us a lyrical introduction to local Métis history, including the story of how she was hushed by her mother as a baby seventy-five years ago: "Be quiet my child so we can listen for the bells on the soldiers' sleighs." This was surely a relic of Frog Lake and Duck Lake, of General Middleton's troops and the Métis rebellion of Gabriel Dumont and Louis Riel. This crumb of history was tucked away in Kelly Lake – the westernmost Métis settlement in Canada.

We also heard the story of when Annie and her "old man" were out hunting for moose, rabbits, and 'chickens' (ptarmigan) and became separated. Annie had her German shepherd dog with her. Suddenly the hair went up on his back. He ran off and barked at four grizzly bears playing in a forest meadow. The biggest grizzly followed him back to Annie. Unable to run away, she stood her ground. Her dog ran towards her with his tail between his legs. Annie raised her .22 and shot the bear twice before it grabbed her. "He took the gun right out of my hands and sat on me. I could feel the bear chewing on my head. My dog jumped on the bear and the grizzly left me to chase the dog. I picked up my rifle to try and shoot again, but my hand was torn. I couldn't even fire the rifle. With a broken wrist, cut leg, and bleeding scalp I walked two miles back to camp." All this happened only nine miles from Kelly Lake. "When I got back to camp I fired my rifle three times so my husband would come. Before he came, the horses were spooked and began to run off. I had to chase them back to their feed. Finally my husband came. He asked me if I had accidentally shot myself. I just said, 'You better take me home.' I sat upright in the wagon next to my husband all the way to Goodfare Corner. From there we went by car to the hospital at Beaverlodge. When we reached the hospital we had to wait two hours before the doctor came at 9 p.m. It took him until 3 a.m. to patch me up. He told me if I had laid down in the wagon, I probably would have bled to death. Sitting up saved my life. Here, give me your hand," she said to John. "Feel my head where the bear bit me." He did.

After tea we said good-bye to Annie and headed down the road to visit David Gray at his trapline cabin on the mine-lease area. It was odd to travel through an area being prepared for major industrial development then to park in front of a log cabin surrounded by trapping gear. David was standing by his woodpile stretching two new beaver pelts on sapling hoops. It was warm by now and he must have been hot wearing a plaid work shirt with the sleeves rolled and a pair of Levis that were both belted and suspendered. John stepped forward and introduced himself. David smiled, shook our hands, and welcomed us inside his cabin for tea.

We followed him through the low doorway into a combination mudroom and all-purpose storage area filled with tools; jars and tobacco tins containing nails, bolts and bullets; traps of all sizes and descriptions; and neatly hung winter clothing. From here another door opened into a one-room interior. The light came through the curtained window facing south over an unnamed creek. The window-sill held candles, a cribbage board, a much used deck of cards, and boxes of wooden matches. Against this wall was a plywood table and two old, wicker chairs with flour-sack pillows. A cast-iron stove with a metal pipe chimney stood against the far wall. A bed with a straw-ticking mattress was wedged against the north wall. That completed the furniture. A rope-and-pulley system suspended a clothes-drying rack not far above our heads. The log walls were covered with old calendars, thumb-tacked notes and a few framed photographs. A low shelf held a line of paperback novels, mostly Louis L'Amour westerns. David set about lighting the fire in the stove to make tea.

"I want to tell you guys about how trapping works." He looked out of the window and said, "You know, there is still survival out there. There are still about thirty of us boys who trap out of Kelly Lake. We are all trapping on lines that were originally registered in the 1930s, back in the Depression. The seasonal routine is still pretty much the way it was for old St. Pierre Gauthier, Narcisse Belcourt, and Eva's dad, Milton Campbell. Preparation for a new trapping season begins in September before the cold weather of winter. We get the traps out of storage, and oil and repair them. If you need new ones, you go out and buy them then. This is also the time to overhaul your Ski-Doo; in the old days you'd be repairing your dog harnesses and hitches. If you need to, you go out and clear new trails and set areas with an axe and chainsaw. Line cabins are spruced up for winter, and stores of dry food in tin cans and boxes are trucked into the cabins. New winter clothing is bought, and last season's gloves, mitts, pants and coats are mended. People enjoy all this preparation; it is an exciting time in Kelly Lake.

"On October 1st the season begins and the trappers start with sets for beaver and muskrat. These furbearers are best taken before the creeks and streams freeze over. By November, all furs are legally open for trapping. Now we can trap for everything: lynx, marten, squirrel, weasel, otter, fisher, wolf, coyote, wolverine and fox. They are not always available in the same numbers, you know. They come in cycles in the bush – I call them fur cycles – that depend on how their predators are doing. The lynx cycle is the most important one for the Kelly Lakers. In the bush the lynx prey upon hares. City guys usually call them "rabbits." Shortly after the hare population peaks, so does the lynx. In the Monkman region, our lynx peak every eight to eleven years. This is important to us because lynx are the most valuable pelts. Recently they've risen sharply in price: in Edmonton the fur buyers were paying four- to five-hundred dollars for top grade last year."

David explained that every year he reports his fur harvest from memory on the British Columbia Fish and Game Branch Application for Renewal and Return of Registered Trapline Holder form.

You have to do this in order to get your licence renewed. Over the years these records build up a very good database for monitoring a region's productivity and capacity. David's records go back to 1943, and graphically demonstrate the lynx cycles he has trapped through his career. In the banner years of 1963 and 1964, he bagged thirty-three and thirty-five lynx respectively. The records also show how David has specialized in red squirrels, in some years trapping more than two-thousand; in 1954 he trapped three-thousand and fifty-six. Martins, beavers, muskrats, and weasels also show up every year in large numbers.

"But let's get back to the trapper's year in the bush," said David. "By mid-December, the men with the longest return trip to Kelly Lake are thinking of Christmas and returning to their families. Most of the boys will have already been home the odd weekend or at least once per month to sell their fur and buy new grub. In the old days the unlucky trappers, the ones whose lines were farthest from Kelly Lake, would only come out once every one, or two, months. Ski-Doos and pickup trucks have changed all that. Today I can get home in thirty minutes! In the old days the trip from Monkman Cabins took two days by horseback. Everyone wanted to be home by Christmas. It was one of the best times of the year!

"Sometime after New Year the trappers went back out to their lines. Then beaver and muskrat are hard to trap because of freeze-up. So you go after other types of fur. In the coldest time of the year the fur is thickest. This is when prime pelts are harvested. Winter fur season closes at the beginning of March. Now muskrat and beaver are open for trapping again. By May 1st spring has usually arrived, and the trapping season starts to wind down. The pelts are getting thinner as the furbearers start to moult for summer. From May to mid-June grizzly and black bear can be taken, and at the end of this period all the trappers are generally out of the bush. I call this the beginning of the summer slack. Today very few trappers bother with bear season, as other jobs have become available after spring breakup.

"Summer in Kelly Lake begins when the trappers return home and continues until they set out for their lines again in late

September and early October. It is a time for relaxing, jobs in the oil patch, logging, and helping the farmers with their harvest. Some Kelly Lake families also created their own summer businesses in guide-outfitting. The Calliou family especially got into guide-outfitting. Johnnie Calliou started out in the 1940s. His sons Charlie and Cliff run the business now. Years ago they maintained a string of thirty or forty pack horses. They advertised their trips and hunts in Outdoor Life magazine. Over the years they built up a lot of good clients, mostly Americans and Europeans. They ran circle trips in the Monkman Pass of two and three weeks. Now Charlie and Cliff run about fifteen horses and they are developing a third generation of clients."

Turning to the future of trapping and guiding in the Monkman region, David raised a lot of concerns. "I am the oldest trapper in Kelly Lake now. As the pace of oil and gas and coal development continues, so does the possibility of a good-paying job. I never made more than eleven-thousand dollars per year trapping. Young guys now can make that in two months in these other industries. Also, as these new access roads are built, more and more people can get into the backcountry and make a mess, or steal your gear. Tourists are worse than wolves! Old Alex Monkman's historic cabin north of Duke Mountain, near Honeymoon Creek, was burned down by somebody eight years ago. You've seen all that remains of the Monkman Cabins community today, just an old stone fireplace and six depressions in the ground where the cabins used to stand. That was where the Calliou, Monkman, Hambler, Gray, Gauthier, and Gladu families lived during the trapping seasons of the 1930s and 1940s. I was born there. It was a beautiful sheltered area with clean water and lots of firewood. It was also a good place to winter the horses because there was plenty of feed. Now I hardly recognize the place."

Game is also suffering, according to David. "I can only harvest one moose and one elk per year, as long as I have the government's hunting licence. Out-of-region hunters, people I don't even see, are taking large numbers of game that really ought to be available to local people. I don't think the hunt is well policed; a lot of meat goes out of here without licences." Luckily the less obvious bounty of the land, especially berries, goes relatively unnoticed. "Blueberries, cranberries, huckleberries, wild strawberries, wild raspberries, saskatoons, wild onions, potatoes and rhubarb are still in good supply in season." David and his son Jarvis continue to harvest the "bush fruits" whenever they get a chance.

Animal behavior is also changing, he said. "I've seen big changes in just the last twenty years, since the 1960s. Bears especially. When I was a boy you never heard stories about aggressive grizzly bears. They kind of minded their business unless your dog went after them or they were poorly shot in a hunt. Since more people have got into the backcountry they fight more. Now I always go out with a gun. You can't predict how they are going to behave anymore. Black bears are starting to be unpredictable, too. Now you really have to keep your senses alert when you go out in the bush.

"When I say there is still a career in the bush for the next generations, I mean that the bush can still provide a good living if you have the skills. In my time there weren't any of these other kinds of jobs, and young men learned from the older guys how to trap and hunt. We had no choice but to go out on the traplines. But you know, people used to enjoy their life then more than they do now. Most of all you didn't need to chase money all the time. Back then you didn't need a job, just a trapline."

Our two hours with David had flown by and the tea had been supplemented with hard-tack biscuits, big hunks of old cheddar, jam and peanut butter. "That's how we eat out here, boys," said David as he came to the end of his reflections on the trapper's life. John was glancing at his watch; I knew that I had to get him back to Dawson Creek airport. Then I was going to return to spend a few nights with David at his cabin, knocking together the coal division's trapper's compensation policy with a view to applying it first of all to him.

I drove John to Dawson Creek, wished him a safe flight back to Calgary, turned around and made it back to the cabin at dusk. David and Jarvis were just finishing pitching an old canvas wall tent. A fire was burning in a ring of rocks, and moose ribs were sizzling under a brushing of barbecue sauce. A case of beer was ready for opening and the boys were all ready to talk some more. "That boss of yours is a good guy, Mike. He listens." I agreed and began to share some ideas. "It's been a long day, but a good one. I was really interested in the description you gave of the fur cycle, Dave. Have you ever figured out what your average annual income is during one complete cycle?" "Nope, but it wouldn't be hard because the fur buyer at Hythe keeps records for all the furs he buys. He's been buying most of my fur for thirty years." "So, if we got those records, and adjusted your receipts for inflation, we could come up with an amount in constant dollars for each year for the past thirty." "Yup, and that would cover about three lynx cycles, too, said David." I explained that we needed to come up with a good system for determining compensation, one that could survive repeated use in different situations, but which had an internal logic. It had to be fair.

David and Jarvis said that all the companies active in the region had different policies. "Most just want to pay the trapper for any damage done by their crews. You know, buy new traps, replace padlocks on forced doors, that kind of stuff." No company was prepared to supplement lost income, or pay a trapper to move if his trapline was being destroyed entirely or partially by development. "You know, us trappers know what we think our line is worth. I call it the 'beer parlour price'," said David, explaining that good lines were always in demand, and most deals on transferring ownership had nothing to do with the government licensing process. "I got offered twenty-five thousand dollars by Billy Warn in a Dawson Creek bar a few years ago, but I wouldn't't sell." That was the amount another trapper was prepared to pay to get the right to register his name on the trapline. Bits and pieces of a policy were now starting to come together in my mind. We ate dinner over a few beers, and started talking about our families and matters far from Monkman bush country. Afterwards Jarvis said I could sleep in the cabin. He and his dad were going to sleep in their old Jones Tent and Awning wall tent. "Dad thinks it will help you to dream like a trapper," he said. And so my first day on the trapline came to an end.

In the morning I started the day by washing in the creek. It was cold, but it woke me up fast. Jarvis had already made coffee and David was cooking bacon and eggs. It was a still, hot July day. Over coffee I began to lay out the basics of a possible policy. First of all, we'd expect the trapper to participate in good faith. He would have to make his trapping-sales records available, and in the first step we would jointly calculate his average annual income in constant dollars for at least one lynx cycle. The current income for the year of industrial disturbance would be calculated next with the working assumption that the usual level of effort was being put into trapping. To gauge one year's compensation for disturbance, the payout would equal the lynx-cycle average annual income, minus the income for the year of disturbance. If the result was negative, the company would cut a cheque to restore the average annual income for that year. If the result was positive, there would be no compensation cheque. David thought about this formula for a while. "It seems fair; at least I'd be sure of my average income, and in some years, that would be more than I would usually make. But what if my line is ruined by the mine? How do we deal with replacement of the whole shebang?" I said that the "beer parlour price" was interesting. "How about if we asked the trapper to substantiate it in writing, perhaps with proof of offer from a third party? Or, how about if we simply said total destruction of a trapline would earn the trapper five times the lynx cycle income average in total compensation, and that a release form would have to be signed?" I explained that, based on yesterday's discussions, it appeared that David's average income might be exactly one fifth of "the beer parlour price" of twenty-five thousand dollars that he quoted. David really liked the "five-times" concept, but he thought other trappers would be reluctant to put their beer-parlour offers in writing. "I'd certainly settle for twenty-five thousand," he commented over the fire. "I'll take all of this back, write it up, and see what John thinks," I said. "Is that okay with the two of you?" It was.

I flew back to Calgary with half my mind in the bush, and half in Lance's world. I was planning to build him a sandbox even though he wasn't yet a month old. And, I had a beautiful pair of beaded moose-hide slippers for Lynn made by Annie.

John was very interested in the trapper's compensation discussion and really appreciated the logic and that it could be replicated. I set to work and wrote up the draft policy. Upon completion I faxed it to the Kelly Lake School, asking the principal to give it to Jarvis and David. Two days later Jarvis phoned me, and said the policy was "just like jam." I asked him what that meant, and he said: "Really good!" He also asked me to apply it to his dad's claim for one year of disturbance, and total loss of the trapline when the mine opened in a year. "I've already asked the Hythe fur buyer to forward you dad's receipts going back thirty years. He said he'd get right on it." Sure enough, they arrived in a week's time. I calculated David's lynx-cycle average, based on three complete cycles, at five-thousand and one-hundred dollars per year in constant 1982 dollars. Armed with this data I went to see John. "Good thought and good work. Now get out there and settle both of Mr. Gray's claims. That will be the real test of your skills." I carefully documented the claim for complete eradication of the trapline due to mine improvements over the following year. I requisitioned a cheque for twenty-five thousand and John signed it. We'd work out the current year's disturbance claim when we were face to face. So it was back to Kelly Lake to settle the trapper's compensation issue and to see how the interviews were coming along. On top of that we had to start writing the social-impact-assessment document. Once again I prepared to leave my young family for a week. Lance gazed at me as I said good-bye to Lynn and headed to the airport.

The road to Kelly Lake was becoming an old friend as I tore over the gravel in my rented pickup. I wanted to have dinner with David and Jarvis at the trapline cabin that night. Once again I pulled in just as dusk fell. I walked up to the cabin door, opened it and called out, "Hello this place." "Come in," said David. "We're having loon soup." I could see he was stirring something in a big black pot on the stove. Just then he pulled out the ladle and with it came the greater part of a bird's long neck. "I hope you like loon soup, Mike."

I said I had never had it, but probably would like it as I could eat anything. It was pretty good, too. We had homemade "many-berry" pie for dessert. "Okay, how was John with our trapper's compensation policy ideas?" asked David. "He liked them, and I have something for you, David." I reached into my briefcase and pulled out an envelope with 'David Gray' typed on the front. David opened it and saw his cheque. "I am very happy to see this." Then he simply creased the cheque and put it in his shirt pocket. He was content to sign the release. We next agreed that his trapping efforts this current year, 1983, were normal, but he thought over all it would be a four-thousand dollar year. "Would eleven-hundred dollars make it worthwhile?" "Yes, Mike, it would." I slept in the wall tent that night, and David and Jarvis in the cabin. We ate a second "many berry" before calling it a day. The next morning I was up early with the Grays and on the road back to Dawson Creek and the airport after a hearty breakfast of toast and trout.

Three years later, in 1986, I got a phone call from Gerry Andrews to tell me that Dorthea had inoperable cancer in her spine, and was in a hospice in Dawson Creek. Once again I had moved on in my career and was no longer at Petro-Canada's coal division, but the old project's relationships still had a strong emotional pull. "Would you like to like to go up and say good-bye to her, Michael?" "Absolutely, Gerry." So we paid our own way to Dawson Creek and met once again at the airport arrivals lounge. Gerry was wearing an old tweed jacket, grey flannels, white shirt and his regimental tie. He had just lit his pipe as I caught my first glimpse of him striding along, now eighty-two. He looked pretty good. I was all of thirty-five, and had just been appointed the executive director of the Arctic Institute of North America at the University of Calgary. We took a cab to the Alaska Highway Hotel for old time's sake, and booked a single room with double beds. "No sense wasting money at either of our ages," said Gerry matter-of-factly. He suggested a nip from the red sock "to brace ourselves for Dorthea." He poured three fingers this time.

We decided to visit the hospital after a light dinner, neither of us with any sense of what we were about to see or find out. We discovered Dorthea in a screened half of a shared room. She was lying painfully on her side with eyes closed. "Dorthea, its Gerry and young Michael. How are you feeling, my dear?" She stirred, opened her eyes and said, "Oh Gerry, it's inoperable. I'm dying. I'm so glad you've both come to see me." "Well Dorthea, you are just going along to see St. Peter a bit before me. I'll be along too, soon enough." "I'm sorry I can't offer you both anything to eat or drink, but I'm barely able to talk. I haven't walked in weeks." "You've put your share of bricks in the temple, my dear. Don't you worry about us. Michael has moved on to a new job. He has the rank of director. Isn't that marvellous!" "I'm sure you'll work hard as ever, Michael. How is that wife of yours, and little Lancelot?" "Both are fine, Dorthea. Lynn sends her love and so does Caitlin who was born last year!" That was all the energy she could muster. We returned to the hotel and had another drink from the red sock. Gerry put on his damn old red flannels and turned in. I lay awake for a few moments then fell asleep thinking of Kelly Lake. We both flew home on morning flights after a sad breakfast. Dorthea died one week later.

12

Planning the Mackenzie Valley Gas Pipeline Through the Sahtu Lands of the Dene

"The next graphic shows where the work camps will be on this spread"

The vice-president of Petro-Canada's corporate office of environmental and social affairs was disturbed about the loss of the coal division from the predictable stable of clients in 1984. The writing was on the wall: more and more divisions of the company were building their own regulatory-approval capacity by relying on external consultants and the call for our corporate office services was in decline. This probably also had something to do with the fact that the corporate office was filled with Liberals, environmentalists, social justice egg-heads and fellow travellers. At least, that was what the hardcore drillers and engineers in the other divisions thought. I knew this because they regularly told me so when we met socially for lunch or went for training runs for the Jasper-Banff corporate relay race.

When I was called before the boss one more time, I wondered what on earth could be next. Certainly not LNG or coal anymore. "I have received a phone call asking if I would agree to your going on executive secondment with the PolarGas consortium, Mike. They are one quarter owned by Petro-Canada, and they need a manager of community programs and northern affairs to negotiate with all the communities from Inuvik in the western Arctic to Zama in northern Alberta. This position has your name all over it!" I listened with interest as the possibility of a layoff was definitely in the offing with plunging oil prices, corporate angst and the failure of coal.

I asked for twenty-four hours to discuss the prospect with Lynn and some of my colleagues.

The reality was if I did not take the job it was unlikely that I would be placed on research duty ever again. Lynn, as always, asked if I would be happy in the new role. My colleagues said that the future was dim if I stayed in the corporate office because there was a rumour that it would be wound up at year-end. So I went in the next day and volunteered for the Mackenzie Valley gas pipeline. The vice-president happily instructed me to fly down to Toronto immediately for introductions and briefings. "And by the way, you will be reporting to the president and CEO. His name is John Houlding." This was certainly a step up. I arranged for air travel after a brief phone call with my new boss. He instructed me to stay in the King Edward Hotel as it was close to Commerce Court West where the project had its offices on the thirty-fourth floor. Clearly, this was going to be a different kind of assignment from Dawson Creek with Dorthea Calverley and Gerry Andrews.

The Toronto skyline loomed large as I taxied into the King Edward from the airport the following day. The hotel was stylish and luxe; my room was beyond anything I had ever stayed in. I straightened my tie, brushed my blazer, and headed over a few blocks to the Commerce Court complex, a tall cluster of glass and stainless steel buildings full of lawyers and financiers. The elevator whisked me up thirty-four storeys into the executive suites where I would shortly meet my new boss.

The environment was very old school. Everywhere there was wool carpeting, teak panelling, and interesting Canadian oil paintings of northern landscapes. Here the secretaries dressed for success, the junior staff called me sir, and my contemporaries eyed me with cool Torontonian guile. I gathered all this while walking to Mr. Houlding's office from the elevator. His secretary commanded an enormous outer office, where I was immediately seated and offered access to a juice and coffee bar in a cabinet. Through open double doors I could just see the man seated behind an enormous modern desk, talking on his phone. He was kind of patrician, white haired, fit looking, probably at least sixty-five, and wearing almost the same blazer outfit that I was sporting. So far, so good. "Come in, Michael! How was your flight?" And so began the new era. John was immediately informal and even fatherly to me. His agenda was to put me at ease while describing the consortium's dream to build the pipeline that had been completely halted in its tracks by the so-called Berger Report in 1976.

Clearly my new role was to win over the Dene communities with evidence that the PolarGas pipeline-engineering group knew its stuff and would put safety first. There would also be a reliance on my decency and perhaps charm. But "win over" it was, as the pipeline had to succeed this time. The consortium had already spent significant dollars on engineering studies of the favoured right-of-way and my duty was to present these to the communities in such a way as to win converts to the cause. At the same time I sensed that discussion of options, or of trade-offs, might be possible in the broader cause of gaining project approval. "The engineers, of course, know the technicalities best," was the prevailing sentiment.

To understand how thorough the work to date had been, I would next meet Ollie Kaustinen, the vice-president of engineering. John took me down the corridor to meet Ollie who, he assured me, "understood the new North." We rounded a corner and entered another massive office, panelled in dark wood, and containing another great magisterial desk. Behind it sat the vice-president of engineering, another sixtyish Toronto executive. He looked up and smiled at me. John made brief introductions and turned to make his exit. "Ollie and I will take you to lunch at the Ontario Club. We'll have to leave sharply at 11:45 to beat the rush." We all smiled at one another; it was now 10 a.m. Ollie ("Call me Ollie") was not very busy at the moment it seemed. His desktop was almost clear.

He launched into what seemed like a familiar speech about the future of the North. First of all, he thought the massive, seven-billion dollar pipeline was going to be built quickly with almost exclusively union labour, and as "most of the Dene would not be union members, employment opportunities would be difficult at best." After that would be the operations-and-maintenance phase, lasting some thirty years, and employing perhaps two-hundred and fifty "O and M types." They would keep the compressors humming, revegetate the right-of-way and undertake aerial surveillance to check for washouts, ruptures and related safety concerns. All those jobs, plus the managerial ones in Inuvik, Norman Wells, and Fort Simpson, would require at least Grade 12 and probably academic math and at least one science credit at the matriculation level. "I don't think you will find many northerners with those qualifications," he mused. I ventured that we could get some recent high school graduation statistics from the Government of the Northwest Territories. On Ollie bored with his cold logic. From his perspective, it was hard to see many tangible benefits for the Dene. In fact, he seemed to think they would be pleased to watch it all pass by like tourists in their boreal forest homeland.

I could see he was now tiring of this topic, however, and wanted to move on to his first love – pipeline engineering. Here, he was on top of his game. Few Canadians possessed more detailed knowledge of pipelining through tundra, taiga and permafrost. He was a master of the fine art of pipeline river crossings. He understood the business right from hot-rolling pipe in the foundry to commissioning the line on opening day. On this last note he poignantly opened a blue silk presentation box on his desk and extracted a Cross pen bearing the logo of PolarGas on its machined-black metal barrel. "I had these made for the pipeline commissioning ceremonies, Michael. They are for the dignitaries who attend on our opening day. We have also got some PolarGas toques, sweat shirts, and some cowboy belt buckles ordered for your new community programs and northern affairs office." "Yahoo!" I thought to myself.

Ollie then led me down the corridor to a large open-plan, fluorescent-lit workspace where a small group of engineers was toiling away, far from the executive suites. I was introduced to the design team by the vice-president who then returned to his work. Here I received good-natured kidding, some free advice about working for John and Ollie, and was questioned about my prior career in

Calgary. I asked how much of the route selection and design had already been accomplished. "We know our preferred route from Inuvik to Zama already," said the team leader. "We always try to pick the straightest possible route because it uses the least amount of pipe. And we like to minimize river crossings; they are tricky to engineer. It is also good to keep the line close to navigable waters so our pipe-supply routes are short and direct. If possible we like to locate our mustering areas and construction camps close to existing communities so that local airports and businesses get fair exposure to business opportunities. I was factoring all of this pipeline-engineering information into my social-engineering head, when I heard Ollie calling me for our lunch. "Come on Mike, time to go over and get a table before the rush!" I walked over to him, saying my good-byes to the design team.

We joined John in the hallway and soon were whisked down to the main floor by a super-fast elevator. The route to the club was mostly underground in a vast interconnected maze of shopping tunnels. We seemed to cross under a main street and pass under a cluster of related buildings before we zoomed back up about forty stories to the Ontario Club. It was filled with white-haired corporate types in blue blazers and grey slacks, just like us. John pointed out the "old boys table," where octogenarians sat together and talked about the old days and today's stock market performance. It was very Toronto, very Caucasian, very male and as blue Tory as Ontario gets.

As soon as we sat down stiff martinis were served miraculously without even ordering. John said it was customary. The menu, printed for the specific day of the week, was provided by an "old-boy waiter." Again John and Ollie's order was customary. In an effort to blend in, I followed suit and we all had steak tartar. Over lunch I was questioned about my first impressions of the PolarGas team and my plans for starting up the northern discussions. John thought that if the project were approved, I should move to Inuvik and, in due course, would become the vice-president of northern affairs. I wondered what Jim Boulding would make of my meteoric ascent up this corporate mountain. I could almost hear him laughing. Somehow it seemed like corporate tribal anthropology to me. And once again I was benefitting by my ability to fit in, to observe closely, and, by the newly learned ability to guard my tongue. I'd actually learnt quite a bit since my LNG days. But I was concerned about the Toronto-centric values of PolarGas, and very concerned that Ollie and I would soon end up butting heads over his perceptions versus local realities.

As dessert was served Ollie dropped his guard. "Mike, I've hired a good, well-seasoned pipeline engineer to travel to the North with you. His name is Ed Mirosh. He'll keep you well briefed on the pipeline technology and will report to me. He lives in Calgary, too, and you can share offices with him." So, it appeared that I'd be monitored by Ollie's guy, while I worked for John. I wondered how this had been worked out between the two of them. Why had they deemed it necessary? Once more I kept my cool. It would be interesting to meet my new engineering partner, to try and figure out the situation from his perspective. But basically I knew that I was being shadowed to keep me from promising too much, or delivering the wrong message. Once again the corporate beast was raising its ugly head. I was starting to see some interesting patterns. There was definitely acknowledgement of the need for corporate environmental and social responsibility, but it was the delivery that frightened the executive office.

After dessert we all filed back to the Commerce Court West building. I kept to small talk, locking up the inner dialogue in my head. I had a second one-on-one meeting with John and explained that our first northern foray should be to Fort Good Hope, home of the strongest opposition to the pipeline during the days of the Berger inquiry and the intellectual and spiritual heart of Denendeh. It was time to return, to explain how things had changed, and to hear about people's hopes and aspirations for Denendeh when the comprehensive claims were all finally settled.

There was much talk in the northern press of the Gwich'in (the northernmost Dene of the western Mackenzie Delta and the Richardson Mountains) going it alone, of breaking solidarity with a

Dene Nation claim process in favour of getting things done locally and immediately. The unanimity of purpose of the mid-1970s was changing, and with it Denendeh. We were now eight years through the key Berger recommendation of a ten-year moratorium to settle comprehensive land claims and to prepare for inclusive northern development. It was time for PolarGas to find out how things were progressing. It was certainly time for PolarGas to show a face in the Mackenzie Valley communities. John listened patiently to my flow of thought. I could see he was intrigued, but it was also clear he was entering new waters. "I appreciate your point of view, Michael. But I caution you not go too fast. We haven't even submitted our application to the National Energy Board for approval. We don't want to raise expectations, only to have them dashed once again." I could see his point. At the same time, people needed to view proposals, to offer local input, and to prepare. I managed to get his approval to go to Fort Good Hope with the design team's maps for the right of way installations fifty kilometres up and downstream from the community. I then asked him about my engineer partner. "Don't worry about him, Michael. You report to me. It won't hurt you to have some expert engineering opinion to rely on, either. But I can see your point of view." There was a sparkle in his eyes as he said this.

I ate alone at the King Eddie (John and Ollie's term) that night. I was surprised to find my bed turned down and a large Lady Godiva chocolate on my pillow when I returned to my room. I wondered what my room in Fort Good Hope would be like. In the morning I took a cab to the airport and flew back to Calgary. For the rest of the week I would move into the PolarGas Calgary office in the Trans Canada Pipeline tower and meet Ed Mirosh. Next week we would plan our first visit to Fort Good Hope. It felt good to be working on a new project and to be free of the stresses and strains of the Petro-Canada corporate office.

Ed Mirosh turned out to be a welcoming, cigar-smoking son of the Calgary oil patch, refreshingly Albertan in his manner – direct and approachable. He was already in an adjacent office when I showed up on Thursday after my return from Toronto. "How did you like the John and Ollie show?" he enquired with a conspiratorial wink. I shared my first impressions with him guardedly, but soon fell into friendly banter about the differences between conducting business in Calgary and Toronto. I immediately realized that working with him would be fun. And his knowing, informal manner would be just what was needed in Denendeh. All that remained was to develop a bond of mutual trust which would happen over time. We set about planning the first trip to the North to visit the Sahtu Dene who live principally in Fort Good Hope.

I asked Ed to order a set of plastic overlays on top of an appropriately scaled map with Fort Good Hope in the centre. The overlays would show the pipeline right of way, the staging areas where pipe and materials would be off-loaded from river barges, the location of compressor stations, the sites of all gravel borrows (pits) to build the right-of-way berm to hold the pipe, and the site of all the construction camps for the spread crews active in the area. My idea was that we would put all of these data up on the walls of the community hall in Fort Good Hope and I would make a clear presentation on the construction impact of the proposed alignment. Ed would follow this with a talk on pipeline trades and unions, and how the dispatch of labour to the work site would probably function in what was assumed to be union project. Eager to get going, Ed ordered the overlays. He also had a chat with Ollie about the union scenario and discovered that Ollie felt the unions should speak about their activities, not the pipeline owner. Given that the National Energy Board's approval was at least two years away and the marshalling of the workforce would only happen after construction contractors had been chosen, it would be late in the day before the Dene learned about the realities of southern hiring-hall practices for operating engineers, teamsters, welders and labourers. I could see that the local workforce needed to be in training much sooner if we were going to be able to offer much in the way of construction employment benefits. And whatever training offered would have to be union sanctioned. But from Ollie's perspective, training was a union and contractor responsibility, or possibly a government one for the

Dene. The upshot was: no union talk from Ed. I called John for advice and guidance. "Go slow Mike. We'll have plenty of time for training after the certificate of convenience is issued by the board. I think Ollie is right on the time issue."

The plastic overlays were a big hit in Toronto, however. Ollie liked the fact that they showed how much work had already been done, and the competence of that work. The young design engineers felt the same way. When the maps arrived in Calgary they were also appreciated for their clarity and accuracy. Fort Good Hope was certainly going to be action central during pipeline construction. Eager to get North, Ed and I planned to leave the following week. I made phone calls to the Dene Nation and the Métis Association of the Northwest Territories, both in Yellowknife, and Chief Councillor George Barnaby and the band council in Fort Good Hope. I also called Antoine Mountain of the Dene Cultural Institute, the principal non-governmental organization in the community. I wanted to get a good turnout for the inaugural project meeting. Judging by the reception to my phone calls, there was definitely interest in reviving the Mackenzie Valley gas pipeline. I also booked us into Fort Good Hope community-owned accommodations.

We winged north with great interest and anticipation the following Monday. This was to be our first joint meeting. Over the balance of 1984 and 1985, Ed and I attended over hundred such meetings together. We flew first to Yellowknife, home of the northern Canadian bureaucracy and a highly profitable gold mine. Next stop on the Canadian North 737 route was Norman Wells, Esso's northern oil production centre since 1929. Here we transferred to a locally owned airline and travelled by Twin Otter to Fort Good Hope. The plane chattered down the gravel strip, eventually coming to a stop in front of a log-cabin terminal. I looked out of the window and saw a real bush community.

Log cabins were the dominant housing structure and there was evidence of the bush economy everywhere. It was early fall, and several moose had been recently harvested. Fish were drying on pole racks, and long nets were visible in the Deh Cho (the Big River in Dene, or the Mackenzie River in English), especially across the mouth of the Hareskin at its confluence with the Deh Cho just upstream from the community. A line of radiant blue-eyed sled dogs, which were chained in the brush close to the airport cabin, howled as we clambered out of the Twin Otter. A truck taxi was waiting to take us to our hotel. Ed and I climbed aboard with two other passengers, a young couple just returning home with a very young infant in their arms.

Soon we were checked into our rooms and unpacking. I had held onto the map tube throughout the long flight and was happy to see it arrive safely in Fort Good Hope. I placed it carefully on my bed and hung up my clothes. Ed and I had agreed to meet in half an hour to walk about the community. Dinner would follow with George Barnaby at the community restaurant. Our walk continually affirmed the bush economy resilience in Fort Good Hope. Every house had equipment for fishing and the hunt stored nearby. There were many strings of dogs tethered in the long summer sun, waiting for the return of snow, lazing about eating whitefish. Lots of new Ski-Doos were parked haphazardly on the dirt pathways between the cabins, also awaiting winter. Many people too had trucks for use when the winter ice road from "the Wells" became operational. It did not take long to realize that the Dene language was still spoken, even by children. It was also obvious that the children were fluently bilingual and very curious about us. "Are you guys teachers?" one little boy asked as he ran by. "Sort of, but not quite," answered Ed, more to me than the child. After about an hour of circling the town we arrived at the restaurant. It was now 6 p.m.

Only one other person was there. He was about forty, Dene, with long black hair and an open-necked white shirt with black pants. He stood to welcome us with a shy smile and an offer of coffee. "I'm George Barnaby," he said simply. We introduced ourselves explaining how we had just spent an hour getting to know the lay of the land. "You have only seen the smallest piece of our land. It extends out from here like the spokes on a wheel on both sides of the river. We travel on it by day, and dream about it at night. It is our homeland." I immediately thought of Judge Tom Berger's report title: Northern Frontier; Northern Homeland.

After ordering Arctic char with beers, we discussed who and what PolarGas was, and why we were in Fort Good Hope. Our formal presentation to the community was the next afternoon. George was eager for us to give as complete a presentation as possible. He had none of Ollie's reticence about union labour, asking about it in some detail right away. "Don't forget that eight years ago this community had an intensive seminar on pipelining during the inquiry. People don't forget easily and you'll get lots of good questions. I hope you are prepared to give lots of detail." Ed commented that he had actually attended some of the Berger sessions and could remember the community interest. I said that we had brought a detailed set of overlays for the presentation. "Good, we are accustomed to working with Mylar overlays in land-claim selection workshops," replied George. Clearly, my technology was appropriate; strangely I had thought it advanced. I could tell George was tired, and he had a lot more on his plate than me with one project. "I'll introduce you guys tomorrow. You'll get a good turnout. Good night."

Ed and I went back outside with the idea of strolling down to the river. He lit up a big cigar. I was lost in my thoughts. Woodfire smoke was wafting about us, the sled dogs were lying quietly by their tethers, and the net floats were bobbing in the Deh Cho. I wondered just how badly any of the members of this community needed a pipeline construction job? If I lived here, I thought, I'd be quite content with things the way they were right now. I asked Ed what he was thinking. "I just like to look at the land," he said. We walked on down to the river's edge, and marvelled at just how apt the name Deh Cho was. After another hour out on the land, Ed and I climbed the ramparts lining both sides of the river and headed back to our hotel rooms.

The night was just a dimmer light than the dawn at this time of the year. I awakened to the sound of giant ravens squabbling about a garbage-burning barrel near my window. I looked at my map tube and realized today was really my first real day of work for PolarGas.

Ed and I had breakfast in the restaurant. There weren't many other options in Fort Good Hope unless you were staying with friends. And right now we only had acquaintances. After breakfast we pulled our presentation materials together and headed up to the band office to find our hall space.

The staff was helpful, and we were assigned the council chamber, which had public seating for seventy-five, and facilities for overhead projection of slides and movies. There were still flip chart papers taped to the walls from a recent strategic planning session for the provision of band housing. I carefully took down a few sheets of housing plans, and proudly put up my plastic Mylars. Ed arranged a few colour photographs of pipeline construction. By 9:30 we were ready for the show, which wouldn't start until 2 p.m. I looked around the hall and imagined it full of eager faces, with question after question about pipeline construction, but still found it hard to believe that the citizens of Fort Good Hope wanted to join in the mad race to modernity.

Ed suggested another walk to get us in the mood for the presentation. Outside the weather was still, with bright sunshine and a blue Dene sky overhead. We walked about the streets noticing the various activities household by household. Ski-Doos were being repaired, fish were being smoked in smokehouses out behind the cabins, firewood was being split for winter, nets were being mended and reset in the Hareskin and the Deh Cho, house additions were being completed before the really cold weather struck and everywhere people were visiting and laughing as the work progressed. I couldn't help but compare this place with my Calgary neighbourhood, where nobody would be around this time of day during the week. Brentwood was a ghost town compared to this. I also was struck by how absolutely functional the yards were. In my neighbourhood the front yards were purely ornamental. If any work was undertaken, it was generally conducted in private, inside, or hidden from view in the backyard. If conversations occur, they do so over lawn mowers or snow shovels as we strive to maintain the formal order of city life.

At noon Ed and I found ourselves back at the restaurant looking at the same menu once more. We talked about what John and Ollie would be doing in Toronto. There it was two hours later, and they had no doubt returned from the Ontario Club or Winston's, another favourite haunt. I decided to ask a tough question: "So, Ed, are you keeping an eye on me for Ollie?" I could see that this directness took Ed by surprise. "Gosh. What a question!" was all he could muster. I could tell by his flustered response that I was pretty close to the truth and that it was a topic we would continue to work on. But, to his credit, Ed was low key and up to the broad and diverse task we had embarked upon together. At 1:30 we walked to the hall, where a few early arrivals were gathering. It crossed my mind that it would be hard to get anyone out to a meeting in Calgary on a Tuesday afternoon. Here it was the chosen time. The band staff had put out the coffee and cookies that we had asked for as part of the hall rental. Ed went over and had one of each as I went through my presentation one more time in my head. More people were coming in now and taking seats near the front of the theatre. At 2 p.m., with standing room only, I stood to make my first presentation.

"Hello and *mahsi cho* (A big thank-you, my first Dene phrase committed to memory) for coming. My name is Mike Robinson and this is Ed Mirosh. We both work for PolarGas, a company that seeks government and local (Ed took note of this word I am sure) approval to finally build the Mackenzie Valley gas pipeline. We are here today to show you our planned route both up and downstream from Fort Good Hope. We want to know what you think of our plans so far and to hear what plans and expectations you have as a community about our project." From here I went over to the base map sheet of our overlay presentation. This blueline graphic showed Fort Good Hope in the geographic centre, and all of the right of way north and south for a distance of fifty miles in each direction. The Deh Cho also flowed almost directly north-south through the centre of the map. I pointed out the Hareskin River, the prominent ramparts and the Richardson Mountains off on the western verge of the map. The small community (population about fifty) of Colville

Lake occupied a prime spot on the eastern edge. Everyone nodded with approval as the geography was pointed out.

Next I pulled down the first plastic overlay that contained the pipeline route itself. It ran north-south on the eastern bank of the Deh Cho, and came within half a mile of Fort Good Hope, again on the eastern edge of town. This graphic was met with a strange silence. "Are there any questions about the right of way and pipeline alignment?" I asked. Again silence. Thinking silence conveyed assent, I pulled down another plastic sheet. This one contained compressor station locations. Ed rose and spoke a bit about how natural gas pipelines required compressors to drive the gas down the line. The one on this overlay was very close to Fort Good Hope. In fact I now realized it was only a few hundred yards from the old folk's home. Ed mused that it might provide a maintenance job or two, and explained that it was like the engine of a 737 jet, "just like the one you ride in to go to Yellowknife." Another call for questions produced none.

On I motored. This next sheet shows you where the barge off-loading will take place. I now recognized that it featured the confluence of the Hareskin and the Deh Cho prominently, right where about ten sets of nets were at this moment. "This is where the big river barges will unload pipe, Bobcats, dump trucks, low beds, camp trailers, food, you name it; all the material needed to construct the pipeline." Again I asked politely for any questions. Again the strange silence persisted. On I ventured.

The next graphic featured gravel borrow locations. There was a big one just north of town. An audible murmur arose as this information was digested. I looked at Ed, who was busily engaged in note taking. "Have you any points you want to make about gravel pits, Ed?" "Only that we will use a lot of gravel in berming certain parts of the pipeline, Mike. We use it to avoid trenching through permafrost. You cannot lay pipe in permafrost because it promotes melting and therefore weld failures, so we either suspend it like they did for much of the Alyeska line, or berm it with gravel. And gravel is hard to come by locally, so we have to make the most of what we have. Any questions from the floor?" None. On I sped. "The next graphic shows where the work camps will be on this spread. Oh yes, a spread is the industry jargon for segment or unit of construction. Typically one contractor will bid on several spreads. Each one has its own camps, its own logistics, and like I just said, maybe even its own contractor. As you can see, PolarGas is proposing a two-thou-sand man construction camp just a few miles out of town, which we think will be good for local businesses while construction occurs in the area. Ed, anything you want to add about construction camps?"

"Only that pipeline construction moves pretty fast, so if you plan a local business to only serve the camp nearby, it will be a short win-dow of opportunity. And don't forget that the workforce will most likely be unionized, so that there may be specific requirements that only unionized companies may bid for certain camp contracts. But you'll hear more about unions when the construction contracts are let, and that's still several years away at this point." I looked hope-fully out at the audience. The silence continued. "Are there any points anyone would like to make about the environmental impacts of the project in your area? Is anything obviously difficult or missing in the planning we have done to date? I do want to emphasize that this work we are presenting today was done without your input. It is based upon what, from an economic, technical and safety perspec-tive, makes the best sense to PolarGas. The shortest line is the most economic, because it uses the least steel pipe. Technically what we are showing you is state of the art for pipeline construction in 1984. From a safety perspective, we are also state of the art for 1984. Are there any environmental questions?" I waited for about a minute, then looked to George Barnaby for his assistance. "Chief Councillor Barnaby, is there anything you would like to say?"

George rose to his feet from a seat near the back of the room. He stood still and spoke slowly, with a hint of passion in his voice. "I want to thank the guys from PolarGas for coming to Fort Good Hope. We have met your kind of people before, back in the Berger inquiry days. The walls of this hall have heard a lot of this stuff before. I am going to say that I am surprised you didn't come to our community before today, because we could have told you a lot of things that would have helped make this presentation more successful for you. When you present information in Denendeh, and there is silence, like right now, you must not think it means there are no concerns or questions. It is because we have many problems with your proposals, and these people do not wish to embarrass you in front of us all. That is not our way.

"But listen to me; I'll talk with you in the way you are used to talking down south. First of all, as I have said already, you should have come here first before you determined your right-of-way alignment. By not doing so you have acted without our traditional knowledge, and as soon as our comprehensive claim is settled, our permission. This is not your land to do with what you wish. Never forget, this is Denendeh first. Next, your compressor motor which whines like a 737 is next to where our elders live. How disrespectful to them. Would you like to have that noise next to your big houses in Calgary? I don't think so.

"The compressor station location you put up there on the wall is totally unacceptable. Because you put it up first, you shamed yourself in front of all these people. The barge off-loading area is right on a spawning area for Arctic char, and right where we set our nets at this time of the year. Making a big mess of such an important location to our country food-gathering is also totally unacceptable. Again, you have shown yourself to be arrogant in not asking us first. That is why you got no questions on that Mylar overlay, Mike. Your gravel-borrow site is the Fort Good Hope cemetery. May your God never rest your soul if you ever start digging there! We bury people there because graves can be dug even in mid-winter. It is the only place around our community where permafrost doesn't lock up the land all the time. Many hundreds of our elders and younger people who went before their time are buried there. You will never take gravel from that place for your pipeline. And putting a construction camp so close to town will find no support from the mothers of our young girls. We have heard about the carryings on of pipeline welders from Texas in Alberta, and we do not accept that kind of behaviour here. We will not accept any road link with any construction camp of that size. We want you to move that camp far away. I hope I have spoken slow enough for you to get all this stuff down, Ed. Just be thankful that I spoke to you in your language. Mike didn't show that courtesy to those of us here who speak only Dene. Because of that I am now going to repeat myself in my language, mostly for the benefit of the elders here this afternoon. George proceeded to speak in Dene for about twenty minutes to a nodding and appreciative audience. Ed and I sat silently until he finished.

When he did, George looked at us, and said, "Don't lose heart because of today. Learn from this experience. You will notice that I didn't say we opposed your pipeline; I just said that we are angry with you for your arrogance so far. That doesn't mean you cannot learn and improve your ways. The challenge you face is to earn our respect and confidence." I got up and thanked George for his patience with us and for his good and direct criticism. "We can take criticism, and we can work with what you have said to us. I am apologizing right now for not coming earlier, but now that we have come, and you have told us how to improve, will you invite us back?" "Yes, of course," said George.

I had anticipated a scathing reaction like George's because I knew no one in the pipeline-engineering side would have approached the community to find out what their needs were. It suddenly crossed my mind that I had just been on the receiving end of a commentary not unlike Ray Williams' when he spoke at the Captain Cook Bicentenary Exhibition opening at the University of British Columbia's Museum of Anthropology in 1978. Ray and George's truth-tellings were both spot-on – the only difference being my role. What a classic paradox.

At this point I turned to Ed and said that we would take all of the comments recorded back to Toronto, discuss them with the design team, and return with improvements for community discussion and further input. Ed simply nodded at me with just a hint of a smile on his face. I knew he was thinking of his report to Ollie. I was already thinking of my phone call to John tomorrow. With that I looked at my watch. It was 4 p.m. I thanked the audience for coming, using *mahsi cho* too much, and asked everyone to please stay for coffee and cookies. Surprisingly, most stayed, and little knots of people formed in front of the overlays to check out the details. A few people introduced themselves and thanked me for "taking harsh words well." Over in the corner Ed, holding a big cigar, waved me over. "What did you make of that, Mike?" he asked. I knew my answer would travel farther than the hall.

"Well, Ed, I think we were honest. And I think we began to earn some local respect today. We have a ways to go, but I think we can do it." Ed took a few puffs and said, "Actually, I don't think it will be a problem to incorporate what we heard into a new set of maps. Design always involves changes. I don't mind telling Ollie that it needs to be done." "Great, Ed. In the long run, this is the only way to operate in the Mackenzie Valley." On that note we rolled up our presentation papers and strolled out into the blue-sky of Fort Good Hope. It was now 5 p.m. We deposited the map tube in our hotel and decided to walk before dinner. We were now becoming a little better known in town. People actually waved or said hello as we went about the community. Ed was visibly at ease; I was too. There is something to be said about confronting your demons. We strolled along the top of the ramparts, and looked across the wide river to the west bank. "I bet there is gravel over there somewhere," said Ed.

Dinner was Arctic char at the hotel restaurant. We had rhubarb pie for dessert with a beer. I was already composing a long memo in my head to John and Ollie. I promised myself that all of this front-end work would be properly documented for posterity and that each promise made would be a promise kept. The next morning we took the taxi truck to the airport and flew back to Norman Wells to catch the 737 home. By the time we landed, I had written the memo to John and Ollie. It was a narrative of the presentation and concluded with George's key points. I hoped it would be received with interest and respect. We arrived in Calgary on Wednesday night. Only three days away, and yet it felt much longer, perhaps a week. My family welcomed me as always, with love and questions. "How was your meeting, Michael?" asked Lynn opening the front door. "It's a longer story than I thought," I said. Lance, now eighteen months, looked at me, and said, "Duckle duckle." "That is his first word!" said Lynn. I wondered what it meant.

The next day I dressed for downtown Calgary and was amused to see Ed in his suit again. "You look pretty dapper, Ed," I ventured. Out came the cigar and he retired to his fancy office to prepare his expense report for Ollie. I wondered if he would write a memo. A phone call was probably all that was needed. I sent my report to John and Ollie by fax first thing. We'd probably hear some sort of response today, I thought. Sure enough, Ollie called me after lunch. "Michael, Kaustinen here, I've just read your Fort Good Hope report and discussed it with John. He asked me to call you and talk about it. I've also discussed your meetings with Ed. You guys did a good job and took the flak that my design guys should have taken. I'll get them working on some alternatives right away. The compressor station can easily be moved, north or south. The barges can also be off-loaded north or south of Fort Good Hope. We actually put the off-loading ramp there because we thought the residents could get some labouring jobs out of it. I'm kind of surprised they don't want the work. The gravel borrow can also be relocated; we already know of some other sites on the west bank of the Mackenzie River. And the construction camp for two thousand men, it can also be moved to the south. But once again, I want you to make sure that the community really doesn't want to run bars, restaurants and dance halls for the workforce. There's lots of good work opportunities there too, you know."

I thanked Ollie for his quick response. "My guys will get a new map tube to you in about a week. Do you think any other community will want early input to final design like Fort Good Hope?" he asked. "I think we just set a useful precedent, Ollie. They will all want equal participation." "Does that mean I have to send Ed out with you to every community from Inuvik to Zama, Michael?" he groused. "Yup, and there are probably a few more communities we don't know about," I countered. "This is going to cost me big bucks,"

Ollie lamented. "Just consider the cost of not doing the work when we get to hearings, Ollie. It's a new world out there now since the Berger days." He fell silent for a while. I suspected he was hoping I'd fill the void with something he could use. I remained silent. "Okay, Michael, get organizing the next set of meetings." Click.

I waited awhile and then strode into Ed's office. Swathed in cigar smoke, he was hard at work writing with one of the Cross PolarGas pens in his ledger book. I told him about my Ollie call and he smiled. "What did you expect him to do? John told him to co-operate with you, Mike." This was useful intelligence. And so we got to work on planning the next set of consultations. Realizing that more community-based expertise was needed I reached out to Elmer Ghostkeeper, an influential Alberta Métis politician, to join us as a consultant. Now the three of us could tackle the formidable task of explaining pipeline construction and operations opportunities to all of the communities along the right-of-way.

By the end of 1985 we had been to every community on or reasonably adjacent to the pipeline route. Many in fact were visited several times. Community negotiations were begun to augment pipeline design with the inclusion of traditional environmental knowledge. Little did we know, though, that another round of changes was blowing in the wind.

13

The 1985 PolarGas Christmas Party in Toronto

"If you have a lifeboat, I'd get into it real soon"

As Ed and I continued our meetings and community negotiations in Denendeh during the fall of 1985, the outside world was whirling about as oil prices fell and frontier projects were subject to closer and closer economic scrutiny. Ironically, the assumed primacy of environmental and social issues was once again replaced by crude economics. My weekly phone calls with John were less and less northern briefings and more and more appeals to me to "slow down the pace of northern of work to better approximate the pace of work in the Toronto office." This had Ed and me in a quandary. If we stayed south, we had little to do but attend industry-wide meetings on northern issues in Calgary, or read in the office. My innate urge to act was dulled by this tedium. My peers in Calgary were all facing the same situation. Weekly there was news of some other project being "downsized" or completely shut down. I was actually told by a colleague that we were lucky to have such a small northern presence, and that "reading in the office wasn't all that bad, given the alternatives."

The year wore on, lightened to some degree by the promise of a big Christmas party in Toronto where the board and the boss would explain the state of the PolarGas universe in a festive atmosphere. Ed and I figured it would be the best indicator of the future and a must-attend event. So we made reservations and purchased tickets. Meanwhile, all of our links to the North were suffering from our absence. With the boys from PolarGas no longer at every community event, difficult questions were being asked about the future of the project.

Christmas season finally arrived and Ed and I flew east to discover our project's fate. We had booked rooms at the King Eddie for old time's sake, and on arrival dressed for success at the party. The event itself took place at Commerce Court West in the PolarGas boardroom, which had been festively decorated by the secretaries. Starting at 2 p.m., the guest list included the Texas-based American partner, ConocoPhillips, the Ontario partners TransCanada Pipelines and Trillium, another Canadian minor partner, Panarctic Oil, and Petro-Canada.

Ed and I arrived to find hordes of consultants, partner vice-presidents, and all of the Toronto staff at the party. There must have been two-hundred people milling around. Someone dressed as a Santa Claus distributed small gifts, fancy Cross pens. Ollie must have re-ordered, I thought. There was an unending flow of booze and cake. All of the corporate and work groups circulated like a colony of penguins. Ed and I were no exception.

Strangely, there was no big speech on the future of the project. John and Ollie were in good form, the Conoco vice-president spoke with me at great length about his Christmas travel plans, and Charlie Hetherington, the corporate grandfather of Panarctic, told his Arctic war stories.

At about 5 p.m. I headed into the executive washroom. A Toronto-based, senior cost consultant at the urinal, turned to face me. "If you have a lifeboat, I'd get into it real soon. This project is toast, Mike. And meanwhile, have a Merry Christmas."

Two months later Ed, Elmer Ghostkeeper and I were quietly laid off. The project slimmed down to a handful of Toronto stalwarts. We managed a farewell tour of the northern communities. At Fort Good Hope, George Barnaby shook our hands and thanked us for the efforts we had made on behalf of the Sahtu Dene. For me there was a special pain in realizing that I had now spent the better part of my thirties working on four energy mega projects that had collapsed in the planning stages because of international economic realities.

It was also hard not to think of the pain that closures and delays caused folks in northern communities who were eager to move on into different kinds of employment. While the bush economy was still strong, I perceived that many younger workers wanted more options and some changes in their lives.

Section 3

Synthesizing Values and Work in Non-Governmental Organizations

After seven years of exposure to corporate life, I was laid off by an energy mega project, and hired as executive director and adjunct professor by a university-based, non-governmental research institute, the Arctic Institute of North America (AINA). Here my values were in direct alignment with my employer's. Ultimately a thirty-year period of productive, happy work in non-governmental organizations (NGOs) ensued. AINA led to the CEO position at Calgary's Glenbow Museum and then to an innovative cultural start-up in Vancouver as CEO of the Bill Reid Gallery of Northwest Coast Art. In addition, I was also volunteer board chair of three national environmental NGOs, Friends of the Earth Canada, the David Suzuki Foundation, and the Canadian Parks and Wilderness Society.

Oh – I also ran as a Liberal in Alberta and lost an election. But that's another story!

14

Starting 'Real Work' up North

My new T-shirt actually said, "Itchin' to be Gwich'in"

After a brief spell in 1986 of consulting for the Federation of Alberta Métis Settlement Associations with Elmer Ghostkeeper, I was hired as the executive director of the Arctic Institute of North America (AINA) at the University of Calgary. Founded in 1945 in Montreal's McGill University as a bi-national, Canadian and American institution, Premier Peter Lougheed had essentially arranged for its purchase and transfer to the fledgling University of Calgary in the early 1970s, where it became the university's first research institute. Since then AINA had become geographically hemmed in and financially constrained. My mandate was to grow the place beyond its walls and to make it more relevant to northerners and students.

I began work on Monday July 1ˢᵗ, and that first week was invited to lunch at the faculty club by Dr. Joan Ryan, a pioneering Canadian applied anthropologist who was tired of teaching at the U of C, and who wanted to practise community-based research in the North again. She had undertaken her MA research in Alaska, and had had a prior career in northern Quebec as a community development officer in the 1960s, working with her public service and academic gurus, the legendary Moose Kerr and Keith Crowe. Joan was a major character on campus whom I already knew through my friend George Calliou, the native affairs advisor with Petro-Canada's environmental and social affairs corporate office. In her unforgettable style, Joan always spoke her mind.

"I am tired of the academic bullshit, Michael. I have been a department head, a full professor with tenure, a chair of every conceivable university committee, and I'm ready to be an anthropologist again. I want to go north and live in a community and train people to do their own research on topics of their choosing. I want you to help me do this while I still have enough energy to pull it off. I'm fifty-five and ready to go. If I take early retirement, will you hire me?"

I didn't have the money, but I sure appreciated Joan's offer. "Let's go out and raise some money and put you to work," I replied. Meanwhile I called James Ross, the young Gwich'in Dene Chief of Fort McPherson, a small community on the Peel River, just south of the Mackenzie Delta in the western Arctic. Towards the end of the PolarGas assignment we had come to know each other and I had a sense that he wanted to work with me on community-based projects.

"James, remember me – Mike Robinson from Polar Gas? Well now I'm at the Arctic Institute at the University of Calgary, and . . . ." James cut in right away. "You know, now you can do some real work, and get your name back." "What do you mean, James?" "When you were with PolarGas you were the 'guy from PolarGas.' Now you can be Mike, yourself. And you can do some work that really helps us." "That is exactly why I am phoning you, James."

I described Joan's talents and her background. "Obviously we'll have to meet her first and you'll have to raise her salary, Mike, but we can supply a house, firewood and hard-working community trainees." I started to sense the old Kelly-Lake feeling as James talked frankly, with a very different tone from when I was a corporate guy.

"You know, Mike. I just took an oil-company guy for a walk down to the Fort McPherson cemetery. I told him to take a real good look at the headstones. All of the names are Gwich'in. Many are people who died way before their time, like my brother and his wife who burnt to death in a house fire. There are lots of babies and suicides in that cemetery too. I told that oilman that he'll never be buried there. Not because we wouldn't take him, but because all of "your tribe" go out and home to die – priests nuns, teachers, do-gooders of all types. You all go home to die. We stay here to die. We have seen all of you before. In residential school, in church, in the RCMP, in government and now in oil and gas. Always lots of sympathy and good talk at the start, eh. But you never really become a part of this place. You are all just visitors. Tourists. Strangers to Gwich'in ways. Do you understand me, Mike?" James' tone was tough, but with an interest and, perhaps, respect for what I was proposing. "Yes, James, I have a good sense of what you are saying."

On October 1st, Joan retired from her academic position, and moved all her books over to the library tower offices of AINA, where she settled in as the senior research associate. She was great fun to have on the floor, bringing a new sense of the North to the place. We started having tea breaks, potluck suppers, and northern community people in for talks when they passed through Calgary. We created a northern students association on campus, and Joan and I started teaching undergraduates in northern studies. Soon AINA's profile on campus started rising, and fund raising, both on and off campus, became easier, particularly with family foundations who favoured a grass-roots approach to community development. The Corazon Foundation, based in Calgary and stewarded by Kathy and David Ashford, was a notable early supporter of our efforts.

Within a few months of my first discussion with James Ross, four of us: David and Kathy Ashford, Joan and I flew north to meet with the Fort McPherson band council. The route we followed was similar to the old PolarGas routine: Calgary to Inuvik by Pacific Western Airlines 737 that departed at 6:30 a.m., stopping at Yellowknife and Norman Wells en route to Inuvik. We were able to rent a four-by-four crew cab at the Inuvik airport and left immediately for a three-hour trip down the Dempster Highway to Arctic Red River, the ferry across the Deh Cho, and the gradual climb up to Fort McPherson on the banks of the Peel. It was June and slowly warming up to the season when everyone wanted to go off to their family fishing camp.

We pulled into Fort McPherson at dinnertime, and went immediately to meet James at the band office. Waiting for us behind his desk, James, twenty seven, jumped up with a smile on his face. He was of medium height, powerfully built, with a baseball cap tilted back over a thick, well-cut head of black hair. He wore a plaid shirt and black jeans, and noticed that I did too. "No more PolarGas belt buckles and toques to hand out, eh Mike?" he said with a wicked grin. "Nope, James, they're all gone. Like the pipeline." "Now we can do some work together that will help the Gwich'in more than the TCPL (TransCanada Pipelines) shareholders," he replied. I introduced David and Kathy. "Welcome to our homeland," James beamed. And then I introduced Joan. "So Dr. Ryan, do you want to come north to save the Indians?" "No chief, I'd rather become Gwich'in!" she countered. "Do you want to put me to work?" James smiled again; he saw what I saw in Joan. She was feisty in the best sense, tough, principled, and under it all had a heart for anyone who had a need for her special talents and abilities. Standing there in her bush clothes, stocky and somewhat worn by the academic battles, she was ready to go to work. She too had a genuine, human smile that James could understand. "Let's go over to my house for supper," said James. "I bet you guys could eat something after your long day of travel." Off we went on foot, with Joan and James in the lead.

James' log house was one of the best in town. It was perched on a hill, with a good view of the Richardson Mountains, the last gasp of the Rockies, which dominated the western horizon. Waiting for us on the front porch were Mary and Rosie, James' wife and mother-in-law. After a warm welcome we sat down at the dinner table almost immediately. We were probably a bit later than expected, as the food was ready to eat. Supper was all country food and vegetables bought at the Co-op. Baked Arctic inconnu (a type of fish also known as a coney), porcupine caribou, potatoes, homemade bread, berry preserves, pies and tea. As each dish was finished, Rosie and Mary brought out the next round to our vocal applause.

After dinner we remained at the table and talked about our joint project. Mary was adamant that the Chief Julius School curriculum had to have more Gwich'in content. "Right now our children are using readers that talk about turkeys at Thanksgiving, have pictures of grain elevators and wheat crops in prairie fields, and warn about the dangers of crossing busy downtown streets at rush hour. They are culturally illiterate when it comes to the Gwich'in world view. If they talk of us at all, they use the language of explorers, calling us *Loucheux* which means "slanty-eyed" in French. Could you help us develop locally relevant curriculum materials for our community?"

Joan quickly and succinctly outlined this problem with references from across Canada. She spoke about how a few First Nations had created local curriculum units that met all of the relevant pedagogical standards, and about how this approach provided students with intellectual incentives to stay interested and in school. Kathy and David next expressed interest in supporting this kind of work, especially if the project featured Joan living in the community, training local people to create culturally relevant curricula. James turned to Joan, again with his trademark smile, and asked if she would mind cooking on a wood stove and using a honey bucket in a log cabin. "That's how I lived on my first job in Nouveau Québec before you were born, James. I am ready to go back to my roots." Everyone in the room was eager to see this happen.

David and I pitched in by doing the dishes. After one last cup of tea, we all were taken to Rosie's house where we were billeted for the night. She had recently lost her husband but was happy to host a gang of Calgary strangers. It was still daylight outside when we pulled the curtains and quickly fell asleep. Fort McPherson already felt like home. Outside the ravens fought with tethered lines of sled dogs for scraps of whitefish, and a vacant cabin awaited Joan close to the clear waters of the Peel.

In the morning we had a series of well-orchestrated meetings with the principal and teachers at the school, and a session with the band council. The Ashfords pledged their commitment to fund Joan's salary and travel costs. I gave the full support of the Arctic Institute as the university and southern home to the project. I could already see undergraduate- and graduate-student support for the work in Calgary, knowing that if we did well in one community, others would want similar projects. Before lunchtime the band council gave approval in principle to our plan. It was now up to us to write it up and formally propose it to council in two weeks. Everyone wanted things to start in September. A sign of how well the community and the Arctic Institute meshed was Joan's gift to me in subsequent days of a T-shirt that had blazoned across the chest, "Itchin' to be Gwich'in."

As we walked to our truck for the afternoon drive back to Inuvik, James came up beside me and put his arm around my shoulders. "This is more fun than arguing with us about compressor station locations, isn't it!" I wondered how he knew that story. "Yes, James, you are absolutely right." "Now you and I can do some interesting work together," he continued. "What do you know about traditional land-use mapping and land-claims negotiations?" I smiled the entire trip back to Calgary.

15

Joan Moves to Fort McPherson

"Home at last"

In late August, Joan and I loaded up a red University of Calgary Chevy Suburban and headed north. Joan had packed her winter survival gear, down coats and sleeping bags, dry food that was hard to purchase in the North, her working library of books and off-prints, essential tools like her personal computer and her axe, her cameras and plenty of rolls of film, but no booze.

For the first time since she left the North in 1969, Joan was going teetotal because Fort McPherson was struggling with alcohol. The band council was dealing with the alcohol challenge after the experience of the Mackenzie Delta and Beaufort Sea offshore-petroleum exploration boom in the 1970s and early 1980s, when there was at least one twenty-four-hour continuous house party in town every day of the week and the month. The net result of all the partying had been community and family violence, fetal-alcohol-syndrome-disorder children, and a conspicuous lack of community and individual savings. By 1987 the exploration activity had all but ceased, PolarGas had gone away, and life had returned to some semblance of normalcy. It was now up to the families and school to socialize and educate the children of the boom, many of whom would never become fully functioning adults because of the ethanol "swimming pool" in which they had spent their first nine months of life.

Joan had given considerable thought to gifts for community people who helped her settle in and start the project (now formally the Gwich'in Language and Cultural Project). She went to Ribtor, a Calgary hunters' and fishers' outfitter, and bought a dozen sharp sheath knives, a few good long-handled axes, some large cast-iron frying pans and pocket watches. All would come in handy later. By the time we headed out of town, the Suburban was completely full, even though it held only the two of us and Joan's gear. She had initially packed for a year's sojourn.

We drove to Vancouver and up Vancouver Island to take the M.V. Queen of the North ferry to Prince Rupert. From here we tacked north on the Dease Lake Highway up to Watson Lake and eventually Whitehorse, Yukon. Here we checked in with the AINA Yukon staff and spent a night at the Kluane Lake Research Station (KLRS). Station managers Andy and Carol Williams, and the rest of the AINA researchers at KLRS were glad to fill Joan in on some local knowledge after which we had symbolic last drinks. Then it was back to Whitehorse and north again to Dawson where we turned east onto the Dempster Highway.

The Dempster is a fitting entry to the world of the Gwich'in. It rises up through the boreal-forested river valleys of the Yukon to run on shale gravel for miles along barren ridge tops that afford vistas to the horizon in all directions. It is not uncommon to see caribou, grizzlies, black bear, wolves, moose, *siksiks* (northern ground squirrels), ptarmigan, geese, Arctic owls, ravens, finning trout and greyling before lunch. As we travelled, Joan mused about the reception we would receive when we finally pulled into McPherson after a 17-hour drive that day. We knew they were expecting us and that a house had been assigned to Joan, but little more.

When we finally wheeled into town, the buzz of flying shale and the hum of the Suburban's V-8 engine were firmly lodged in our heads. We had long ago crossed the Arctic Circle and were accustomed to twenty-four-hour daylight in late August. We pulled up to James' home and he came out to drive us the symbolic last hundred yards to the project house. The three of us squeezed together on the vehicle's front bench as we bounced over the rutted road to a two-storey log cabin on the banks of the Peel. The truck stopped. James turned the motor off. "Home at last," said Joan.

Immediately in front of the porch was a large jumble of six-foot sawn lengths of black spruce and pine. "Mike, one of your jobs tomorrow will be cutting those lengths into stove wood for Joan," said James. "Come on, let's have a look inside," he beckoned as he got out of the vehicle. The front door was unlocked. We walked into a clean-smelling space with no room divisions. To the right was a kitchen area, with an electric fridge, wood-burning stove, locally cut and manufactured pine cupboards, and an aluminum sink on a long counter centred on an east-facing window. A large plastic cistern held enough water supply for one week. The floor was covered in yellow linoleum. To the left was an open closet, and a living room furnished with a red sofa, two large easy chairs covered in green, and an Ikea bookshelf with no books. A Co-op calendar featuring Nova Scotia outports was the only wall art. The far left corner was curtained off with a red bed cover suspended on a wooden pole. Joan walked over and pulled it aside. Facing us was a tall metal toilet bucket containing a Hefty garbage bag suspended under a small leatherette toilet seat. "Pretty nice!" said Joan. I noticed there was an adjacent wooden stand containing a clock radio. "You turn on the music when you pull the curtain," said James matter of factly. We continued the tour upstairs where there were two bedrooms, both containing new single beds, freshly made up for us.

James had to go, but explained as he left that various community members would come to see us with food and offers of help. We thanked him and began unloading the truck. It was now after midnight. After getting the basics into the house and upstairs, we were both ready to pack it in for the night. In fact we were both upstairs in our pyjamas as someone walked into the living room below. "Hello you guys," called an old man's voice. I went downstairs to meet the new neighbour, Peter Vittrekwa, who was holding a large metal cookie tray with a clean wash cloth draped over its contents. I accepted the gift and pulled back the cloth to reveal a dozen dinner rolls just out of his oven. "In case you are hungry," he said. 'Thank you so much neighbour!" I replied. "I'll help you cut your wood in the morning," he offered going out of the door.

I wondered about this kind offer as Peter was evidently well into his eighties. When I went upstairs Joan was snoring her way into a deep sleep. Soon I was too.

The morning came late for both of us. The bedside clock said 9 a.m. Outside I could hear someone sawing away at our wood pile. Downstairs I heard music coming from behind the red curtain. Joan must already be stirring, I thought. At fifty-six she was holding up pretty well to the rigours of travel. At thirty-six I was feeling stiff and tired from the road and last night's hauling stuff out of the Suburban. I dressed and went downstairs to make tea. I was startled to see a recently gutted caribou bleeding on the yellow-linoleum floor in the kitchen. "Don't be worried about the caribou!" called Joan from behind the honey-bucket curtain. "Ernest Vittrekwa just dropped it off for us. He "knocked it down" at Rock River yesterday. We can butcher it this morning any way we like. That's the Gwich'in way." "Okay, Joan. Tea or coffee this morning?" We agreed on tea. Joan asked how much water there was in the kitchen cistern. I could see in the morning light through the heavy white plastic that it was about half full. "Good, after tea we can have baths," yelled Joan. Just then I saw a metal washtub under the sink. It was big enough for one human. "Aha," I thought out loud. I put on the tea and headed out onto the porch just as Joan emerged from the honey-bucket area to wash her hands in the kitchen sink.

Out in the front yard Peter was hard at it with a clutter of small stove-length rounds at his feet. "How long you been shacked up with your woman?" he asked as he moved his Swede saw back and forth over a six-foot log. "Actually, Peter, I work with Joan, but I don't live with her." I could see how this was puzzling the eighty-plus, master caribou hunter, a man used to dealing with observed facts. I stumbled on with further comments about my work, but none of it seemed to be getting through. Just then Joan arrived with tea for both of us. I could see Peter was pleased to take a break. I introduced Joan as my work partner, and Peter held out his hand in welcome to Fort McPherson. "Can you help me with a few questions, Peter?" Joan enquired. "Yes," he replied. "When does the water-truck man come by to fill the cisterns? And when does the honey-bucket man come to take away the honey bags?" "Water on Tuesday; shit on Wednesday," replied Peter. "Same man does both jobs." "Thank-you," Joan replied, the proud possessor of a story she would tell for years afterwards.

16

Danny Murphy's Island
"What date was the map printed?"

As Joan and her community trainees began work on the Gwich'in Language and Culture Project GLCP), James Ross and the Fort McPherson band council became increasingly disenchanted with the Dene Nation's two southern regions, Deh Cho and Akaitcho, who did not support the 1990 negotiated Dene-Metis final agreement. The initial idea was that one grand claim would be easier to negotiate than many smaller comprehensive claims. However, as the Gwich'in saw it, legal and consulting fees were getting out of hand, and progress was dismally slow. Things came to a head in 1988 when James got up at the annual Dene National Assembly and effectively set the stage for the Gwich'in going it alone to negotiate their claim with the federal government. The Gwich'in subsequently broke with the Dene Nation negotiation process, and created their own negotiating team. As they began to settle their own comprehensive claim, the Gwich'in took on increasing responsibility for tasks normally reserved for southern experts. In this atmosphere the word "consultant" took on a pejorative aura, so that Joan and I were careful to describe our working relationship with the Gwich'in as "trainers" and "partners." It helped greatly that our salaries and costs were born by a foundation and the University of Calgary.

While Joan lived in Fort McPherson, I travelled back and forth while the Arctic Institute's community-based projects began to multiply, and our teaching and supervisory role developed at the university. When I was in Fort McPherson, however, I was often asked by James to sit in on meetings because he wanted me give him an opinion on strategy issues involving members of what he always referred to as "your tribe, Mike." Sometimes I was asked merely to sit in and to observe quietly from the back of the room.

One such occasion remains vivid in my memory and also in the minds of many Gwich'in. It involved land selection as part of the comprehensive land-claim process. James was chairing a community meeting with a panel of federal government representatives who had just flown in from Ottawa. The object of the meeting was to settle the ownership of Husky Lake, long a Gwich'in harvesting area for whitefish to feed the dog teams in winter. And, even though Ski-Doos were now prevalent, many elders believed that the negotiations should not be based on the current economic situation. After all, they had spent their youths in the Depression years relying on whitefish.

I remember seeing the federal representatives arrive, as they always did, in a brand-new rental truck just earning its first dents and mud. The head negotiator, Danny Murphy, was the driver and four other experts sat with him in the cab. They got out at the door of the Chief Julius School auditorium and proceeded to unload the tools of their trade: map tubes, tripods and flip-chart pads, boxes of coloured inks and pens, roles of masking tape, and cameras to record the process. They were all dressed in brand new casual wear, a mixture of Eddie Bauer and Mountain Equipment Co-op. A friend with a great deal of northern experience of such meetings calls it "contrived casual." They exuded a sense of purpose as they set up their gear; their first task being to put a long-folding table between themselves and the audience.

A school janitor had filled the hall with folding chairs and small groups of elders and students were beginning to file in and sit down. There was not much talking. In the back of the room where I sat there was noise coming from the kitchen, still shuttered from view, where several women were making coffee, tea and bannock for the audience. James strode in from outside and went over to Murphy with his trademark smile and baseball cap in place. "Hello, Danny. We are expecting a good turnout here today. Who have you brought with you?"

The four experts were introduced: a land-use planner, a fisheries biologist, a mammalian biologist, and a lawyer, all from Ottawa. They were clustered together in a little knot smiling politely as they were introduced. James said he would introduce the Gwich'in experts as soon as they arrived; some were travelling in from Eight Mile and Rock River bush camps where they lived at that time of the year. Others were already seated in the hall. Rosie Firth, Emma Robert, Neil Colin and Margaret Patterson were introduced along with Dr. Joan Ryan as the GLCP team. The Chief Julius School students were introduced along with their teachers. Finally the elders from the bush camps entered the hall. The old men walked ahead of the women and sat in the front row; the women sat cross-legged at their feet. They were all dressed for riverboat travel in warm, practical wool and canvas clothing, with the women wearing silk head scarves in purple, yellow and blue patterns. They smelt of wood smoke and sat silently waiting for the meeting to start. One of the women lit a pipe and was smoking while she looked around the room.

Sensing it was time to start, James walked to the centre of the room directly in front of the bush elders and welcomed them back to Tetlit' Zeh, the Gwich'in word for Fort McPherson. He next introduced the community elders who were present. The GLCP workers were then introduced; they would tape the meeting and maintain the community record of the event. Tomorrow they would broadcast the results in Gwich'in on community radio. James then turned to the panel seated behind the table at the front of the room and recalled everyone's name and area of expertise perfectly. He explained that they all lived in Ottawa, a place far away from Tetlit' Zeh, and had travelled here so that the Husky Lake ownership issue could be settled. He then asked Murphy to open the meeting for the federal representatives.

Murphy rose from behind the table and thanked everyone for attending the meeting. "The comprehensive land-claim process is long and thorough. We act in each negotiation with the knowledge of precedents already set. We try to be fair. It is important for you all to know that the federal government negotiators represent the interests of all Canadians, and that certain rules must be followed. One of them is that half the shoreline of each lake, and half of its lakebed in a comprehensive claim area must be retained for what we call the Crown, in right of her Majesty Queen Elizabeth II. So, in the case of Husky Lake, the matter before us today is to determine what shoreline and lakebed allocation must be made in the Crown's interest. We understand that the lake is important to the elders because of its fish, which up until the 1970s were used to feed your sled-dog teams, especially in winter. Mr. Fetzell, seated to my left, is a fisheries biologist, and he can help us with his expertise on whitefish if you have any questions. But now I would like to hear from you, especially the elders who have travelled in from bush camps to attend this meeting."

James rose from his chair and addressed the crowd. "Now it is our turn to speak," he said.   It would be good to hear from our elders, and you may speak in our language if you wish." One of the old men from Eight Mile immediately began to speak in Gwich'in. In response to his words, James directed everyone's attention to the big map of Husky Lake hanging at the front of the room. After about ten minutes the elder stopped and nodded to James. James stood up again and walked over to the map. "Mr. Vittrekwa lives at Eight Mile on the Peel River over here. He lived through the great Depression when people had to rely on the bush economy to get them through many harsh winters. No one had any money at that time. You couldn't just go to the Co-op or the Bay store and buy dog food. You had to put out nets under the ice to get whitefish and other fish species for the dog teams to eat. Mr. Vittrekwa thinks that we should not rely on the Whiteman's economy too much. He doesn't trust it because of his own experience in the 1930s. He thinks snow machines are very expensive to buy and operate. He thinks the Gwich'in should always keep their dogs as Depression insurance. That is why we must always keep our whitefish. Also, Mr. Vittrekwa doesn't understand why the Queen needs whitefish. Perhaps you could explain why, Mr. Murphy?"

Murphy rose once again, cleared his throat and took a sip of water from the glass in front of him. "Mr. Vittrekwa has made a good speech. The Queen herself probably doesn't need any whitefish. She acts through her public servants to protect the interests of us all. Husky Lake is a beautiful lake, and we of the federal government want to preserve access to its waters for the public, so they too may camp beside it and fish in its waters."

James got up and spoke to the elders in Gwich'in. They looked at him intently. When he finished, another old man asked a question in Gwich'in. James translated: "Does the Queen know that the whitefish swim about in the lake, and that they do not stick to one part of the lakebed? Even if the Gwich'in give up their ownership of some of the lakebed to the Queen, it does not guarantee that her nets will always catch fish Do you have an answer for this question, Mr. Murphy?"

Murphy stood up looking a bit confused. "Yes, our experts have studied whitefish. Mr. Fetzell here is an expert on whitefish, their life cycle, their habitat, their . . . Would you like to respond to the elder's question, Mr. Fetzell?" The young fisheries biologist got up and began to speak about his qualifications. It seemed he thought that he was about to give testimony in court. "I have a PhD in sub-Arctic aquatic fisheries, and have published fourteen peer-reviewed papers on the topic." At this point Murphy asked his expert if he knew that whitefish swim around in Husky Lake. "Yes, of course I know that whitefish swim around in their lake habitat." The response was a bit terse. James immediately got up and broke into Gwich'in. The elders started to laugh. James turned to Murphy and explained that the elders were pleased that the Queen's expert knew that whitefish swam about in the lake.

Sensing it was time to frame a question, James turned again to Murphy: "Danny, the elders assembled here do not want the Queen or any of her subjects fishing, swimming or camping in or about Husky Lake. They just want this lake left alone as whitefish habitat. As Mr. Vittrekwa has said, it should be viewed as Depression insurance, and left that way, as you guys say, in perpetuity. We can provide you with another lake for camping and fishing in our territories, but not this one. So, can you please respect this one request of our elders who have travelled a long way to come to this meeting and make this point?"

Murphy stood up again. "James, since we are now on a first name basis, I must thank the elders for coming such a long way to make their point about Husky Lake. We of this panel have also travelled a great distance to come to this meeting. Unfortunately we cannot break precedent on shoreline and lakebed division. The Gwich'in must decide what shoreline and lakebed they want. Husky Lake must be divided. That is the way this process works, Chief. And you know that as well as we do."

James gave a short translation in Gwich'in. He looked upset and the tone of his voice was not happy. When he finished translating the men from the bush camps rose one by one and walked out of the hall. The women stood up and followed their men. James turned to the federal panel. "Well, you have insulted our elders and as you can see they have left. I do not think the Queen would be happy with this result. We are going to have a one-hour recess so we can caucus with our elders. You may have tea at the back of the hall." With that he walked out too.

The federal panel stood up as one looking decidedly unhappy. They trooped to the back of the room where the kitchen shutters had now been opened to reveal tea pots, coffee urns, mugs and big plates of fry bread. Several jars of homemade preserves were open and ready for spreading on the bread with plastic knives. The students and other members of the general audience were now stirring. Still, the federal representatives were glum. I refrained from introducing myself and sat down with Joan to have a tea. "They were totally inconsiderate of the bush elders! What a bunch of bureaucratic twits! I hope they don't think that they are representing me!" Joan was in fine form. We wondered what James and his team would salvage from this mess. Neither of us had been invited to the caucus, so we would just have to wait and see. I looked at my watch; it was 4 p.m.

At 4:30 James and the elders reappeared for an attempt to resolve the Husky Lake debacle. There was a humorous glint in James' eyes. He seemed pleased with what he was about to offer. "Please sit down everyone," he called out into the hall. Chairs squeaked on the linoleum floor, voices muted, and last sips of tea and coffee were swallowed. "I have an important announcement to make from the Gwich'in negotiation team. We have been instructed by the elders to make Mr. Murphy's team a counter offer. We are prepared at this time to give the federal government this large island in the Deh Cho, just downstream from the confluence with the Peel River, in exchange for all of Husky Lake. He pointed out the island on the big map hanging above the federal panel's table. "As you can see it is about the same size as Husky Lake, about twenty-five-square kilometers, has good canoe beaches for campers, lots of easy-to-burn driftwood, and the prevailing river winds keep the bugs down. It is just the sort of place the Queen would like to camp. And it has no hills or mountains, making walking easy for city people. You will notice that it has no name, and we would like to propose one: Danny Murphy Island!" This was a masterstroke. Danny himself was seen to smile. His panel members were absorbed in recording James' words. You could see their interest in what was being proposed. "What do you think, Mr. Murphy?"

All eyes were on the senior federal negotiator. He once again stood to address the hall. "Well Chief Ross, this is indeed an interesting proposal. Quite unique; I have never had to deal with anything like it before. If you don't mind, I would like to caucus with my team for ten minutes." "Go right ahead, Mr. Murphy. Take your time," said James. With that the experts gathered away from the table in the corner of the hall. The land-use planner was consulting the lawyer, who was talking with the biologist. Murphy was bending the ear of the mammologist. Soon they had all come together, keeping their voices low. They consulted the map, measured the island, and then sat down again behind their long table. It was 5 p.m.

"Elders, Chief Ross, band councillors, you have given us a very interesting compromise to consider. As chief federal negotiator, I have the ability to set precedent from time to time; to exercise some creativity in the cause of completing the land-selection process. This power is of course not to be abused; it must be used rarely; it must result in a just outcome for the Crown as well as the beneficiaries of the claim. I hope you will be happy that I am convinced that this is just such a case. I accept the offer of "no name island" in exchange for Husky Lake. I cannot, however, accept that it be named after me. Administering that right is the responsibility of the federal top-onymist in consultation with the territorial government's toponymy committee. You may of course propose a name to this committee process." Murphy sat down to loud applause and smiles in all quarters of the hall.

James stood up and faced the federal panelists. "This is a good day for the Gwich'in. It is also a good day for you guys. Instead of leaving Tetlit' Zeh full of angry people, you will leave us happy because of your visit. So thank you for your generosity of spirit. All of the elders here can now go home to their bush camps happy in the knowledge that Husky Lake will always be Gwich'in. Now I know that you will be wanting to drive back to your nice hotel rooms in Inuvik, and we all wish you a safe trip home." While the federal experts began taking down their maps, Murphy came over and shook James' hand with great energy. "Good-bye for now, James. We'll see you again next month to discuss mineral-rights allocations." "Good-bye Danny."

And that was it. The people all went home for dinner, and James made sure that all the bush elders had a place to stay for the night in Tetlit' Zeh. I hung around to walk home with James after we had stacked the chairs. "How did you ever come up with that compromise so quickly?" I asked. "Mike, you know how practical we Gwich'in are. Now go and look at the right-hand, lower corner of the big map." I walked over to check it out as instructed. "What date was the map printed?" "1976," I called back. "Remember the big floods of 1980? The island washed out that year."

17

"This Is Mike, He's Our Consultant"

I had no idea how to reply

As our work with the Gwich'in evolved, so did our understanding of their culturally complex homeland and their relations with their neighbours, the Inuvialuit, the Inuit of the Western Arctic. The Gwich'in and the Inuvialuit exemplify the French anthropologist Claude Levi-Strauss' dictum that cultural groups sharing a common border both aspire to be different from and better than their neighbours. I think this is a fair observation to make in the western Arctic. Both groups had settled their comprehensive land claims with the federal government by 1984, but the western Arctic claim of the Inuvialuit was settled first in 1982. The Gwich'in would argue that their claim took longer because they were less reliant on consultants of all types; the Inuvialuit would argue that their early start reflected their superior state of organization. This competitive spirit continues today; it especially finds play whenever the two groups come face to face in negotiations with their common foe, the Canadian federal bureaucracy in all its many-headed forms.

"Mike, we'd like you to come to Edmonton on Friday and be our consultant!" It was James Ross on my office phone, in an especially fine mood. "Hi James. That's only three days from now. I think I can fit it in, but wonder what level and kind of expertise you need? I am probably not the person you are looking for." "Mike, you are perfect. Wear that old, brown tweed jacket, and bring your black briefcase and glasses. You'll also need a couple of those yellow legal pads and some pens. We want you to just look like a consultant, okay?" I realized that this was a unique opportunity to see the Gwich'in in

155

action again, probably against the feds. "Who am I going to meet besides the Gwich'in, James?" "The Inuvialuit and all their consultants, and a Department of Indian and Northern Affairs (DIAND for short) specialist panel on self-government. Robert Jr. and Willard (both were members of the Gwich'in land-claim negotiations team) and I will be holding down the fort for the Gwich'in. Then there'll be you, our consultant. But you probably won't have to say anything." How could I not agree to go on those terms? We decided to meet in the appropriate hotel lobby on Friday at 8:30 a.m. James hung up and I contemplated the theatre of the absurd that I was about to observe. I wondered what level of expertise would be on show for the Inuvialuit. I had a much better sense of what to expect from the Ottawa bureaucrats.

I flew up to Edmonton dressed as James had specified with two new, yellow legal pads in my black briefcase. I found the hotel and my Gwich'in clients in the lobby. "Hi Mike! Are you ready to go to work?" laughed Robert Jr. I assured him I was, I just didn't have a clue about the exact tasks. "Perfect," said Robert. "We'll see just how fast you are on your feet." We all walked down a carpeted causeway to the convention centre, where we soon found our room. It was set up for three panels of ten people, so the Gwich'in would have six empty seats. We were the first group to arrive. "Make yourself comfortable, Mike. Pour some water into the glasses. Get out your pads and pens. Put on your glasses. The show will start very soon," said Willard. James was smiling his Gwich'in-devil smile. Just then in walked a large crowd of suits. "Look, Mike, it's the Inuvialuit consultants," whispered James.

There were six of them. They were all men and all were attired at a high level of Harry-Rosen splendour. All had computers and were busily engaged in opening brief cases stuffed with files. I looked sadly at my yellow legal pad with no notes of any kind defacing its top page. I reached down, picked up my ballpoint pen and clicked it open. Ready for work. James suddenly nudged me: "Look, here come the DIAND guys." Sure enough, another ten panelists had appeared. Men and women this time, all dressed in Ottawa style, not corporate exactly, and with a bit more individuality. Some were excessively casual, jeans and no tie; others were suited up for a big day of self-government negotiations, I guessed. Next the four Inuvialuit delegates arrived. They exchanged good mornings with the Gwich'in before taking the four centre seats at their table. The chair of the day's activities was one of the DIAND panelists. I leaned over to James, who was seated to my left, and whispered, "Do you know any of the government folk?" Never seen any of them before. Nor do I have the faintest idea what this day is about. DIAND invited us because our comprehensive claim is complete and they want to tell us how to govern the Gwich'in. We've been self-governing for thousands of years! They should be learning from us." Just then the chairman called the meeting to order.

"Good morning everyone, welcome to the DIAND self-government workshop for the western Arctic. I'd like to begin the day by asking for formal introductions of the Inuvialuit and Gwich'in panels. The Inuvialuit delegation may begin." So we began without hearing who the DIAND chair was, or any of his panelists. The ranking Inuvialuit panelist from Inuvik introduced the three other community representatives from Holman Island, Sachs Harbour and Tuktoyaktuk. He then introduced two lawyers, a land-use planner, a political scientist, a geographer, and a hamlet manager. All were described by their long affiliation with the Inuvialuit and their university credentials. "Now we'll hear from the Gwich'in panel," the no-name chair announced. James cleared his throat and introduced Willard and Robert Jr., explaining their roles in negotiating the Gwich'in claim. He also detailed their entrepreneurial activities as regional small-business owners and mentors to other Gwich'in beneficiaries. Then he turned to his right and said with a smile, "This is Mike. He's our consultant." That was it. I smiled at the twenty-four people and looked down at my yellow legal pad.

What followed was very boring. The federal chair began describing self-government as he saw it, as yet another layer on top of band councils, settlement councils, regional claims organizations, the territorial Legislature and the federal Parliament. It seemed vaguely to be yet another form of regional government that he was describing, but it was not really clear to me. Or to James. "Just what is this guy getting at? Doesn't he realize we have just settled our comprehensive claim? This is most confusing," he whispered. Then he said, "Mike, take some notes on your yellow pad. Look like you are fascinated." I took some notes. On and on the chair droned; it was like an undergraduate political science class at a provincial community college. I wondered if he realized that the three Gwich'in delegates sitting before him were fresh from closing a multimillion-dollar claim, with complex co-management rights and fee-simple title to an enormous piece of the western Arctic. Just what was the purpose of it all?

Finally at 10:30 a.m. the monologue stopped, and a coffee break was called for by the chair. James walked over to him and asked if his group were flying back to Ottawa tomorrow, Saturday. "No, we've booked a trip to Jasper for the weekend. No point in flying so many people out here without having a chance to see the local scenery!" "How much did this seminar cost you guys, anyway?" asked James. "I don't know, he replied."

Just before the panels returned to work, James leaned over to me and said, "Isn't it amazing that we negotiated our claim with these guys? Now you have some sense of what our work is like every day. How do you like being a consultant? Is it fun?" I had no idea how to reply.

18

"You Have Been Referred"

It had been a long day, we had a reservation

As the Gwich'in began to implement their economic-development policy after the comprehensive land claim was settled in 1992, they realized they needed to look at business successes outside the western Arctic. They were very interested in tourism, given that ecological and cultural tourism were growing world-wide. In the absence of oil and gas, tourism seemed a logical way to build on the existing Gwich'in strengths of hospitality to strangers, traditional knowledge of their homeland, and its outright splendour. The Arctic Institute of North America at the University of Calgary was asked to help increase their knowledge of the sector by organizing three visits to family-owned tourist operations in British Columbia: the Rocky Mountaineer railtour company owned by the Armstrong Group, the Strathcona Park Lodge And Outdoor Education Centre now run by Myrna and her son Jamie Boulding (after Jim's untimely death from cancer in 1986), and the Yuquot bed and breakfast owned by Terry and Ray Williams. Four young Gwich'in lads led by James and Robert Jr. came down to Vancouver to accompany me on the site visits.

The Rocky Mountaineer is a major Canadian tourism business that provides all-daylight dome car and coach rides through the Rockies from Vancouver to Banff, Jasper and Calgary. Peter Armstrong, the Vancouver-based, founding entrepreneur and conceptualizer of the service, met with the Gwich'in and talked about the fundamentals of his business. He stressed the importance of a business plan, a strong governance board, adequate start-up financing, and marketing. He also expressed his concern about luring significant numbers of tourists to the North. Load factor (the percentage passengers or visitors compared to capacity) for all tourism products, and guest-service training were very important things for the Gwich'in to consider. We met with him in his executive office at the train station. The Gwich'in were attentive and focused; part of this concentration was due to the fact that Peter is my brother-in-law, and James and Robert Jr. knew that a few favours had been called in to get a briefing from the CEO and president. At the close of a two-hour discussion, the group toured the head office and met key staff. Everyone was impressed. However, James, always the pragmatist, said that it was "a little bit more of an operation" than the Gwich'in currently wanted to own and operate. Well educated but somewhat in awe of the Rocky Mountaineer's style, we headed over to Vancouver Island and Strathcona Park Lodge.

Strathcona was created by the legendary outdoor education pioneers, Jim Boulding and his wife Myrna. With her oldest son Jamie, Myrna now continues the work. Located on the shores of Upper Campbell Lake, Strathcona featured funky log architecture, home-style, organic cooking, and guides steeped in local knowledge. It attempted to reflect the region as well as being environmentally conscious in all aspects of its operations. In many respects its offerings were more complex than the Rocky Mountaineer's, including student programs as well as tourism experiences in a variety of carefully thought-out packages. The Gwich'in immediately liked the location and the environmental sensibilities of the Bouldings, and appreciated the cultural sensitivities of the staff. Here they saw the potential of one family running a lodge with up to fifty seasonal employees. The fact that the operation was now over twenty years old was also noted. A successful passage of the business from the founders to their children was also under way. Both James and Robert Jr. liked what they saw. After a day watching kayaking, canoeing, sailing, ropes-course activities, hiking and rock-climbing instruction, the Gwich'in thought they could aspire to this kind of adventure lodge in their part of the North.

The final site visit, to Ray and Terry's B and B at Yuquot, alias Friendly Cove on European maps, involved a van ride to Gold River from Strathcona, and a trip down Muchalaht Inlet in the Uchuck III, a converted Second World War minesweeper now serving as a coastal freighter. Everyone was looking forward to this part of the trip because Ray and Terry were a Mowachaht First Nations couple in the tourism business. The trip took three hours and involved all the senses as new landscapes unfurled before Gwich'in eyes. Robert Jr. quickly spotted herring balling up clear across the inlet, James saw salmon jumping half a mile away and everyone wanted to know what a sea otter looked like. As the Uchuck finally approached Yuquot, all of the Gwich'in leaned over the gunwale to catch a glimpse of the last standing totem pole. Ray and Terry's house was the only one occupied in the village, because the Department of Indian And Northern Affairs had moved everyone else up the inlet to Gold River adjacent to a smelly pulp mill and closer to the wonders of mainstream society with its roads, muscle cars, and bingo halls.

Ray was at his makeshift log wharf as the Uchuck slowly nosed in to drop us off for an overnight stay. Everyone packed their gear down the gangway as Ray manoeuvred his wheelbarrow dockside to help carry gear up to his house. We could all see Terry drinking a coffee in the shadow of their front porch. As the group walked carefully along the floating logs, a loose board flew up and pitched Robert Jr. into the water. He quickly recovered and Ray helped him haul himself back onto the logs. "Oops, sorry about that!" quipped Ray. "I'll have to nail that board down better for the next guys!" Robert took the dunking in his stride, marching off the wharf with a big smile on his face. The rest of us were soon in Terry's kitchen drinking strong black coffee and eating her trademark sockeye sticks.

The two days were low-key, casual, and a great deal of fun. Terry spoke about how she cooked for tourists; Ray explained how he ran his fishing-guide business; and everyone marvelled at their son Sanford's Mowachaht masks and bent cedar boxes. When guests came to Ray and Terry's, they heard Mowachaht spoken and were encouraged to learn and speak as many words as possible. "At least *klakow* for thank-you, *kakawin* for killer whale, *Yuquot* for this place, and *toot'sup* for sea urchin gonads!" said Ray. Long walks along the outside beaches, homemade blackberry and huckleberry pies, salmon-fishing excursions, storytelling and humour were a part of the every-day experience at Ray and Terry's. We even visited the burial cave to hear the story of why Ray and Terry fought to stay at the village when everyone else moved to Gold River. The elders of long ago simply told them to stay, to speak their language, and to protect the village from its enemies. This they did and still do. Leaving was difficult, and we all wanted at least another day at Yuquot when the seaplane came to pick us up. But it was time to return to Vancouver, and then Tetlit' Zeh and Calgary. Ray and Terry made us all promise to return as we walked down to the beach to the waiting Twin Otter.

We picked up our van at Gold River and drove down island to Nanaimo to catch the ferry to Horseshoe Bay and Vancouver. As we travelled I asked each participant to choose his favourite tourism business and to tell us all why. Everyone said it was Ray and Terry's B and B. Most had the same reason: "It reminds us of home. It's not all perfect." said James. "We understand their world, and they understand ours. Even though we are Gwich'in and they are Mowachaht."

As we neared Nanaimo I took a short detour to drive through a planned retirement community still under construction. Every house was the same, row after row. I explained that the baby boomers would soon be retiring down south, and this is how many would opt to spend their retirement – playing golf and watching television. "I hope you don't do that, Mike. And if you lived in one of these houses, how would we ever find you?" said James.

Vancouver loomed out of its smog on the ferry trip home. We drove through rush-hour traffic to get to our hotel located on the Granville Mall downtown. After parking in the underground lot, we hauled our suitcases and duffle bags into the well-lit lobby where a black-suited clerk eyed us suspiciously. "Hello, may I help you?" he said to no one in particular. "Yup," answered James, "We're the Gwich'in group from the Northwest Territories. We have a reservation for seven people tonight." We were all tired and looking forward to showers, dinner and sleeps. "Well, it is after our 4 p.m. check-in time, and I am sorry to tell you that you have been referred." I vaguely heard this from my position at the back of the group and started to push forward to find out what the hell was going on. It had been a long day, we had a reservation and no one had said anything about a 4 p.m. deadline. And what in god's name did a referral mean? I thought it was a medical term. James held me back as I approached the clerk. "Just watch this, Mike. It will be part of your Gwich'in education. It happens all the time to us. We are being sent to the Indian hotel." "What . . . the Indian hotel? You must be joking," I sputtered. "Nope. Just watch and listen. It will be full of people like us, smell of beer and tobacco smoke, and have cigarette burns in the carpets." The clerk meanwhile had prepared a map for us. "Your new accommodation is at a hotel on Kingsway, not too far from downtown." God, the hotel was miles away, and it was already 7:30 p.m. I took James' advice and shut up. We all packed the gear down to the parking garage and got back into the van. I could see that Robert Jr. was enjoying my anger. "Loosen up, Mike. It'll be fun and more like Ray and Terry's than that stuck up place we just left!" I drove us to the hotel parking lot on Kingsway.

When we arrived, you could tell it was a down-market establishment. The building fronted a busy street, it needed painting and the neon sign on the roof actually said "Hot l." There was no underground parking, so I swung the van into a parallel-parking spot behind the building. Just as we were preparing to get out, another vehicle, an old Ford sedan with Washington State licence plates, pulled in beside us. It was filled with African Americans. "Look, Mike," said Robert Jr., "They've been referred too!" Our van rocked with laughter, leaving the American group wondering what the joke was.

19

Gwich'in Economic Development Theory
"How much are them whitefish?"

Neil Colin was one of the best Gwich'in storytellers and was one of Joan Ryan's trainees in the Gwich'in Language and Cultural Project in Tetlit' Zheh. As the only male, Neil was often called upon to provide fish and caribou for feasts and celebrations. He grew up in the Gwich'in homelands before the construction of the instant town of Inuvik in 1958, with its northern store, hotels and restaurants. In those days it was customary to barter for whitefish down at the Peel River's bank in Aklavik, especially on the long, warm days of summer.

Neil can take it from here: "This guy was selling fish down by the river. He had a nice big wooden box full of whitefish. They were fresh caught, just out of the net, and a line of people had formed to buy them. Two guys were in front of me. The first one says to the seller 'How much are them whitefish?' The seller replied, 'One buck.' The first guy gave him a dollar and picked a real good one out of the box. The second guy then moved up, and he asked, 'How much are those whitefish?' The seller said, 'Fifty cents.' He picked up a real juicy one in return for a fifty-cent piece. I was next. 'How much are them whitefish?' I asked. The fish man said, 'One dollar.' I asked, "How come the second guy paid only fifty cents?' The fish seller replied, 'I couldn't help it; the fish came from his net'!"

Neil often told this story at economic development conferences, long a part of Mackenzie Delta life in the 1970s and 1980s as its residents prepared, and then prepared again, for the appearance of the mythic Mackenzie Valley gas pipeline. The story conveys the essence of how the Gwich'in view western economics, where something belonging to the land (and therefore in this case probably to the Gwich'in), is sold by someone else, who reaps by far the biggest profit on the sale. A big energy company selling Mackenzie Delta gas down south is equivalent to a local person selling whitefish from someone else's net and pocketing the cash. Whenever Neil tells this story to a Gwich'in audience it always gets a big laugh.

20

Kittygazuit Summer

"Dad, it isn't 2 a.m. yet; that is my bedtime if you know."

In the summer of 1992 the Robinson family went on a northern vacation, flying to Whitehorse and then driving to Dawson, Fort McPherson, and Inuvik. Lance and Caitlin were now ten and seven respectively, and their parents thought it was time for them to see where their father disappeared to so often. The final destination was the Binder family whaling camp, about one kilometre south of Kittygazuit (locally called Kitty), a storied, old Inuvialuit whaling camp on the Beaufort Sea coast, some twenty-eight kilometres west Tuktoyaktuk. To be fair, the idea for the trip to an Inuvialuit family's whaling camp came from Lloyd Binder, president of the Arctic Institute of North America Student Association, and just wrapping up his BA in economics at the University of Calgary.

"It is time you had a northern vacation with your family, Mike. Northerners need to see you here in your leisure time, too," said Lloyd over a beer at the faculty club. He was already well established in life, married with two sons and a daughter, and well into a career with the Government of the Northwest Territories. In fact he was head of economic development and tourism in the Inuvik region. Even more to the point, he was a multi-lingual, creative soul who brought multiple perspectives to any discussion on the future of the North.

Lloyd did so by birthright. His mother, Ellen Binder was the daughter of Mikkel Pulk, a Kautokeino Sami reindeer herder from Norway. Mikkel and a small group of Sami herders travelled from Norway to the Mackenzie Delta in 1929, and then went by land to help with a reindeer drive that was in progress to move thirty-four hundred reindeer from Alaska to the western Arctic. They were also to teach pastoral-reindeer herding to the Inuvialuit, a people whose culture was, in large part, based upon hunting caribou, essentially the reindeer's biological cousin. This ambitious and fundamentally difficult idea was hatched in the Ottawa bureaucracy at a time when famine struck the Mackenzie Delta in the mid-1920s when the Bluenose-West caribou herd changed their migration route, commercial whaling in the Beaufort Sea was in steep decline, and the delta communities were still recovering from the horrendous influenza epidemics of 1902 and 1918. For both the Gwich'in and the Inuvialuit, this was a time of bare survival. The introduction of Alaskan reindeer was a potential solution to all the problems facing the delta peoples. The Canadian government hired the best herders in the world, the Norwegian Sami, to drive the reindeer to the Mackenzie Delta. Andrew Barr was the first leader of the drive, and Mikkel Pulk became the chief herder when the reindeer were established in Canada.

But the story actually goes farther back than that. It probably begins in czarist Russia in 1892, when one-hundred and seventy-one reindeer were imported to Alaska from Siberia. In 1902 the czar prohibited further exports, but by then one-thousand, one hundred and twenty-eight reindeer had been imported into Alaska. By the 1930s, some sixty thousand reindeer were grazing on the Alaskan tundra and it was from this stock that the Government of Canada purchased its three-thousand, four hundred animals in 1929.

Lloyd's father, Otto Binder, an Inuk from Kugluktuk, met Ellen when she was a young teenager herding reindeer on the tundra with her family. He earned her father Mikkel's respect by demonstrating a strong work ethic. The young couple married, forever bonding the Sami and the Inuvialuit in the Binder family. For his part, their third son, Lloyd, learned Samigiella, English and Norwegian – he now speaks French and German was well – and he aspired to buy the reindeer herd from its then Inuvialuit corporate owner. Lloyd wanted to return to the Sami herding techniques of his maternal grandfather, build the herd up to its former numbers, and make it commercially viable. He hoped his BA in economics would advance his dream by enabling him to create a practical financial plan that would attract funders.

"The connections of the Arctic Institute board could be very helpful to me, Mike, but I don't want you to do anything until you get to know our extended family better. The best way to do that would be to bring your family to Inuvik this summer to vacation with us. Would you like to come to our whaling camp near Kittygazuit?" I said "Yes!" immediately. I knew the anthropologist and adventurer in Lynn would approve.

To be fair, the Binder's whaling camp draws on the Inuvialuit side of their family's biculturalism. Richard, Lloyd's older brother, really runs the camp with his wife, Olive. They extended the formal invitation to us and our friends the Ellis family from Vancouver. On July 4th, 1992, we all flew to Whitehorse and then drove the Dempster Highway from Dawson City, through the Gwich'in homelands to Inuvik, to join up with the Binders at Lloyd's house on the appropriately named Inuit Street. Here we checked our gear, bought some mosquito netting and black-fly dope at the northern store, and prepared Lance and Caitlin for the day-long boat trip down the east channel of the Deh Cho, under the lee of Richards Island to Kitty, which is located on a small bay protected by two headlands. Just north of Kitty in the open Beaufort Sea, swims the massive pod of western Arctic belugas, now numbering more than forty-thousand whales. Every year in July, the Inuvialuit whalers return to camp locations that are probably over thousand years old to practise their whaling skills. The Binders are continuing their father Otto's family traditions at their camp...

The Western Arctic Claim of 1984 (the Inuvialuit comprehensive land claim) created a sophisticated co-management system to preserve and enhance the country-food harvest of the Inuvialuit beneficiaries; beluga co-management is core to the process. In essence, co-management means government scientists and Inuvialuit harvesters sit in committee to determine harvest quotas and to discuss practical conservation measures. Co-management is a Canadian invention with roots in the Northwest Territories that date back to the creation of Fish and Wildlife officers to regulate hunting and trapping in the 1940s. Today, in a comprehensive and sophisticated manner, it guides implementation of settled northern land claims whose first priority is the preservation of culture, language and the country-food harvest. By going to whaling camp each year the Binders celebrate their connection to the land and the ocean. They always get at least one beluga to process and to take home for eating over the winter months which means they literally celebrate the ongoing success of their land claim. The involvement of their children guarantees that the beluga-whaling tradition will be passed on to successive generations.

The final leg of the trip to the camp began when Binder family friend, Floyd Roland, brought his fibreglass cabin cruiser to the Inuvik docks and we began loading the gear over his stern. Hiram, Richard's first cousin and "No. 1 camp man" had already set off in a long, low skiff, almost awash in food, tools, tarps and tents. It was a clear blue-sky day with little wind and Hiram was confident he would be safe. Richard's eighteen-foot, tin whaling boat was the third vessel in our armada that was transporting seventeen people to Kitty that day. We were all launched and speeding down the east channel by 1 p.m. We saw the occasional trapper's cabin, and a few incoming boats as we passed from the taiga boreal forest and shrub zone into the low-rolling tundra of the Arctic plains. Caitlin and Lance used the opportunity to get to know 'Little Richard' Binder (Richard and Olive's son) as we splashed along. The Ellis family, with their three daughters Viveca, Leslie and Claire, were also extremely attentive to their new friends in the extended Binder family.

Soon we were leaving the channel and encountering a low-wave action on the Beaufort Sea. Floyd kept up the speed while the coastline passed by in fast motion. We saw flocks of snow geese, ptarmigan and Arctic terns in large numbers in the shallows along the beaches. Suddenly, Richard slowed and started rounding a low headland to starboard. Floyd followed him into a broad and sheltered bay. On our right was a series of silver-weathered tent-cabin frames and erect tipi poles. Richard powered up onto the beach sands and jumped out of his boat to tie up. Floyd nosed in second and soon we were all standing on the gravel bench known for centuries as Kittygazuit. Hiram had already unloaded his boat and he had set up a net in the shallows before a creek mouth to the south of camp. The next two hours were spent stretching canvas over familiar structures and creating three-walled tent cabins (for girls, boys and the kitchen), and two tipis for smoking whitefish and beluga-whale meat. We set up our Mountain Equipment Co-op tent that looked like a blue igloo on the tundra. Caitlin, Lance, the Ellis girls, and Little Richard found a sheet of plywood to sit on, and immediately began playing *napatchuk,* an Inuvialuit children's game that involves knocking a sharp dart-like object from each joint of your body onto the plywood so that the point lodges on each landing. I wondered how this game was played five-hundred years ago before plywood was invented. Lloyd pointed to all the driftwood on the beach and said, "There is your answer."

Coffee was brewing in the kitchen tent and we all trooped over for dinner as the prevailing Kitty winds began to fall. Just as quickly, hordes of black flies, mosquitoes and 'no-see-ums' swarmed in. It was instantly obvious why the tents all had elaborate screen doors and windows. Lance burst into laughter when he saw his sister's anorak change colour from blue to black as an icing of flies and mosquitoes hitched rides on her back.

We crowded into the kitchen and sat around the central picnic table. Lloyd pointed out the monster-sized ketchup, mustard and relish containers on the table. "Do you know what size these condiment bottles are, Caitlin?" "No," she answered shyly. "Why, they're Inuvialuit size!" was his reply. Everyone laughed. Hiram and Olive were cubing some white meat on the counter. Each piece was literally dice-sized, and again Lloyd asked Caitlin, "Do you know what they are preparing for us?" "No," she answered. "Why, it's beluga *muktuk* – the skin and adhering blubber. It's really good with soy or HP sauce!" Soon we all were eating beluga, some of us for the first time. It was really good with HP sauce. After finishing the *muktuk*, Olive served fried chicken that she had prepared in her Inuvik kitchen. "I hope the hunters in this camp will have good luck, because this is the last of our town meat." "Don't you worry, honey. Whale and fresh white fish starting tomorrow," said Richard.

After dinner the men washed dishes in a tub of hot water, then headed down to the boats to check the whaling gear. Floyd had to get going back to Inuvik, as he had only come along to carry the guests and children to Kitty. We thanked him and paid for his gas. Grudgingly, he accepted. Hiram went over to check his fish net. He soon returned with four nice whitefish. "Lots of bones," he said, "but good to eat all the same." Lynn looked at her watch. Unbelievably, it was midnight, yet the sun was high in the sky and it seemed to be about noon. Sure we were getting tired, but it was invigorating to be here and to be a part of all the action. "Caitlin, it's time for pyjamas and stories in the tent," I called. She was busily playing *napatchuk* with Viveca, Leslie and Claire. "Dad, it isn't 2 a.m. yet; that is my bedtime if you know!"

It wasn't long before exhaustion set in. The first night at camp ended at about 1 a.m., as we all tucked into our intriguingly named Polarguard sleeping bags for the night. My last memory of that day is of looking at thousands of bugs jostling for position on the mesh tent door. Thank god they were on the outside. Soon we were all asleep, oblivious to the flies outside who wanted in so badly.

We all slept in to accommodate a very late night. I was up at 9 a.m. and off to visit the tundra toilet. It wasn't as protected as the tents and there was no excuse for loitering because a particularly vicious group of black flies inhabited the cesspit. I could see that Hiram was already up and checking his net again. I walked along the point and looked over to the opposite headland that formed the eastern entrance to what I now recognized as Kitty lagoon. The opposite shore was also flat, and beckoned across about a quarter mile of water. I bent over and felt the temperature of the ocean; it was actually warm. The sandy shallows appeared to extend for some distance offshore. The whole appearance of the beach suggested

Club Med Kittygazuit. I took off my clothes, leaving them in a pile on the shingle, and ran in for a swim. It was delightful, reminding me of Spanish Banks in Vancouver when I was a boy. "So this is swimming in the Arctic Ocean," I said to myself.

Back in camp Lloyd and Richard had stirred and were down by the tin boat checking the whaling gear. Rifles for the kill shot, boxes of shells, two harpoons, polypropylene rope to tie the whale to the boat, life jackets, spare motor parts, binoculars, first-aid kit, and grub boxes. There was an air of order, mission and efficiency. "Mike, the co-management regulations don't permit you to actually go whaling with us, but you can be involved on shore before and after as much as you want. I hope that is okay," said Richard. "I am here as your guest, and what you say goes," I responded. I was secretly sad and glad, almost in equal proportions. "Today we'll be out scouting for a good whale. We may not actually harpoon it, if we find it," Richard said, explaining that generally females, especially nursing mothers, and all calves were off limits. The ideal beluga was an adult male, but generally not an ancient one. "We like to go out and scout around a bit first. And this year the co-management regime is enabling a total harvest for Inuvialuit beneficiaries averaging between a hundred-and-fifty to a hundred-and-eighty belugas. There is no quota, and beneficiaries are able to take what they need. I thought to myself that one-hundred and fifty to one hundred and eighty out of forty thousand was a good ratio. It certainly seemed to favour the belugas.

We all had breakfast together in the kitchen tent. The whalers, Richard, Little Richard, Lloyd and Hiram were planning to be on the water at 11 a.m. The rest of us were going to tend the net, go for walks, and play on the beach. Caitlin and Lance were already outside, transfixed once again by *napatchuk.* Lynn was taking photographs. I was just watching all the activities. Once again it was a clear, blue-sky day. Suddenly we heard a strange noise. It was a rhythmic clatter on beach stones across the bay. I looked up just in time to see three caribou running across the southern horizon. Hiram was close by. "If I had my rifle, I'd knock one down, but I don't. It's in the tin boat for whaling. That's okay; it is good to know they are nearby."

At 11 a.m. the whalers departed, all smiles and expectation. Lance, Caitlin, Lynn and I decided to hike along the coastline to the east of Kitty. We wanted to experience the tundra and its life in all its forms. We packed a lunch, mindful of the fact that we had just finished breakfast. The day was getting all screwed around once again as we attempted to accommodate twenty-four-hour daylight. We set out in anoraks over T-shirts to combat the ever-present bugs and with our new bug hats, which had curtains of see-through gauze hanging from their brims. We sprayed everything with Muskol bug juice for extra protection. Nobody liked the chemical doping, but it really we had no choice, especially with a ten and a seven year old. I wondered how the Inuvialuit of old dealt with the problem. After about half an hour we were rounding the shoreline to the opposite headland.

The east shore of Kitty's horseshoe bay was rolling tundra and the shoreline was fast eroding at the water's edge. We could see odd, small rises here and there across the eastern headland covered with bunch grasses and wildflowers. We walked up to the first rise to investigate. Looking down we saw a bleached wooden drum hoop; the skin cover had long ago rotted away. Next to it was a four-segment, socketed whaling harpoon with its whalebone point still intact. Underneath these artifacts in a shallow excavation was an articulated human skeleton lightly covered in mosses, its white skull looking up at the sky. We had rounded the bay to find the Kittygazuit graveyard. We walked to the next mound and found a complete kayak frame, again only missing its skin cover. Its owner in life lay beside the kayak in death. We walked about carefully for an hour, viewing the remains of more than thirty burials, each one containing the remnants of the tools of life as lived on the Arctic Ocean long ago. At the far edge of the cemetery we decided to walk back along the shoreline. Lynn bent over and picked up a long, thin bone. She inspected it closely before laying it down exactly where she found it. "It's a human ulna," she said quietly. "What's an ulna?"

asked Lance, full of ten-year-old interest. "Show me your forearm," replied his mother. He rolled up his sleeve and held up his little arm dutifully. "It's that bone there in your wrist," his mother pointed out. "How did it get there on the beach, Mom?" he asked. "It is part of a human skeleton that has been washed out of its grave by the waves." Caitlin asked if her mom could point out where her ulna was too. She rolled up her sleeve and was shown how to find it. She quickly rolled her anorak sleeve back down as the bugs began to gather on her skin.

We continued our walk along the coast for another hour. The bugs were warming to their task and soon we all had to put on gloves to protect the last bit of exposed flesh. We were all still talking about the Kitty graves when we rounded a small point and came face to face with a long beluga skeleton washed up on the beach. As we approached we could see a yellow rope knotted through its jaw. It appeared to have been towed here after it had been shorn of its flesh. We'd ask Richard later if it was one of his catches from last year. The rotting muscle and ligaments gave off a piercing smell that increased in intensity as we approached. I took out my Swiss Army knife and cut a series of teeth from the whale's lower-jaw bone. They all bore distinctive wear markings, perhaps indicating the mammal's age. I put the teeth in a small plastic bag I carried for taking interesting specimens back to camp. In the back of my mind I thought they would make a unique necklace. I wondered if Lynn would wear it. "Its beluga teeth from Kittygazuit; thank you for asking," she would say.

By now the children were hungry and tired of the walk. It was after 3 p.m. We sat down for lunch on a grassy viewpoint overlooking the Beaufort. The children asked all sorts of interesting questions and the topics were as varied as the morning's (or was it the afternoon's?) adventures. I thought to myself that the experiences of the last four hours probably would never be forgotten. How often could a family say that about one outing? I noticed Caitlin was looking upwind with great interest. "What do you see, Cait?" I queried. "Dad, there are some little, brown teddy bears playing over there."

She pointed to the next grassy swale about fifty yards from where we were sitting. Sure enough, two barren-land grizzly cubs were playfully rolling and running about. They hadn't noticed us yet, perhaps because we were downwind. There were no trees to climb and nowhere to hide. We were absolutely exposed and had no bear spray and no gun. I gathered up the picnic containers near me and quietly said to Lynn, "Time to get out of here." "Why? We are just starting lunch. Don't be so rushed." I pointed out Cait's find, and Lynn too realized it was time to retreat. "Why can't we stay and watch them some more, Daddy" Caitlin pouted. "Because their mother is nearby, and she will not be happy," I said. We went back to Kitty, glad that the grizzly family was playing east of us and not blocking our route to camp. All the way home I kept checking over my shoulder, just in case.

We were back in the kitchen tent in time to help Olive with some basic dinner preparation and to see the tin boat full of whalers slowly round the Kitty headland. It was towing a long, white beluga lashed to its starboard side. "There will be work for everyone tonight," said Olive with a knowing smile. I imagined she was right. We all raced down to the boat, eager to see the whale and to share in the success of the hunt. Richard, Little Richard, Lloyd and Hiram were already out of the boat and unknotting the haul line to pull the beluga up onto the beach. Little Richard, all of twelve years old, was especially happy. So was his dad. It was Little Richard's first beluga, a major step in an Inuvialuit's coming of age. "He killed him with two shots," remarked Richard proud of his son. Olive and Richard's cousin, Jean, were coming down the path with sharp flensing knives to begin the process of removing the blubber. They would use several different methods of meat preservation. *Muktuk* and brown muscle meat for camp dinners was a priority. The white sealer buckets were ready for salting blubber. The smoke house was prepared for smoked-meat production, and some flesh would be wind dried on pole racks. Everyone in camp had their favourite recipe for beluga dinner. By the end of the evening all of the meat had been flensed from the whale's carcass by the two women. The men helped by hauling the slabs of blubber to the different processing locations. It was hard work, but everyone knew their role and there was plenty of humour to leaven the tasks. By 2 a.m. most of the day's work was complete. Our family was instantly asleep as soon as the tent door was zipped up and heads were on pillows.

I was up at 10 a.m. and went to the kitchen tent to find Lloyd making tea. "Good morning Mike," he whispered, careful to let the others sleep. "I want to talk with you about an idea I have had for some time." Over tea Lloyd began to describe how he had met Nina Afanas'eva, president of the Russian Sami Association at a conference in Kautokeino, Norway, the year before. He had been impressed by her embrace of *perestroika* and *glasnost,* and her awareness of the Inuvialuit co-management process. She clearly wanted the Russian state to give the Sami a better deal and was wondering if Canadians could help her in any way. Lloyd was convinced we could import the Canadian concept of co-management to Russia, along with traditional land use and occupancy mapping – if we could find the money to fund the project. He asked me to help with developing a plan. I thought it was a wild shot, but certainly worth trying. "I'll develop the project plan, if you'll prepare the first draft budget, Lloyd," I ventured. I had no idea of costs in Russia or Scandinavia, but I knew from the Arctic Institute's work in the North and provincial mid-Norths that such a project required an invitation from the community. It also had to be participatory, run over multiple years and needed top-notch trainers committed to the entire project cycle from start to finish. The back of my mind registered that Joan Ryan was unavailable because she was still working in Fort McPherson. We'd have to staff a potential Sami co-management project with new people. I impulsively asked Lloyd if he and I could do a lot of the work. Lloyd said he could get a leave from his government job to help establish the project for the first year, but beyond that would be a struggle. I wondered if my board would be willing to let me play a major research role in a Russian project and how Lynn would feel about such a commitment, which undoubtedly would take me far from home for large blocks of time. What about our inability to speak Russian? There was lots to consider. And we hadn't even had breakfast yet.

Soon the camp started to awaken. Hiram and Richard began making their morning black coffee. Rachel, Lance and Caitlin were pouring milk on cereal. Olive was getting out the frying pan to cook bacon and eggs. Jean was lighting the cook stoves. Little Richard wanted only his *muktuk*. The Ellis family was happily offering to help breakfast along in any way possible. My mind was in Russia. Lloyd could see I was intrigued. He was smiling.

After breakfast Lloyd and I reported for smoke-house duty. We cut driftwood for the fire, making sure it produced the right kind and amount of smoke, and then we hung *muktuk* outside to prepare it for cooking and muscle meat on the racks inside the smokehouse. All the while we continued our talk about the Russian Sami. "I think their herding culture is more intact than the Norwegian Sami; we could be the first researchers to tell their post-*perestroika* story to the world," said Lloyd. I was increasingly excited about the possibility of introducing what we were now calling participatory action research (or PAR for short) to the new Russia. "How do we get in touch with Nina to see if she would be interested in working with us," I asked. "We can reach her through a Finn named Leif Rantala, who translates extensively for the Russian Sami in Murmansk, Lovozero, and Jona, their political headquarters, and the two main herding communities in the Kola Peninsula," said Lloyd. "In fact, he already thinks Nina would go for such a project." Lloyd was farther down this path than he had let on.

The rest of our time at Kitty was consumed with various country-food preservation projects. We ate different cuts of beluga every day, and all of us began to feel like Kitty was where we really lived. The swimming continued, Lance and Hiram became fast friends and net tenders, and Caitlin, Viveca, Leslie and Claire all became *napatchuk* experts. The parents thoroughly enjoyed the camp, pitching in with the daily chores. Lynn worked closely and happily with Olive on women's tasks; camp was well ordered along gender lines with the women allocating all the roles. I helped 'the boys' out as much as possible. Soon it was time to return to Inuvik with of our pails of cooked *muktuk*, smoked meat, and ice-cellar frozen raw *muktuk*. Two weeks had gone by like two days. The Binders had given us all a wonderful gift. Lance summed it up saying, "I am now an apprentice Inuvialuit, Dad."

21

Sami Potatoes

Taking the western Arctic concept of co-management to Gorbachev's Russia

In order to take the western Arctic concept of co-management to the Russian Sami, predictably our first need was financing. I remembered the extraordinary relationship that the International Centre at the University of Calgary had developed with President Mikhail Gorbachev and had heard rumours that a trust fund for joint-venture research in Russia was being established there. The story of its creation is almost unbelievable. In 1990, in the very early years of *glasnost* and *perestroika* (literally translated as "open government and economic reform") Gorbachev had weathered a threatened military putsch at his summer villa on the Black Sea. Fearing the worst, or at least planning for it, his staff had made a series of phone calls to university presidents around the world. The object was to secure a possible chair or fellowship that Gorbachev might escape to – if the old guard rose again and he was able to flee. The U of C was on Gorbachev's list because of his fond memories of a tour of Alberta when he was secretary of agriculture in the final years of communism. He was hosted by Eugene Whelan, then Canada's minister of agriculture, who was celebrated in many rural Albertan communities with Russian-Canadian roots. Pierre Trudeau Canadian the prime minister, also developed a strong relationship with Gorbachev.

Seeing a landscape that reminded him of home, and enjoying Trudeau's company, Gorbachev formed some positive opinions of Alberta and Canada. In his darkest hour he hoped Alberta might help him out. Strangely, of all the calls made by his staff to university presidents, only Murray Fraser, president of the University of Calgary, returned their call. And he did so on his cell phone from the beach in Waikiki, because his vice-president academic, Joy Calkin, thought the call might be legitimate and it was worth bothering her boss on a long-delayed vacation. Fraser agreed to do whatever he could to get Gorbachev a chair and a safe passage to Alberta. For his part, Gorbachev never forgot Alberta after he survived the early threats to his reforms. His first research initiative in the West was therefore in Alberta, at the U of C. The Sami Co-Management Project was one of the first generation of projects funded in 1994 by the University of Calgary-Gorbachev Foundation Joint Trust Fund. It was largely underwritten by Gorbachev who donated his speech fees.

Lloyd had been correct about Nina Afanas'eva wanting to embrace co-management. She was also eager to earn some foreign currency for her organization. The herding communities themselves were enthusiastic about meeting Canadians in the new spirit of *glasnost*. Ours would be the first western research partnership ever conducted in the Kola Peninsula. Leif Rantala, the Finnish translator of English, Samigiella, and Russian, agreed to join the project and work for travel and accommodation costs. Lloyd was also right about his ability to get a leave of absence from his government post, but only for the summer of 1995. For my part, I was able to convince the Arctic Institute of North America's board that an academic sojourn in Russia would be good for their executive director. Lynn enthusiastically supported the project, in part because her mother's family was Russian, originally from Kalmykia, and in part because she was able to accompany me to the project start-up discussions in 1995. Rarely does a project come together so well. To be honest, we also had a fair amount of naïveté on our side about the conditions we would face in the Kola.

Lloyd, Lynn and I set off for Rovanjiemi, Finland, in early June. We met up with Leif at the airport and began the process of learning how tenuous academic research work would be in the 'new Russia.' Leif went so far as to give us new Russian joke books to prepare us. He had a Finn's instinctive interest in Russia, tempered by the fact that his father had "killed quite enough Russians in the Second World War." He was skeptical about the impact of Gorbachev's reforms in Siberia, and in fact said the Kola Sami's lives were becoming intolerable because of *glasnost* and *perestroika*. "As you will see when we get there, nothing works properly anymore. In fact, most of the state's institutions are withering away." We had already decided to rent a four-wheel-drive truck from Lloyd's uncle Helge in Mertejarvi, a small Sami village in northern Sweden, and so the next piece of business was driving north with Leif in his vintage Toyota. We arrived at Helge's farm the next day and saw that he had put considerable thought and preparation into our trip because he believed we risked being killed by roadside pirates on the road to Murmansk.

After a traditional Swedish Sami dinner of salmon, smoke-cured reindeer and *mesimarja vedelma* (Arctic bramble berry and raspberry) schnapps, we went out to Helge's garage to inspect the truck. It was a Saab with almost military bearings. Helga said we shouldn't assume that gas would be available, so the back was filled with topped-up jerry cans. The same logic applied to water, so five large canteens were strapped in as well. He added five tanned-reindeer hides for good measure, "in case you get stranded and very cold." There was a comprehensive first-aid kit under the front seat, "and space for a machine gun if you have one. And you should." Clearly Helge was expecting the worst. "Why do you care about the Russian Sami? They can easily cross over our border if they want to; they don't really need your help." Lloyd and I attempted to explain our plans for introducing co-management to Russia. Clearly the Russian Sami already knew of the Canadian policy and practice in the western Arctic, and dreamed of implementing a shared, progressive land-and species-management policy in their homelands. We stressed it was really '*glasnost* and *perestroika*' for the Sami. Helge wasn't impressed. Lynn tried to change the topic by asking Uncle Helge if he still had reindeer. "I just keep a few for pets now," he replied.

We slept that night at Helge's, wondering if we'd ever see him again given his bleak prognosis for our survival. In the morning we headed out for the Finnish border town of Ivalo, "the doorway to Murmansk," as it advertised itself. Here Leif parked his car to join us in the truck. We arrived just before the only grocery store closed and we rapidly shopped for last-minute survival rations. Lloyd stocked up on his favourite cheeses; Lynn bought sliced meats; and I grabbed a handful of Finnish chocolate bars. Leif watched all this effort with a bemused grin. He had just returned from Murmansk last week. "It is all not so bad as Helge thinks," he said quietly. By the time we had shopped and taken our purchases to the truck it was 6:30 p.m. "The border is now closed," observed Leif looking at his watch. As a result we spent an unscheduled night in the Ivalo Motel. We watched television and marvelled at a world, where, as Leif was constantly pointing out, "everything still works."

We arose early and had a quick breakfast at a restaurant across the street. We then jumped into Helge's truck and began the drive to the Russian border crossing. As we left, I noticed several very fancy late-model BMWs in the motel parking lot. "They are the cars of new Russians," explained Leif. "No doubt purchased with Mafia money." We were soon at the border. There were no other cars going in; several beat-up old Ladas were leaving Mother Russia. A well uniformed guard wearing white gloves beckoned us forward. He lifted a black and yellow zebra bar and Lloyd drove us into the customs area for inspection. Another guard informed us in Russian (thank god for Leif), that we must now take all of our luggage and open it for the guards inside the building. As we were getting our bags together, another set of guards approached the truck with two mirrors fitted to long metal poles. They proceeded to screen the underside of the truck for what? Bombs? Hidden chambers full of money? Weapons? No one explained. Inside the customs house, still more guards went through all of our luggage. All questions were in Russian. Leif had quite a long series of questions put to him about our work and for the first time we invoked Gorbachev as our project's patron saint. "They are not impressed by Gorbachev," said Leif. "He is too far away in Moscow." After much scrutiny of our visas and letters from Nina and her Lovozero and Jona colleagues, we were finally told to go on our way. I observed Leif putting several packs of Marlboros on the customs counter, which he contrived to forget as we walked out to the truck. "That is how things are done in Russia," he said softly.

We were soon speeding along a well graded gravel road through boreal forest. Russian boreal forest. After about twenty minutes, Lloyd suggested a stop to have a beer and toast Mother Russia and our project. We pulled over to the side of the road, opened four beers, and began a series of toasts. After about twenty minutes we were back on the road to Murmansk. Leif explained that all of Russia has a sixty-mile defence zone, which we were now transiting. "It is the first part of their national defence system, and they take it very seriously. Soon you will see barbed wire fences with raked sand on one side so they can track footprints of Russians who are trying to escape!" joked Leif. Sure enough, around the next bend in the road we came to a very elaborate wire fence with raked white sand on the Russian side. Up ahead we could also see a sentry box and another zebra-bar barrier across the road. "We must stop here and hand out more cigarettes," said Leif. Lloyd pulled the truck over. No one was in the sentry box, but soon a very young, conscript border guard bounced up a flight of steps from a hut just out of sight of the road. He asked for papers and looked at his watch. "This is not a good sign," said Leif. "The border guards at Ivalo stamped our time of entry on the visas. We have arrived here twenty minutes slower than we should have because of stopping for the silly beers." The guard asked us all a pointed, angry question in Russian. Leif replied. "He thinks we have hidden something on our way here. Stuffed something in the bushes." I told Leif to explain we had stopped for a brief picnic, nothing more. Leif soldiered on. Cigarettes were produced. More discussion ensued. Finally Leif turned to me. "It is okay to go; he was just wanting his *blat* (bribe) to let us pass."

The rest of the ride was relatively uneventful. We eventually left the forest and began driving through an area of old gravel pits, broken mining machinery and broken little towns. "This is an area where the worst fighting against the Germans took place in the Second World War. Many Russians come here on the weekends to look for war souvenirs. The Great Patriotic War they call it. My father still remembers the lines of Russians coming forward with their rifles, only to be gunned down by Finnish machine guns. Pretty soon another line of soldiers would advance without guns. They simply picked up the still hot guns of those who had fallen and fired until they too were killed. My father was sickened by all of the Russians he killed." Leif fell silent.

Immediately ahead we could now see Murmansk. Soon we were in the outskirts. It loomed as a sprawling city of bland, grey-concrete apartments. Most were six to eight storeys tall. They were festooned with erratic television antennae and clotheslines. Every private balcony had some distinctive use. Some were glassed in to form an extra room, others held elaborate outdoor gardens, and still others were loaded with boxes and furniture that wouldn't fit inside the tiny suites. Everywhere there were clusters of shambolic homemade parking garages adjacent to the base of each apartment in which to store Ladas. As we drove by these garages they also seemed to be shelters for male socializing. It was Saturday afternoon and public male drunkenness was all about us. We trundled around the inner city in Helge's army truck as Lloyd tried his best to follow Leif's directions to Nina's Sami national headquarters building.

Quite unexpectedly, a small blue Lada in front of us pulled over to the side of the road. Its occupants jumped out just before it caught fire and ultimately blew up. We were shocked. All except Leif who said in his now characteristic deadpan voice: "You see, the unexpected is always happening in Russia. It is quite normal for such things to occur." Finding a city of four-hundred thousand north of the Arctic Circle was a shock to Canadians. Seeing it through Leif's eyes gave it an even more exotic flavour.

We finally started to enter the old town in the centre of Murmansk. We could not see the inlet that formed the harbour, but we knew from the large numbers of uniformed Russian Navy sailors on the streets that their ships must be nearby. Here the buildings were much older, lower in profile, and strangely French in design. Naval flags and symbols were everywhere on lampposts and billboards.

Some featured imperial eagles clutching rockets and lightning bolts in their talons. Fancy wrought-iron gates protected landscaped inner courtyards from strangers. Here and there military police stood guard before imposing doors high enough to ride a horse through. This was evidently the central administration district for the Russian Naval Command, and its star attraction, the North Atlantic Nuclear Submarine Command. Leif was fascinated by the Russian military, and pointed out the differences in sailor's uniforms and insignia as we drove along the main street.

"The well-fed and largest sailors are in the Submarine Corps. You can see how well tailored their uniforms are and the pride with which they wear them. Their "boomers" (nuclear ballistic submarines) are all based here. If there is ever a third world war, these are the young men who will kill all the Americans and quite a few Canadians I am sure. The more ragged looking ones are from the surface fleet. They do not get paid as well, and even their food is poorer. They are generally very skinny. But at least it is a job." Leif's naval lore was fascinating and betrayed eclectic interests beyond Sami culture in the Kola Peninsula. "Finns have a special interest in Russians," he said. "Sometimes in our history we are loving them; sometimes we are killing them. It is most complex."

At the imposing but decaying Arctic Lights Hotel we finally turned away from the waterfront. "Nina's place is now very close. We must park immediately, Lloyd," said Leif. "That hotel is the best in Murmansk. It was built for *apparatchik* Muscovites in the 1970s. Since *glasnost* and *perestroika* it is where new Russians stay. We will not stay there. I have made us reservations in a small hotel for real Russians. We must now walk over some rubbish to get to Nina's." Leif was accurate. The Sami national headquarters was located in a ruined building that seemed to have been semi-deconstructed by a work crew who suddenly abandoned their job. The sewers were off-gassing terribly as we approached a green metal door on the ground floor. Leif knocked and spoke loudly in Russian. From inside we could hear metal bolts being slid back and muted voices.

The door swung open and a thin, short man in a threadbare suit welcomed us with a strangely lopsided gold-toothed smile.

In minutes we were standing amongst ten Sami workers in a green painted room filled with files and clusters of small desks and chairs. Just off it was a small kitchen, and down a dark hallway was a tiny bathroom. "This is a typical Russian family apartment," said Leif by way of explanation. He then introduced us to a fifty-ish woman with closely cropped brown hair and lively brown eyes. She too was very short, under five feet tall, but possessed a commanding presence. "Michael, this is your partner in Russia, Nina Afanas'eva, president of the Russian Sami Association," Leif stated formally. Nina stepped forward and gave me a hug, and started into a long welcoming speech in Russian. Leif reminded her we were unable to speak Russian. Nina laughed at her assumption. We were all introduced, with special attention being paid to Lynn, whom Leif explained was "a Russian who had lost both her mother and her language at a young age." Immediately a unique form of pathos engaged the Sami as Lynn and Nina exchanged hugs and kisses. "Lynn, we could all see your Russian features as soon as you walked in the door," said Nina. Next it was Lloyd's turn. Nina and her team marvelled at his height and good health, meaning that he was well fed and had all his teeth, Leif explained. "It is unusual for forty-ish Sami men to be so strong and fit," said Leif to us as an aside. "Many are now dead by Lloyd's age." Pavel, the man who had opened the door, said he would make tea. "This means the Russian Sami want to hear in detail of your plans," observed Leif.

During tea, the Sami talked about their dire plight since the introduction of economic reforms and openness. It was immediately clear that while the West was enthusiastic about Gorbachev and his vision for a capitalist Russia, neither were well received in the Kola by the Sami. In fact Nina said that she welcomed us and our planned research, but she was "very angry with Mr. Gorbachev. I will take his money, but not his ideas." Murmansk is experiencing some marginal benefit, Michael, but wait until you see Lovozero and Jona. They will tell you a different story."

I began our first face-to-face meeting by asking Lloyd to outline the practice of co-management in the western Arctic. Lloyd
began with the story of the czar's reindeer brought to Alaska, the
story of his great, great grandfather's voyage to work on the Alaska
reindeer experiment, then the story of Mikkel Pulk and the Canadian reindeer project. He walked us through the negotiations and
the concluding western Arctic claim of the Inuvialuit. He went into
detail about the composition of the co-management boards, used
beluga co-management as a key example, and talked of how important traditional land-use and occupancy maps are in all stages of
the process. "By making detailed maps of how you use your land,
you are preserving wisdom about land use and you are preparing to
negotiate with governments and industry about the future pattern
of land use in your region. Good maps lead to good negotiations.
For instance, when you map precisely where the reindeer migrate
during the year, you can show calving areas, nursery zones, coastal
rearing areas, and ultimately the overwintering forest lands. When
you negotiate, in your case perhaps with the military, you can then
explain why nuclear wastes cannot be stored here, why low-level
strafing run practices must not occur in this part of the tundra, why
roads should not be built near a certain lake and so on." Lloyd was
wisely using three examples Leif had told us were of critical current importance. Unbelievably, a young Sami herder from Lovozero
had recently been machine gunned in the midst of his reindeer by a
military helicopter gunship. Spent nuclear fuel rods from the aging
"boomers" were being encased in concrete and left on the tundra
not far from Murmansk, and unspecified wastes were being poured
into tundra lakes.

The Sami were transfixed by Lloyd's speech. When he had finished, however, Nina responded by saying: "This all sounds like a
fairy tale to us. What makes you think the Russian military or commercial interests will respect our rights in the way you outline in Canada?" Lloyd responded that we must all think like Confucius when
he said, "The longest journey begins by taking the first step." I said
"And that is what we are doing here right now: taking that first step!"

It was getting late. I said that we would like to take our Sami partners to dinner. Leif explained where our hotel was, and asked Nina for the name of a good nearby restaurant. She explained that the Sami could only afford to go out to dinner with foreigners who paid the bill. She then gave us the name of her favourite restaurant in Murmansk, The Bear. She also said that I had been invited to lunch tomorrow by Galina Andreeva, chairperson of the Murmansk duma's (legislative body) committee for science, education, culture and nationalities. She had heard of our project from the Gorbachev Foundation in Moscow, and wanted to meet me alone before we went to Lovozero to start our work. Nina gave me a fancy printed invitation. "You must be careful at this lunch, *Mikhail,* as this woman will attempt to befriend you and turn you against us. You must be very diplomatic." I said that I would wear my suit and be on my best behavior. Then Nina said, "Good, as you will be the guest of Galina's husband, who is the Captain of the *Novosibirsk,* one of the newest nuclear submarines based in Murmansk. The lunch will be in the captains' mess at North Atlantic Submarine Command. Be careful or you will end up at *Lubyanka* (the notorious Stalin-era Moscow prison)!"

We had a good dinner at The Bear, but we were all tired and at 9 p.m. headed to our "typical Russian hotel." The place was on the terrace overlooking old Murmansk, and from our windows we could see the waterfront and military ships of all descriptions loading, unloading and rusting quietly side-by-side. I laid out my blue suit for lunch tomorrow and amused Lynn by talking loudly for the supposed microphones installed in our room by the KGB in the days of old. We were soon sound asleep.

The morning gave us new views from our room. Outside on the street corners were Romanies – men, women and children – begging for rubles in Asian 'Stan clothing distinctly different from the ubiquitous Adidas track suits and runners that so many Murmansk citizens of both genders preferred. (The Sami collectively referred to anyone from the cluster of former Soviet Union's eastern republics as 'Stan.) Nearby were the new signs of capitalism, *Milky Businesses,* essentially kiosk stores, privately entrepreneurial, selling vodka, cigarettes, candy, magazines and newspapers. Underneath us somewhere, the hotel restaurant was booming out the latest global pop tunes, especially Barbie Girl, an awful example of western progress. We dressed and went down for breakfast. Lloyd was just ahead of us in the buffet line-up. "I hope you want a big cucumber sandwich. And a nice tall glass of Israeli pineapple juice. Oh, and a sardine or two. That's about it." He was accurate as usual, that's exactly what we got.

Leif joined us for coffee as we ate breakfast. "Tell me, just who is this Barbie Girl person?" He had a son, but no daughters, then we filled him in on our whole family. It was odd to have such loud, aggressive music for breakfast, but we sort of got used to it. We next had a brief reunion with our Sami national headquarters team, where Lloyd began to explain just how the traditional land-use maps are developed.

Lynn went to the department store behind the hotel, while I began to prepare for my lunch meeting. I selected from my luggage two *na pamyat* ('for the memory of this visit') gifts, purchased in Calgary on Leif's advice, for Galina and her husband. I chose two fairly elaborate Timex watches, gift boxed, to ensure I would not be forgotten. At 11:30 I went downstairs with Leif. He called a cab for me, and explained where I needed to go. It turned out that submarine command captain's mess was in a French colonial two-storey, yellow-stucco building only three blocks below our hotel.

I was saluted into the mess as soon as I presented my engraved invitation to lunch. Inside the building I was immediately met by a young woman in naval uniform who said, "I am your translator. My name is Lieutenant Kondrashov." We walked down a long corridor and into an anteroom just outside the mess. Here Galina was waiting for me, formally dressed and smiling. "Hello Professor Robinson," she called out. I responded in English, and soon realized that the hello was as far as we were going to go in English. Lieutenant Kondrashov effortlessly began the process of formal translation. "We will shortly be joined by my husband Sergei, and then we shall go in for lunch. Until then let us talk about the Sami that you so dearly wish to study." I remembered Nina's warning, and thought about how to respond.

"We are so fortunate to have Mr. Gorbachev as our principal project sponsor. He is personally interested in the progress of the Kola Sami, especially in the process of co-management." I could tell that Lieutenant Kondrashov was having difficulty with translating co-management, so I stopped to explain the concept in more detail for her. She then began a more exact translation for Galina, whose face betrayed, or perhaps deliberately conveyed, a kind of low-grade anger at this point. "Professor Robinson, the Murmansk duma has the best interests of the Sami in heart and mind, and I do not understand why they need your assistance?" I followed up with some detail about participatory action research, which necessitated another long discussion with the lieutenant. Galina didn't like this tack either. Just then Sergei arrived, wearing the full-dress mess uniform of his service. He was trim, muscular, erect and smiling with a full mouth of gold caps. He linked arms with his wife and me, and we walked as a troika into the mess. Or what I thought was the mess. It was in fact a private dining room, and what appeared to be five other captains were already seated. As we entered they all stood to attention and saluted me. I saluted back as a Canadian. Lieutenant Kondrashov explained that I should sit first. The others would then follow. I sat down in a French provincial gold-leaf chair. Then they all did the same. Formal introductions followed at the table. I was lunching with a duma cabinet minister and six 'boomer' captains. They were the cream of the Russian Murmansk naval operations establishment.

Lieutenant Kondrashov introduced me to the menu. It was printed in my honour, she said, and it contained three separate entrees, with three accompanying wine selections, and three desserts. All eyes were on me as I gazed at the incomprehensible choices. Again the lieutenant came to my rescue: "You may select from sole, salmon or veal, Professor Robinson. Each dish comes with the perfect wine." I selected the salmon and a *Sauvignon Blanc* from France. At that moment all of my tablemates closed their menus with approving words. "You have also selected the lunch for everyone at the table," she said with a smile. "That is the custom of the submarine captains' mess," she further explained. Sergei then looked me in the eye and said in perfect English, "Professor Robinson, please tell us all why you have selected Murmansk *oblast* (province) for your research project?" This caught me completely by surprise. I launched into my spiel on comprehensive land claims in Canada, and the participatory action research methodology. All was translated by Lieutenant Kondrashov, presumably for all but Sergei. It took the entire entree, which was served immediately (implying that the kitchen had three sets of entrees already prepared), to explain. Or did I explain? The concepts were quite foreign to Russian academia, let alone the navy or the *duma*. I also got the impression that here too Gorbachev was somewhat suspect as a research funder. Nevertheless, I stuck by my script because I was greatly indebted to his largess to even be in the room. As I spoke our wine glasses were continually refilled by stewards who hovered over our shoulders almost after each sip. Pretty soon it became evident that not much work of any substance was going to be done after lunch. I hoped no one here was piloting a submarine out to the Barents Sea this afternoon.

And that was about it for content. There were no probing questions. Galina was letting her husband do all the talking. I began to think that maybe this formal lunch was in some way intended to show me that not all of new Russia was suffering, and that the North Atlantic Nuclear Submarine Command had an important diplomatic role to play, almost akin to the czar's navy in pre-revolutionary times. It was not lost on me that these gentlemen ran boats that targeted all the major cities in North America, including maybe my own. Sergei raised his glass as the entree was being cleared away, and toasted "the enduring happiness between Russia and Canada, and great success to the Kola Sami project!" I responded with a toast to "my host and hostess and the gallant captains of the North Atlantic Nuclear Submarine Command." I then rose and gave everyone at the table an Arctic Institute pin, and my hosts their *na pamyat* gifts. The captains immediately placed the pins in their lapels. The Timex watches elicited a strong *karusho* (very nice) from Sergei, and Galina gave me a hug. Sergei rose, once again bid me good luck with the work, and the lunch formally came to an end. Galina told me to call her if I had any problems during my stay in the *oblast*. Lieutenant Kondrashov then escorted me back to the main doors, and I exited rather drunk into the afternoon air.

I walked back to the hotel, and found no one home. I then returned to Sami national headquarters in the wrecked apartment building. Everyone was there awaiting my return. Nina was very interested in what had happened. "They were trying to figure you out," she surmised. "Do not underestimate them. Right now they are writing a report on you for the *oblast* Governor, Mr. Komarov." Leif added to this translation, "Komarov is the Russian word for mosquito." I appreciated his humour more and more. "Will I have to give him some cigarettes?" I asked. "Worse," Leif added. "You must go and see him at 4 p.m. He has commanded Nina to bring you. Take lots of money." Nina looked at me and smiled. "This is the Russian way. You must first meet all the Sami's enemies before you meet the people themselves!" I then realized that a new person was in the office, an elderly woman with a tired face and a very kind smile. Leif saw my need for an introduction. "This is Dr. Tat'yana Louk'yanchenko of the Moscow Institute of Ethnology, a lifetime scholar and friend of the Sami. She has come at Nina's request all the way from Moscow on the overnight train. She is very tired, but came here to meet you before going to sleep."

I could see a kindred spirit in Tat'yana. We quickly got to know each other in fractured English and Russian. She was a Sami stalwart, tough and yet gentle to the needs of the people in these rough times. She was also a victim of *glasnost* and *perestroika* in that her salary was frozen, inflation was rampant in Moscow, and her institute was no longer seen as a necessary part of academic life. She now financed her Sami research with her own meagre savings. "I am here to help you in any way I can, Michael and Lloyd." We welcomed her aboard. "How would you like to start with a meeting with the governor?" I asked.

At 3:30 Nina, Tat'yana, Leif and I trooped over to the *duma* offices, just a short walk from the Sami national headquarters. The security was way less intense than submarine command, and soon we were seated in over-stuffed visitor chairs just outside the great man's office. His secretary made us tea. Nina was obviously annoyed and angry at "this unnecessary and stupid visit." She was also annoyed at the *na pamyat* gift box that I brought along with me. "Completely unnecessary," she groused. Tat'yana was serene and quiet. I guessed that she was prepared for whatever might transpire. After a wait of about ten minutes, Komarov appeared at his doorway. He was about fifty, heavy set, with a big head and bushy eyebrows, and a rumpled brown suit. He looked pissed off. "Come in, great friends of our Sami," he commanded. I caught the condescension before Leif finished the translation. His office was furnished in old-fashioned Soviet brutalism. Garish, angular furniture, odd clocks, a television on four legs, lots of little banners marking exchanges with other *oblast* officials, and a meeting table with six chairs. After we sat at the table. Komarov lunged right to it. "I only learned of your so-called project from Galina Andreeva last week. You have no permission from the *oblast* to conduct research with the Sami, and I do not recognize Mrs. Afanas'eva's organization. I could throw you all out today if I wished. Mr. Gorbachev is no longer in power, and I am not required to consult him in Moscow about how I run my *oblast*. I am suspicious of your intentions. What do you have to say for yourself, Mr. Robinson?"

I started down my familiar path once again about the Gorbachev Foundation, participatory research, and co-management. Komarov glazed over. Nina fired a short burst of angry rhetoric at Komarov. He shot back. Tat'yana attempted a long reconciliation. Leif translated at breakneck speed, pausing from time to time to say something like, "Michael, this man is very powerful, try to get Nina to stop making him angry." It was all surreal and beyond me. Finally Komarov summarized his requirements of us: "You will report in detail all of your plans to Sergei Semyashkin, my deputy of Sami affairs. He will be my eyes on you while you are in the Murmansk *oblast.* You must obey him." I rose with my *na pamyat* box, and offered it to the governor. He opened it roughly and was startled to find a big, gaudy Sports Timex. "*Speciba. Karusho.*" And that was it. The governor did not return the gift, instead he ushered us to his great doorway. We collected our coats and escaped to the street.

"Semyashkin is a fool," said Nina. "I refuse to talk with him." Tat'yana was more accommodating. "Michael and I will pay him a visit." Leif said that he had met him and he knew "precisely nothing about the Sami." We made our way back to Sami national head-quarters to have tea and calm down. Tat'yana got on the phone and lined up a meeting with the governor's Sami expert for the next day at 9 a.m. Lynn and I decided to go for a walk. Lloyd said he would join us for dinner at 7 p.m. Leif just wanted a break from translat-ing. "Meetings like that one with Komarov are very exhausting for Finnish translators!" They were exhausting for all of us. But luckily, if all went at least okay with Semyashkin, tomorrow we would soon be driving Helge's truck to Lovozero. Only one more night in Mur-mansk. It passed uneventfully.

Next morning Tat'yana and I met in the hotel lobby and decided to walk to Semyashkin's office. Tat'yana had been there once before. The Romany were begging all about the hotel parking, including a legless grandmother on a wheeled sort of skateboard who held an armless little boy. Farther down the street on a prominent corner, two well-dressed currency changers were flaunting enormous wads of rubles and big pistols holstered to their belts John-Wayne style. Sailors on leave were strolling by in twos and threes. We found Semyashkin's *duma* office building and climbed the stairs to his cluttered room. He was working alone. Seeing us approaching he quickly got up from his desk and thrust out his hand in welcome. He was a pathetic figure. His worn out suit, yellowed-white shirt, filthy tie and ill-fitting glasses didn't do much for first impressions. Tat'yana explained that we were about to go down to Lovozero, and had dropped by to pay our respects. "You needn't go there," he responded. "I am the *oblast* expert on the Sami. Why not just stay here and interview me. It will cost you much less money and it will yield superior results. Besides, the Sami do not like foreign researchers, and my reputation with them is superb. Even the governor knows of my reputation as a Sami expert." We told him that we had just had an audience with Governor Komarov, and that he had spoken highly of him. In fact, we felt that we must visit him to pass along this observation. We also noted that the Sami national headquarters and Mrs. Afanas'eva were supporting our research, along with Mikhail Gorbachev. As a result we were going to Lovozero tomorrow. "That is a big mistake. Lovozero is very dangerous. There are many thieves and witches there. Take my advice and avoid it at all costs." At this point we said that we had to leave, but would stay in touch as our research developed. Mr. Semyashkin walked with us to the door. "Do not worry about us!" said Tat'yana. We hurried down the hallway, and made our way down the stairs to the street.

"I told you he was a donkey!" Nina reiterated as we debriefed her. "What an arrogant little man!" I certainly shared her opinion, but we had to work around Komarov somehow. Just then Lloyd pulled up in Helge's truck. All of us would be riding in it to Lovozero, including Tat'yana and Nina now. We added their suitcases to the pile in the back, wedged in amongst the gas cans, the water canteens, and the five reindeer hides. There was barely enough room in the crew cab for the six of us, but we all sardined in, and Lloyd headed south from Murmansk. The road started as an expressway, but soon became a paved two-lane highway. We quickly exited the grey concrete core of the city, and found ourselves in a zone of milky businesses, conurbations of private Lada garages and males partying. The road signage was confusing, but somehow Lloyd kept us going south into the looming boreal forests. There were very few cars or trucks on the road. Occasionally we passed a group of men with walking staffs and shoulder bags heading out on mushroom-picking expeditions. Every fifty yards or so we passed a trapper who advertised his presence by hanging sable pelts on a pole with a crude 'For Sale' sign. Similarly, every so often a sign would appear with *Suomga* written in charcoal letters. Leif was tempted and we stopped to buy a Kola salmon for our colleagues in Lovozero.

Most jarring to me were the enormous military installations we passed. The first was a Bear bomber base, according to Leif. Here in the taiga forests whole families passed their days maintaining aircraft that now rarely flew the old sorties to the Canadian Arctic. Leif explained that "there is no money for fuel and the mothers of this base recently staged a sit-in to protest that their husbands' salaries have not been paid for four months." Crazily, perhaps, I photographed the base as we sped by in our Swedish army truck. Farther down the road we passed an enormous long, low SAM bunker. "This is to shoot down the American Cruise missiles that are fired by their "boomers" at Moscow, which is just six-hundred and twenty miles south of here. If it all still works." said Leif. Everywhere technology; everywhere technology breaking down. Lloyd looked at the gas gauge, and concluded it was time to refuel. We pulled over to the side of the road. Leif reached into his briefcase and pulled out his work gloves. We lifted a heavy gerry can out of the back of the truck and Leif poured its contents into the gas tank. "One down and four more to go," he noted. "It is impossible to buy gas in Lovozero. If we get stranded we may have to order gas from Murmansk. Very expensive. I hope Mr. Gorbachev gave you gas money!"

Shortly after we started up again, a welded iron sculpture of a reindeer appeared to our right. It had a sign hanging below it. Lloyd slowed down. On our left another sign lay in the ditch. Leif noted, "The one on the right welcomes us to Lovozero; the one on the left said 'Good-bye,' but it is ruined." We took a right turn and drove through a small gap in the forest. Lovozero was immediately in front of us. It was just like a mini-Murmansk. There were four, five-storey apartment buildings, and a brand new one that seemed to have been halted in mid-construction. A small cluster of private garages were off to our right. The Lovozero River ran through the middle of the town, and the main bridge across it was closed to car traffic. "It is broken," said Leif. We stopped in front of the first apartment building. Nina said, "This is where Larisa Avdeeva, the president of the Lovozero Sami lives. She will welcome us and show us our rooms." Just then Larisa appeared at the apartment's front door, surrounded by her chosen trainees: Pavel, Andrei, and Nadya. "All of Lovozero welcomes you!" she said. We conducted formal introductions on the spot. Larisa then took the four Canadians to a recently redecorated suite in her apartment block. Tat'yana and Nina would stay with her. We all agreed to meet at Larisa's at 6 p.m. for dinner.

Lynn and I decided to go for a walk in the village. We started down the main street, and soon became aware of the surprised gazes of the neighbours. A few said "*Dobre dien*" (good day), but most remained silent. Everyone was thin, way thinner than us. There were a very few shops, and the few manufactured goods on display were all made within the old Communist bloc. The food store was like the buffet in Murmansk: mostly cucumbers, Israeli pineapple juice, and tinned sardines from Spain and Norway. There were a few Russian sweets and some tins of milk, but that was about it.

We walked on past several private houses in the oldest part of the village backing onto the river. Each one had a prominent potato plot in the front yard. They were beautifully raked and weeded. Ahead of us we saw Nina strolling by herself. We caught up and struggled to make sense to each other in a crazy mixture of *Russki*-English. She pointed to the privately owned houses with some of her contained anger: "*Mikhail, Russki kartochka.*" By this she meant I am sure, "Michael, those are ethnic Russian's potatoes." For some reason they were able to have houses while the Sami had to make do with small flats. And they relied on one basic vegetable staple: the potato. We walked onto a broad field system at the edge of the village. Here the Sami gardens stretched in all directions. Several elderly women were hoeing and weeding many different crops. At the very edge of these fields was the open tundra, and many hundreds of reindeer were visible. "*Mikhail, Sami kartochka!*" said Nina, pointing at the reindeer: "There are the Sami potatoes." We smiled and walked back to Larisa's for dinner.

22

A Walk Through Lovozero with Larisa

"What is good for the reindeer is good for the Sami"

Larisa was eager to start the project, but before we began she wanted the Canadians to see her community through her eyes. Leif explained that it was the custom of the Sami to take all visitors to the Lovozero museum first. It was located in a nondescript office block in the centre of the village, and the curator, Mrs. Sergovina, was awaiting us at the front door. She explained that during Stalin's time all villages made and kept up-to-date lists of births, marriages and deaths. Everyone was tracked in an orderly fashion, and the habit carried over to the creation of village archives and museums of different ethnicities. As a result each village had its own museum. Lovozero's was of course dedicated to Sami history, beginning with the Sami origin myth of Myandash, reindeer man. Myandash had a Sami mother and a reindeer father and he could change back and forth, from one form to the other at will. The early Sami often made rock carvings, or pictographs, of Myandash's birth, and a large boulder bearing this story was in the front lobby of the museum. The carving depicted Myandash exiting his mother's birth canal with reindeer antlers and four legs reaching for the ground. Mrs. Sergovina stopped to make the core point of the Sami origin myth: "What is good for the reindeer is good for the Sami."

Her tour took us to the photo archives of Sami history from the 1920s to the present. Much time was spent illustrating the change that the Russian Revolution brought to the Sami. We learned that the individual extended-family reindeer herds were replaced with Soviet Brigade Units of reindeer, each with its own military command structure. In this way family ownership came to an end and the people became collective owners of the resource. Many herders rebelled against this enforced change and in the early years of Sovietization, many of them were shot, usually in front of their village mates, and often in a schoolyard for the children to bear witness. In the face of this violence, many Sami rituals and traditions went underground, including the use of Samigiella, the peoples' language. "Just a decade ago I could not tell you this story," said Mrs. Sergovina. "But today the practice of *glasnost* enables me to tell you the truth. Unfortunately, as you will see later, all of *glasnost* is not perfect."

Another focus of the photo archives was the Great Patriotic War. The Sami were often on the front lines fighting against the Germans. Their knowledge of the landscape was put to good use in stopping the Nazi thrust to capture Murmansk. A special section of the museum was created to honour the forty-four Lovozero Sami who were killed in the Second World War. Each year on Armistice Day their photos are put on special display in the school. "Everyone still knows their names and remembers their sacrifice," said Mrs. Sergovina.

The final part of our tour included Sami handicrafts and clothing. "Lovozero still makes reindeer boots, pants and tunics for sale, and we hope tourists will come from Canada and around the world to buy our products." Larisa thanked Mrs. Sergovina for the tour and for sharing her detailed knowledge. Leif commented that since *glasnost* and *perestroika* began, the museum's government support had come to an end. "The curator now volunteers her expertise. Probably her salary goes to Semyashkin now!" he said by way of black humour.

We walked around the back of the museum and entered a side door into a large factory space where about twenty Sami were making reindeer clothing. Larisa introduced us to Andrei Zolotuhina, the foreman. "We are fully engaged in making reindeer boots today. They are excellent for walking on cold snow and are guaranteed to keep your feet warm," Leif translated. We looked at the boots. They had hide soles and smelt quite strongly of reindeer musk. I thought they would need pretty extensive rebuilding to become everyday wear in Calgary. Lynn said she would like to try on a pair. We were sent to the storeroom next door. Here we saw literally hundreds of pairs of boots piled to the ceiling awaiting buyers. Leif continued, "They simply come to work each day and make more. They do not have a marketing department. I doubt if they even get paid anymore. This is an old Soviet concept: mass production for the masses whether they need the boots or not. You should also buy a reindeer suit to go with the boots, Lynn." She asked Andrei what the boots would cost. "They are two dollars American," he replied. And so she bought a pair. They did not have my size.

We were next taken to a section of the warehouse that was equally filled with reindeer-hide pants and tunics. "They make them for the herders, too," said Leif. "How many herders are there in Lovozero now?" I enquired. "About eighty," said Leif. "There are enough suits here to fit eight hundred herders," he added. Seeing that we were not buying complete outfits, Larisa suggested that we walk on.

Back on the main street we passed a big line-up of men and women in front of a closed door. "What are they waiting for?" I asked. "This is the village bakery; it will open at 11 a.m. It is the only place people can buy bread," replied Larisa. I noticed an old man in the queue wearing a chest full of medals on the lapels of his old, blue-suit jacket. "Why is he wearing his medals?" I asked. "That is because the government no longer pays the veterans' pensions. He is protesting by wearing all his medals," said Leif. "Many of the surviving veterans of the Great Patriotic War now spend their days marching up and down the main street, trying to shame their government into paying their pensions."

We walked on towards the broken bridge over the Lovozero River that divides the town in half. It is an important division these days, because it determines if you get heat in winter or not, said Leif explaining that in even-numbered years the flats on the north side of the river get heat from the central boilers. In odd years, the south side gets heat. "That explains why you see so many stove pipes sticking out of the balcony windows. People have built stoves into their flats so they can have fires, cook and stay warm. It also explains why there are so many terrible apartment fires." Larisa noted that it was important for old people to have friends on the other side of the river, "so that when it gets very cold in winter time, they can go and stay with their friends who have heat. That is one way that *glasnost* and *perestroika* is bringing us together!" Larisa said it would be good to speak to some of the pensioners, therefore she had arranged for us to meet some in her mother's apartment after lunch.

Lunch was served in Lovozero's *Dom Kultura,* or Culture House, where the Lovozero Sami Association also had its offices. Here we met again with Pavel, Andrei, and Nadya, and talked about our methodology for land-use mapping. As we ate cucumber sandwiches on Borodino bread with tea, the fire-hall siren went off and a bell began to peel. Nina went to the window and pulled the curtains open. "An old Komi woman has died," she said. The Komi are also reindeer herders, but their main villages are far to the east of Lovozero. Leif explained that the small Komi community in the Kola is the continuing result of Stalin's policy of moving ethnic groups, so as to prevent any one group's regional dominance and to promote the idea of a Soviet Union comprised of many contributing ethnicities. Larisa called us to the window to see the funeral march pass. The deceased was lying on her back on a flatbed truck. She was dressed, as she died, in a brown dress. Behind the truck, arm-in-arm, walked her closest women friends. Behind the women marched the Komi men, also linked arm-in-arm. A small disorganized crowd followed along.

Lloyd and I decided to join the procession to witness the funeral for the balance of our lunch hour. We walked to the Lovozero cemetery, where a grave had already been dug. The funeral party had placed the deceased in a wooden box which was being lowered into the grave as we arrived. The older women were crying; the men were stoically silent. There was no priest in attendance. Soon shovels full of soil were raining down on the box. The hole was quickly filled up. When this task was complete the crowd dispersed. That was it. We walked back to the *Dom Kultura.*

"It is time to meet the pensioners," said Larisa, and so we followed her to her mother's apartment. "She is fortunate to have a ground-floor flat, so she doesn't have to take the stairs all the time. She is looking forward to meeting all of you," Larisa said as she knocked on the door. Grandmother Avdeeva opened the door with a smile. Behind her we could see several other older women having tea. We entered the tiny apartment, and Leif and Larisa organized the introductions. Soon we were being told about a pensioner's life in Lovozero. Much of the talk focused on the chaos at the hospital. Lovozero's only doctor was an alcoholic. Sometimes it was actually fatal to go for treatment after lunch by which time he had started to drink. Most weekends he drove the ambulance to Murmansk to party, leaving Lovozero without a doctor and an ambulance, so it was best not to get ill on the weekends. When the doctor could see you and he was sober, there was often only a diagnosis. Treatment generally required drugs, and the pharmacy had closed the previous year. And so you learned you had become diabetic, only to find out that insulin was unavailable; that you were asthmatic, but cortisone was unavailable; that you were suffering from pneumonia, but antibiotics were unavailable. Even if you had a suspected fracture, there was no film for the X-ray machine. If you were actually admitted to hospital, it was generally a death sentence. Death was actually a release that followed a period of bed rest as your condition worsened and your pain intensified. The hospital kitchen served only cucumber, potatoes, bread, jam and tea. If you wanted reindeer meat, you had to bring it yourself, and most of the time the staff ate most of it before it was served to the patient. It eventually became hard to hear and I asked the women about their grandchildren, hoping for some respite from their anguish. The net effect of what we had heard was shocking.

They were all happy to talk of their grandchildren, hoping for the best for their lives in the new era. They knew that reindeer herding would only appeal to a few, and that Lovozero couldn't provide much by way of employment for the rest. They would have to go to Murmansk, or south. Most of all, they hoped that they wouldn't get drafted into the army for service in Chechnya. One Sami boy had met this fate and his mother never heard from him again. The army was no place for an eighteen-year-old man. As for granddaughters, all the grandmothers wished them well in marriage, and all wanted grandchildren. The problem here was the quality of Sami and, even worse, ethnic Russian, men. To start with, ever since *glasnost* and *perestroika* had begun, local jobs had started to disappear. Most of the available local employment was in government agencies, and many of these were now "kaput," Nina's favourite descriptive word. Many men were unemployed and drinking heavily as a consequence. Their life expectancy was low, about mid-fifties in Lovozero. They had completely lost their identity as productive males.

Larisa noted that women retain much of their self-identity even without work. "As mothers, nurturers, cooks, nurses, teachers and older daughters we have many family identities and roles in the extended family. Many of us also work outside the home to compensate for our unproductive men. Sami women are exceptionally strong. Just look at my mother. She is still beautiful and productive at seventy-five, and she has already outlived my father by fifteen years." Grandmother Avdeeva smiled at this compliment, saying, "I wish you all well in your new work; please also tell Mr. Gorbachev that we need a new doctor in Lovozero!"

We all rose to leave with much to think about. The long day of visits and experiences was nearly over. Our last stop was with Mr. Mohammed, Lovozero's village engineer, who had the responsibility of maintaining all government infrastructures. "He is one of two local Muslims," said Larisa. "The other is the prosecutor in Revda. Both of them are very competent men. They only drink in public to be sociable. Unlike the rest." Mr. Mohammed greeted us in his office, in the newest building in the village. His secretary immediately brought out wine, chocolate and cake. "Welcome to little Lovozero, home to so many nationalities, and especially the Sami." We began talking about our day, and the many cultural experiences that Larisa had shared with us. We also talked of the obvious impact of *glasnost* and *perestroika,* and asked Mr. Mohammed to share his hopes for Lovozero's future. "I am generally hopeful of the future," he said. "The old way was completely at odds with reality. There was no real economy, projects were dreamed up that were disconnected from real need. You saw the reindeer-boot and herder-suit factory. That is a good example of the old paradigm. At least now you have to establish there is a need or a market for your ideas. Certain problems will take a while to solve. Certainly there is a need for the protein from the nine reindeer-brigade units, now some sixty-thousand head in total. But that segment of Lovozero's economy will only employ about a hundred men. More are contracted for the annual butchering and packing, but that is seasonal work. We need to build a tourist sector and create more local service businesses. We need to explore locally for oil and gas. We need to build a professional public service. And we need to look after our pensioners better. Over the next few years we also need to improve basic infrastructure in places like Lovozero. That is my role."

We talked about the half-finished apartment block and the broken bridge over the Lovozero River. "Yes, those are my embarrassments. We ran out of money. Or perhaps Russia ran out of money. We are waiting for a response to our request for more, but we know that the new Russia has many such needs. Our time will come. Meanwhile I must do my best with what I have. Have some chocolate. May I pour you another glass of wine?" We ate and drank with some sadness and some hope. The chocolate reminded me of home, and at the same time of the pensioners who had not had any for years.

The violence of poverty and the disintegration of the functioning state were evident in every interaction we had during our introduction to Lovozero. I hadn't really expected to find such anguish tucked into a remote corner of a newly energized Russia. And yet all the Sami we met were eager to start work on the project. They at least had hope for their future.

23

Sami Cultural Days

"You have to think like a reindeer to be good at this event"

Every year the first week of July is given over to the festival known as Sami Cultural Days. Larisa and her team said we should take the day off work. "We want the Canadians to compete with the Sami!" The point of the festival is to resurrect Sami feats of strength and endurance, and eventually to select the best Sami man and woman on the basis of traditional skills. There are "reindeer running" contests where men and women run through a narrow course in the trees with a broom handle straddled across their shoulders to replicate antlers. The trick is to gauge the openings between trees so as not to collide violently and get knocked to the ground. "You have to think like a reindeer to be good at this event," said Pavel.

Another race was simply rowing a boat out to an anchored buoy in the lake, then rounding it for home. Andre said it was based on the boating skills the old Sami had to master to get reindeer across rivers during the annual migratory trek to the Barents-Sea coast with the mothers and fawns. Both men and women tried their hand at the boat race, one at a time. There was also an arm-wrestling table, with two wooden handgrips for the left arms and two strong wooden chairs for the contestants to sit on. Only men queued for this contest, which drew large numbers of competitors and quite an audience. "This is something you would be good at," said Leif to me. "Because of your good diet and large size." I hoped this was a compliment.

A type of football game was also in the offing for boys' and girls' teams. It was played with a feather-stuffed, leather ball traditionally at reindeer camps. Large audiences of parents gathered at a clearing in the forest to cheer on their children. All of these activities took place in a kind of park just outside Lovozero on the road to the lake, and many families had erected their *chooms* (a Sami reindeer hide or canvas tipi) to live there during the festival. Barbecue fires were everywhere and elaborate reindeer dishes were available when you paid anyone a visit.

A stage had been erected in the centre of the festival grounds, and Sami singers were featured at intervals throughout the day. *Samigiella* songs were very popular, especially *joiks* which were often very humourous or sexual in tone. Many elders spent the festival in chairs by the stage, and sang along with the performers. There were also other performers, including an obese middle-aged Russian who dressed like a Cossack. He played an accordion and sang songs like The Volga Boatmen to a very enthusiastic reception. In some of his sets he did variations of the Cossack kick dance, which inevitably left him too winded to sing for some time afterwards. I asked Larisa why the Sami had a Russian Army imposter singing at their festival. "It reminds the old people of their youth," she replied. He was inevitably swarmed by pensioners in between songs with requests for old favourites, and even autographs.

At some point in the afternoon of the first day I decided to go to the arm-wrestling table. Leif came along with me in case I needed translation or moral support. As I arrived in the line-up, people began to talk about my size. Leif wondered if I should compete. I wanted to. And so when my turn came, I sat down opposite a much smaller Sami herder. At the signal to start, I immediately realized that I could easily take my opponent. I feigned a contest for a few minutes, and then ended it with a strong surge of effort. The crowd cheered my victory, but Leif noted the defeated Sami had said under his breath as he was leaving the scene, "It is only because of your fucking diet." The next three contestants all lost the same way. Leif said I should stop. The crowd no longer was on my side. It was time to find other activities.

The rest of the afternoon passed pleasantly enough. For a while I held the row-boat race best time, but by four o'clock five other rowers had posted better times. I was useless in the reindeer race, falling badly many times as my pole collided with tree after tree. Around 4:30 p.m. I was met by a small crowd of Sami men who made it clear I should return to the arm wrestling table. Leif said a new contestant was asking to wrestle me. We walked over to the table where a very large crowd had assembled. As I approached I wondered who my competitor would be. The crowd voluntarily parted to reveal a red-bearded Russian of about three-hundred pounds wearing a submarine command sailor's uniform. Well fed, muscular, a hundred pounds heavier than me and trained to kill. He was there to avenge Mother Russia in Lovozero.

The crowd were all smiles as I sized up my opponent. I sat down on the chair and grabbed the left hand grip. I noticed my opponent wasn't bothering with the steadying influence of the grip. He smiled wickedly as we grasped hands. The Sami started a countdown from ten, which Leif repeated in English in my ear. At "one" his grip tightened incredibly and I braced for the worst. He wasn't playing around. My arm was nearly dislocated from its socket as he ended the contest in the first second. Russia was avenged. The crowd cheered wildly. I smiled in defeat and rose to massage my arm. Before I could say anything, my victor got up, was taken to a waiting car and whisked back to base. He had been brought all the way from Murmansk to teach me a lesson in national humility that I will never forget. Leif capped it all as we walked back to Lovozero that night: "Sometimes you Canadians remind me of your neighbours, the Americans." I think the word I am looking for is "cocky." He was right.

As evening fell, Larisa came to our apartment and said the dancing would begin in the *Dom Kultura* at 8 p.m. We had no idea about dancing, and Leif said he was tired from translating all day. Lloyd was up for dancing, as was Lynn. We decided to go without translation. The building was full when we arrived, and a village band was playing Sami folk music to an empty floor. Soon a young troupe of male and female Sami dancers entered from the wings and began a long performance of traditional dances. Larisa and Nadya's children were among the best. The old folk were present in large numbers, but declined to dance. The room got hotter and hotter. The faux Cossack next made an appearance and reprised his kick dance for the crowd, who demanded an encore from the exhausted performer. We worried for his health, but he obliged his audience.

The next performers were the Komi ladies, many of whom Lloyd and I had seen at the Komi elder's funeral. Larisa explained that they only perform with other Komi women, and unlike the Sami, do not perform with men. They began a repertoire of extremely complex dances, all led by an older woman who really knew her moves. The Komi women were entrancing, dancing sometimes hand-to-hand, sometimes with linked arms, and always with rhythmic swirls and cross-overs. There were twenty of them on the floor, and they suddenly moved their focus to the audience, and immediately to Lloyd and me. We were seized by the dance elder and coaxed onto the floor and into the dance. The band picked up the tempo and all we could do was play follow the leader, who in fact was grasping my hand. Lloyd was transfixed by the dance; I was trying not to make a complete fool of myself. We both threw ourselves into the task. I became hotter and hotter, sweating through my dress shirt while the Komi ladies stepped, threaded, and thought their way through dozens of dance movements effortlessly.

After about twenty minutes, the Komi ladies released us to our chairs. Larisa looked at me and said, "They are just showing off to the Sami women." Lloyd and I offered to dance with the Sami women, but they declined. "It has been a long day; I do not wish to dance," said Nina. Tat'yana said, "Tomorrow is about time to start the work, isn't it Michael? We should all go and get good sleeps." She reminded me of many of my teachers. And she was right.

24

Mapping the Kola Peninsula
Murmansk Duma acknowledges Sami rights

We formally launched the project with a meeting that included the elders of the two main Kola villages, Lovozero and Jona to explain to them what we were doing and what we hoped to produce. We asked for their frank endorsement which they gave before any work was began. After two mapping teams were formed, the initial training sessions were held. The Lovozero team was led by Larisa Avdeeva, president of the Lovozero Sami Association, and included Pavel Fefelov, a former instructor of reindeer herding at Lovozero's vocational school; Andrei Gavrilov a retired hunter and fisher; and Nadya Zolotuhina, who taught the Sami language in the Lovozero elementary school. The Jona team was led by Tat'yana Tsmykailo, president of the Jona Sami Association, and Yulia Sergina, a senior-high-school student; her father Vladimir, a reindeer herder; Vladimir's sister, Alya Sergina, a social worker; and Valery Sotkoyarvi, a local hunting guide and Sami spiritualist. Two new Canadian staff joined us at this juncture, Karim-Aly Kassam and Terry Garvin, from the Arctic Institute of North America's headquarters in Calgary. Lloyd was unable to work with the team after his initial leave from his Northwest Territories Government job to help launch the project. Our primary task consisted of preparing the first traditional land-use maps at a species level of data and description ever prepared in Russia. Every day during the summers of 1996 and 1997 the Lovozero and Jona teams met to interview older herders, current herders and harvesters of edible plants, wildfowl, fish, and fur bearers. The work followed a methodology developed and refined in Canada by the Arctic Institute and Aboriginal communities in northern Alberta and the N.W.T. Central to this method is the premise that resource harvesters are the true experts; university personnel are simply trainers, administrators and writers.

The teams first prepared species lists for all known harvested resources in the Kola and developed detailed harvest location and use descriptions. A series of black, adhesive-backed icons were created for each resource, and were positioned on the maps to indicate precise harvesting locations. Each icon strived to look just like the resource it represented. The little reindeer icons were the most evocative. Similar icons were prepared for herding infrastructure like barns and corrals, and another set for spiritually significant sites. Reindeer icons were always the first ones to be placed on the maps. The colour maps at a scale of 1:200,000 were sourced by Leif and Nina in Murmansk. Leif commented to me that, "I think they are old KGB maps – we found them in a bookstore!"

Once a particular group of resources was completely mapped, say swans and ducks, the village elders were asked to a "validation tea," at which they were shown the progress of the overall project, and asked to inspect closely the particular group of icons being validated that day. The object of this exercise was to weed out any misplaced or erroneous icons, and to develop a consensus that the map was now ready for the next group of species, infrastructure or spiritual-site icons to be applied.

Strangely, when we began the validation process in Jona, the elders were always late for tea. We tried to schedule them for 3 p.m. on Fridays, but they never came before 4:30, and quite often many of the women arrived in tears. After two such late starts I asked elder Matryona Sotkoyarvi, Valery's mother, why so many women were weeping? "It is because JR is so mean to Sue Ellen. We are all upset about what is happening in the village of Dallas!" It turned out that Norwegian television was broadcasting reruns of the Texas soap opera, Dallas, at 3 p.m., and all women gathered at Matryona's to watch it on her television before coming to the validation tea. No amount of explanation could convince any of the Jona women that it was just a pretend story. They took the events at Southfork seriously, as if it were another village just down the road. To cope with JR's weekly antics we moved the validation tea to 4:30, and I began each one by asking, "Has JR been a better husband this week?" The women would then give us an update on the latest happenings in Southfork before the validation work could start.

A separate 1:200,000 map was prepared for 'brigade units' of reindeer. We decided to use the old Soviet term because it was still in use for the nine migratory channels, or routes, taken by the sixty-thousand Lovozero reindeer on their annual circuit from the overwintering forests, to the calving areas in the tundra, to the lichen-strewn coast of the Barents Sea. This map clearly demonstrated the large extent of the Kola Sami's land-use pattern, and provided graphic evidence of potential zones of conflict with known military bases, spent nuclear-fuel-rod storage sites, proposed new mine locations and the inevitable plans to expand roads and runways to improve access to all parts of the Kola. The map also revealed the importance of the north flowing rivers in the Kola, which acted as natural fences for the annual migratory cycles and served to distinguish the traditional boundaries of the brigade units. The Sami elders were especially glad to see this map as it presented a very clear case for their claim for special-use zones to protect the reindeer.

Along with the maps, very clear notes were taken and verified in community validation-sessions where a broad cross-section of people was invited to attend readings, and to criticize what was said. Some of these readings produced new information which was included to bolster and expand what had already been noted. The community readings also produced the idea of a "friendly" book in Russian, which initially had been conceptualized around the creation of the annotated maps, and academic papers for scholarly journals. "It is not enough to only create maps," said Nina, "We must also have a popular book for schools, for bureaucrats, for politicians, but most of all, for the Sami ourselves!" So we added the book to the agenda. Karim-Aly and I agreed to write it, and the Jona and Lovozero teams agreed to listen to every word and make sure it was truthful and to the point. The Gorbachev Foundation agreed to underwrite the costs of translation into Russian, plus a hardcover production with colour photographs.

By the end of the summer of 1997 the work on the maps was drawing to a close and the book writing was gearing up. Nina and Larisa were adamant that it was time to show the maps to *oblast duma* officials. "We need to get the process of co-management under way, or at least committed to before the project officially ends. We need to request a session with the *duma* committee responsible for project approvals and land-use planning. And we need you, Mike, to make a speech on how the process works in Canada so they can see we are proposing a real method that has already had success in a northern country," said Larisa. Once again we all agreed that this was a wise course of action. Nina said she would request the *duma* meeting; Larisa said she would arrange a prior briefing for the mayor of Lovozero, who was an ethnic Russian with good *duma* connections. If all went well, Larisa would invite the mayor to speak on our behalf to the *duma*. Then the project had a dreadful day.

Valery Sotkoyarvi and his mother Matryona were project stalwarts in Jona. Matryona was a key elder, predeceased by her husband, a famous herder. Valery was the star Sami bear hunter on the Kola, and widely sought after as a guide and spiritualist. They lived together in a Jona apartment famous for its bear-skull decorations and bear-hide rugs. All of the bear lore on the maps had been placed or verified by Valery. On a Friday evening after project payday, there was a knock on their door. Neighbours heard Valery answering the door and then a shot. Valery's mother came to his aid only to be shot as well. Mother and son died together in their hallway. A subsequent police investigation found that Valery's weekly earnings of thirty-five dollars (U.S.) in cash had been stolen along with his prize rifles. No suspects were ever apprehended. Leif said that, "Known Mafia hoodlums were to blame, but no one has the courage to name them." Everyone close to the project was affected by this double murder.

I was struck by the fact that I had just paid Valery for his week's work; it was impossible not to feel some element of economic responsibility for their deaths. I wondered if I had ever met their killer(s). The impact of their deaths brought home the horrible irony of the new Russia: *perestroika* and *glasnost*. The Jona and Lovozero teams met in Lovozero and decided to dedicate the book to Valery and Matryona. We would continue as they would have wished.

Two weeks later the maps were finished. Master copies were made for both villages and Sami national headquarters. Karim-Aly and I had blocked out the book and were assigning chapter responsibilities. Nina had a date set with the *duma* committee in a week's time and tomorrow we were meeting with the mayor of Lovozero, Nikolai Brylov. We decided to present to him as if he were Governor Komarov. Larisa, as president of the Lovozero Sami Association, was going to have the lead role. Nina would preside over the agenda as the emcee and I would speak about the Canadian experience of co-management. We were set.

The appointed day arrived. The maps were spread out on a boardroom table. Nina and Larisa wore their traditional Sami costumes, and Leif and I were clear on our roles. The meeting was a huge success. Mayor Brylov could himself authenticate the maps as he was an avid fisher and hunter, he also picked berries and went out for mushrooms. His own favourite spots were well defined on the maps. "I will be pleased to speak on the value of this research at the *oblast duma,*" he said. Nina told him the date. He promised to attend, "and attest to the quality of the work." This was a small but significant victory.

The two weeks before our date with the *duma* flew by. The Canadians were preparing to return home and finish the book. We were already calling it by its final title, Sami Potatoes. The Sami, however, were increasingly nervous. Their entire history of interaction with the Russian state had not been characterized by either kindness or victories, and neither were expected now. The Canadians saw the empowerment engendered by the project starting to ebb. Some of the team even started questioning the need for the *duma* meeting. "Why should we go and be insulted?" asked Alya. Nina was recalling the meeting at the start of the project with the governor.

"He will never support the Sami. He will support that dreadful Semyashkin before he supports us!" But some of the retired herders were in favour of "A Sami last stand, like in the movies of John Wayne," said Pavel with a grin on his face. "We must go in with our guns drawn!" Western popular culture was finding new fans in Lovozero. For my part, I said that the practice of co-management required government support and partnership. We had no choice but to give the *oblast* officials our best presentation and hope for their co-operation in some form.

We drove to the meeting in Helge's truck, with a presentation team that included Nina, Larisa, Tat'yana of Jona, Leif and I. Alya, Tat'yana of Moscow, Pavel and Andrei came along as supporters. It took most of the day before the meeting to drive north to Murmansk and we overnighted at our old favourite hotel. All of the Sami wore traditional dress and I unpacked my trusty blue suit. We walked down the hill to the *duma* chambers, past the now familiar gangs of money changers, Romany 'Stan gypsies, and milky business entrepreneurs. Nina and Larisa appeared stoic. Leif was in a good mood, "hoping for the best." At the front door there was a long period of security checks, resulting in the issuance of officially stamped papers with the time and room number of our hearing. As we entered the august committee room I put on my mock "serious Russian duma face." Nina saw me and started to laugh. Larisa did too. It broke the ice.

Many of our old friends were already around the table: Galina Andreeva, minus her husband Captain Sergei; Sergei Semyashkin, with a big welcoming grin; Governor Komarov's secretary, but no governor; Mayor Brylov of Lovozero, ready as promised to support us; and Vice-Governor Vasili Kalaida, sitting in for Komarov who was "in Moscow on business." We spread out our beautiful maps and notebooks for all to see. As we were setting up, a crowd of new Russian media types arrived with television cameras, tape recorders, and flash cameras. They took pictures of everything in a rather chaotic moment as Kalaida read his agenda document. He looked very serious. I turned to Nina and said, "Now there is a good *duma* face!" By now, she understood this in English. The session then began.

Kalaida gave a long opening speech about the traditional importance of Sami culture in the Kola. He referred to the *oblast's* responsibility for Sami affairs, and the office of Semyashkin. He spoke of
the "recent difficulties initiated by the reforms of Mr. Gorbachev,"
and the problems facing the *oblast* government because of financial
constraints. He then turned the microphone over to Mayor Brylov,
commenting: "The Mayor of Lovozero, a good friend of this *duma*,
has some words he wishes to say about the Sami-mapping project."

Brylov then began to speak out strongly supporting our work.
By the looks on Nina, Tat'yana, and Larisa's faces, I could tell things
were progressing well before Leif finished translating. Brylov com-
plimented the mappers, said the data was well presented and accurate, and that the Canadian experience of co-management would
be good for Russia! As he spoke Semyashkin's jaw began to drop.
Brylov went on to say that he hoped the *duma* officials would now
consult the Sami maps before any new project was considered in
the Jona or Lovozero regions. He concluded by pointing out Larisa,
and speaking about the fine work she had done as Sami association
president in Lovozero.

We were then asked to begin our presentation. Nina gave a very
political speech and took several wicked swipes at Semyashkin. She
concluded by praising Gorbachev for "risking his own money on
the project when the *duma* refused to even support basic needs
like bridge repair in Lovozero." Next Larisa and Tat'yana presented
the maps, paying careful attention to the media. They were thorough and pleasant, being sure to add that a co-management regime
for the Kola would reflect well on the fortunes of the Murmansk
oblast. They both thanked Mayor Brylov for his support and his
expert knowledge. Brylov beamed from his chair in the audience.
I concluded the presentation by talking of the success in Canada of
co-management and the promise it represented for the Kola.

Kalaida once again took the microphone. "Thank you Mr. Robinson. The state has not served the Sami well, and our next steps
must be concrete and pragmatic." He then mused aloud about the
need for a county legislative enactment for the maps to ensure that

their details would be publicly held and kept current, and in order to make their use compulsory in national development planning. He went on to say, "Concerning co-management, I agree with Nina Afanas'eva that national resources are meant for everybody and must take account of the traditional resource use of the "Small Peoples." I acknowledge and respect those who made these maps." We stood and applauded. Nina looked at me with astonishment.

25

I'm Dreaming of a Sami Christmas

"Which one is Rudolph?"

When I was growing up in Vancouver, the first step in the annual Christmas ritual was a visit to Santa's Toyland at Woodward's department store. Here there would be a line-up of children and their mothers, all intent on the big moment when the child sat on Santa's knee and was asked the magic question, "What do you want for Christmas?" Sometimes the answer was delivered from memory or sometimes from a written list, but it was always given in the belief that at least some of the wishes would come true. The next step was the photo, when mothers could rejoin their children with Santa in a smiling tableau that could even become the family Christmas card. I remember that the photo was always taken by the elf. Santa's elf sometimes worked alone, but I also remember at times multiple elves. Some worked the line-up, keeping spirits bright; others gave out candy canes as you left Santa's throne. All the elves wore green and red, generally green leggings, red jumper tunics, strange curl-top shoes and a funny red-and-green hat that sometimes had bells on it. The elves were always shorter than Santa and were associated with his reindeer in some way. On one particularly fine Christmas, the Woodward's Santa even had live reindeer at his faux North Pole workshop. Children could pet the reindeer under the supervision of the head elf, who was constantly asked, "Which one is Rudolph?"

When I arrived in Finland in 1995, I was quickly made aware of the local Father Christmas industry, even though it was June and not December. As we drove with Lloyd and Leif across the country we passed several Father Christmas "parks," each one with a reindeer corral, sleigh rides in season (pulled by eight reindeer), a restaurant and the inevitable gift shop, full of elfin regalia. The standard gifts included the traditional Four-Winds hat, which is generally rendered in red and green felt, reindeer bells for all occasions, Norwegian and Finnish Christmas sweaters in reds, greens and blues, and curl-top, reindeer-hide shoes. The reindeer herder's knife, bone-handled and long, sheathed in reindeer hide, was also a big seller. Leif explained that the Finnish Father Christmas always lived in the forest with his reindeer and his "little helpers." Father Christmas himself was traditionally cast as a tall, white-bearded Finn, who wore a red suit trimmed with white fur, usually ermine or rabbit. When questioned about these little helpers, Leif said they were, "forest folk, gnomish, and always much shorter than the big Finnish Father Christmas. They were light complected, generally had dark hair, and were friends of the reindeer." It was obvious to me who they were; they were the Sami.

As we began our work in Lovozero, we discovered that the Four-Winds hat was a traditional Sami herder's hat, that 'boat sleighs' were pulled by reindeer up until very recently, that curl-top, reindeer-hide shoes (that resembled tiny boat sleighs) were available in the Sami clothing factory shop, and that Sami herders' knives were still made by many local artisans for sale to Finns and Norwegians. Whenever the Sami men and women donned their traditional formal dress, it was predominantly made of red and blue felt, accented with black leather belts and bells. All this made the Sami-Santa's elf connection even more obvious to me.

Seeking official confirmation of my hypothesis, I sat down for tea one afternoon in the summer of 1997 with Nina, Larisa and Andrei. I told them the story of my early visits to Santa's Toyland at Woodward's. "Surely the Sami are Father Christmas helpers? You know the Father Christmas parks in Finland that get so many tourist visits in December; they must be based on some kind of Sami connection to the Father Christmas or Santa Claus traditions in Europe and North America? What do you think?" I asked.

Nina was quick to respond: "The idea that the Sami would take orders from an old Finn is quite preposterous, Michael." Andrei sounded off too: "Those helpers are tiny little dwarfs, not strong Sami herders. Your idea is ridiculous." Larisa nailed the argument shut: "Why do you westerners always think that we should fit into your myths? The Sami have their own sacred stories and characters, and they have nothing to do with Finland or that department store you went to as a child with your mother!" Enough said.

26

Book Launch at Gorbachev's Moscow Office
He had a Russian copy of Sami Potatoes under his arm

In the summer of 1998, Karim-Aly and I took a completed draft copy of Sami Potatoes to Lovozero for a final read through and critique. Tat'yana of Moscow and Leif read it page-by-page in Russian to the Sami team members. We made thorough notes on the feedback of required changes and additions. An English edition was published in the fall of 1998. It was then translated and sent to the Gorbachev Foundation's offices in Moscow for production of the Russian edition. This publication, beautifully illustrated and bound in hardcover, was finally released in the spring of 2000. The foundation offered to pay to bring the project team to Moscow for a formal book launch. After a flurry of emails to one another we agreed to meet there in June.

The trip was a first for all of the Sami team members. None had been to Moscow before. They fretted about cash and their safety. "What if we run out of money down south?" worried Nina. "I dreamt of Lubyanka prison last night," added Larisa. Alya advocated going and having a good time until the money ran out. Tat'yana had never been farther from Jona than Murmansk. Andre and Pavel were united in their desire to meet a person as interesting and as historic as Gorbachev. Karim-Aly and I were eager to meet him too. We all arranged our tickets. The Canadians flew from Calgary; the Sami took the Moscow express train from Murmansk.

We all gathered at Gorbachev's concrete-and-brick compound in downtown Moscow's *Arbat* district. Boris Yeltsin, Russia's first president, was rumoured to have given Gorbachev and his institute the apartment and office complex as a tribute for his efforts as president of the former Soviet Union. We were among the guests being housed for a variety of projects. The Sami were astounded to be given their rooms and we were all lodged close together. Meals and transport were provided and we were also treated to a cultural program that included the Bolshoi Ballet's production of Prokofiev's Romeo and Juliet at the Kremlin's Great Hall of the People. After the performance we all walked through Red Square and gazed at St. Basil's Basilica, architecturally lit beneath a full Moscow moon. Strangely, perhaps, I think we all felt a sense of ownership in this moment. We were guests of Gorbachev, participants in making history, and knew we had introduced a radical new idea to Arctic Russia.

The book launch was held at the Gorbachev compound on the third day of our visit. We had not seen the Russian edition of Sami Potatoes. Only Karim-Aly and I had ever met Gorbachev before, and then briefly at the 1998 convocation address he gave at the University of Calgary. Everyone was eager to meet him and see the book. In the afternoon we all gathered at the Gorbachev Foundation conference centre. Someone had stacked piles of Sami Potatoes about the room on tables and chairs. We eagerly picked up copies and autographed them for each other. The media soon arrived, pressing Nina and Larisa for interviews. After about twenty minutes of disorganization, book give-aways, and interviews, four tall bodyguards swept into the room and walked about the perimeter looking at everyone. At some discrete signal, the main doors were thrust open and in walked Gorbachev in his trademark blue suit, white shirt, and tie. He had a Russian copy of Sami Potatoes under his arm.

Gorbachev walked over to the Sami, who were all in their national dress, shook hands and had a few words with each team member separately. His English was not fluent, but he congratulated Karim-Aly and me on a creative project "that has given Russia some new ideas." He urged the Sami to push on with co-management and to teach other Siberian cultures about the importance of traditional land-use mapping. He then spoke formally to the audience of media representatives and academics from Moscow University. "Read this book. Write about it. Talk with your students about it. Congratulate the Sami on their hard work and achievements." After taking a few questions, he apologized and left to make an address to the Russian Duma, and its new president, Vladimir Putin. Before leaving he encouraged us all to stay a few more days as his guest and to enjoy Moscow.

Pavel said it was the most important day of his life. Andrei said he needed a beer. Nina commented that Gorbachev was "much shorter in person than on television," and that he was also kinder to the Sami than she expected. "Perhaps I should not blame him for all of the problems of *glasnost* and *perestroika!* I am glad now that we took his money!" she laughed. Larisa wanted to take "boxes and boxes of this lovely book home to Lovozero." Tat'yana of Jona said, "This project is the light of my life!" Tat'yana of Moscow said that "it sounds as if Gorbachev understands co-management better than my colleagues at the Institute of Ethnography. He should be lecturing for us!" Leif, ever the stoic, said that "everything has worked out better than I expected. I worried this project would be a total failure. Luckily it has not been at all normal."

27

A Ski-Doo Ride with the Chocolates

While the Sami work progressed, so did AINA's in the Canadian North

While the Sami Co-Management Project ran its course from 1995 to 2000, the Arctic Institute of North America's growing cadre of research associates continued to work with small Indigenous communities in the western Arctic and the provincial mid-North. When possible, I visited our new participatory action research (PAR) projects, met with the community workers and local government, and spent time with our Arctic Institute research associates. In this spirit I was introduced to the Dene community once called Snowdrift, but now known as Lutsel K'e, by Dr. Ellen Bielawski. Here, I began to learn about the impacts of climate change which was already apparent in the early 1990s to members of the bush economy in small northern communities.

Lutsel K'e on the southern shores of Great Slave Lake, south and east of Yellowknife, was confronting strange changes in weather patterns. Elders began reporting variations in ice thickness in 1995, when "the two Basils" went through uncharacteristically thin ice on their Ski-Doos and drowned in the lake close to their homes. Ellen, an Institute research associate with strong PAR skills, was asked to work with the community to create a study of the impacts of warmer weather on hunting and trapping. As a result she agreed to move to Lutsel K'e to organize the project.

As was now customary, I was invited to meet with community leaders at the project's outset and to tour some of the local areas of concern. In early November, just after freeze up, I went to Lutsel K'e to see Ellen, who had already established an office in her log cabin, and acquired a brand new Ski-Doo for project work. After an initial meeting with the band council and elders, a trip was planned with Archie and Alice Chocolate to "have a picnic on the land" as Ellen put it. The Chocolates were senior members of the Lutsel K'e trapping community, who were well aware of the perils of travelling on thin ice for long distances. They would lead us on the picnic trip, taking the opportunity to talk with us about trapline life in the age of climate change.

Ellen scrounged a Ski-Doo suit for me because Archie judged my winter clothing inadequate. When I asked how far we would be travelling, he thought it would be about thirty-eight miles round trip. "We won't be going too far tonight," he said. "We just want to show you some of our trapline." I wondered what a really long trip would be. Ellen was eager to see how the new Ski-Doo would perform, but in deference to local custom said that I should drive. I replied that I had never driven a snow machine before. She said, "Great. What a wonderful place to learn!"

As it turned out, we couldn't start until 3 p.m. for a variety of reasons, chief of which was finding me mitts and a toque to stay warm at minus five-to-twenty degrees Celsius. "It can really cool off after the sun sets, so you need to be well prepared for cold," cautioned Archie. The Chocolates provided the grub for the trip and promised strong tea and moose ribs "cooked to the fire" when we arrived at the picnic site. Ellen and I packed survival rations of chocolate, dried fruit and nuts along with generous amounts of fire starter, spare socks and mitt-liner gloves. We finally headed out of Lutsel K'e with me in command of the Arctic Institute's Ski-Doo, and Ellen riding pillion. We followed Archie who was towing Alice in a toboggan laden with their gear in canvas duffle bags. Light was falling as we hit a well-used trail out of town. Evidently we were off on an evening picnic in the boreal forest in November. I wondered how cold it would be and concentrated on staying up with Archie as he sped along the hard crusted surface.

We were soon in the forest surrounded by willow and black spruce. Up ahead I could see that Archie had switched on his red taillight. I looked for the light switch on the Ski-Doo and turned on our lights too. Suddenly Archie veered off the trail into a grouping of willows. I could see a small hatchet in his mitted right hand. He made a slow approach to something on the ground, and raised the axe. Soon he was raining blows down on an animal caught in one of his leg-hold traps. He next emerged from the thicket. In his hands was a mature wolverine, a stocky and ferocious, flesh-eating mammal. I had only heard of wolverines once before, but knew they were rare and required careful handling on the trapline. They also fetched a good price with the fur buyers. Archie called to Alice to open one of the duffel bags, which she did in the back of the toboggan. He dropped the wolverine in head first, then Alice synched up the bag's drawstrings. Within a minute we were back on the trail to our picnic. Archie shouted at me: "Go fast on the big lake up ahead in case the ice is thin." I heard him loud and clear.

It was starting to get colder. We followed Archie and Alice in single file through a darkening boreal landscape. Suddenly we burst out onto a broad, open, white expanse. As I followed the Chocolates I realized that we were now crossing the big lake. How thick was the ice? Archie was racing his machine, gaining traction on the newly fallen snow, and not ever looking back at us. I thought way too much about "the two Basils." All sorts of fears crowded my brain. Thin ice. Freezing water. Certain hypothermic and/or drowning death. Ye gods. And then I noticed that Alice was waving her hands up ahead. I think she was also screaming, but her cries were muffled by the roar of Archie's Ski-Doo. I picked up speed and raced to the toboggan where Alice was attempting to stand up. We drew abreast of her and saw that she was pointing to the duffel bag that held the wolverine. The animal had miraculously survived Archie's head thumping, and was chewing its way through the confines of canvas. Next stop would be Alice's lap.

I pulled down on the throttle and shot ahead to a position abreast of Archie and we waved for him to stop. He looked startled but immediately pulled over. Right in the middle of the newly frozen lake. "Ye gods again," I thought. Within a few seconds Archie sized up the situation and grabbed his small hatchet from his Ski-Doo satchel. He walked back to the toboggan and rained a second series of blows down on the wolverine. The animal was smacking its jaws together and spraying blood all over Alice. But soon it was definitively over. With the wolverine now truly dead our expedition resumed its course over the thin (I assumed) ice for the distant shore.

The rest of the trip was relatively uneventful. It was pitch dark and cold, but we found a small lake and followed Archie to his customary camping spot beside the remnants of a recent fire. Alice jumped out of the toboggan and got a large axe out of another duffel bag. She went down to the shores of the little lake and whacked a hole in the ice to get water for tea. Archie took his hatchet and cut a large number of spruce boughs to start a cooking fire. Once kindled and lit, he pulled a wire grate out from its snowy hiding place and set it over the fire. Soon Alice was spreading a large number of moose ribs out on the grate and suspending a billy can of water on a wire over the flames. Dinner was ready within twenty minutes.

After a feast of ribs and tea under a wide starry sky it became increasingly cold. No matter how close I sat to the fire, my back would not warm up and my fingers were numb. I said to no one in particular that I was getting cold. Archie perked up, and said it was "probably time to head back to Lutsel K'e." Ellen and Alice agreed. I looked at my watch; it was 7 p.m. We pulled the fire apart and threw snow on the burning embers. Then it was onto the snow machines which magically fired up right away, dimming another fear of mine that we might have to spend the night out here. Archie watched as Alice got into the toboggan, and then pulled back out onto the freshly travelled trail.

As the return trip began, so did the snowfall. Slowly at first, and then larger and larger flakes blew into our faces as we raced along. Archie was going much faster and I had to pay close attention to stay up with him. Sometimes I was afraid that I would lose visual contact with the little glowing-red tail light in front of us. Ellen said nothing as we sped along, leading me to think that she was falling asleep. The noise of the motor was lulling. I became tired and the cold was enervating. On we pushed. I was dreading the big lake crossing. Soon we breached its shoreline. Archie was speeding over our old tracks and clearly getting ahead of us. If we went through he wouldn't know for some time. We'd be gone before he could do anything. The two Basils, Ellen and Mike. That would be it.

There was of course no choice but to press on through the flying snow and cold. The big no-name lake stretched on seemingly forever. The Ski-Doo, however, was fast and reliable, and Archie's red light was always visible far ahead. And then he disappeared. Gone. I could still make out his tracks in front of me. We followed on blind instinct. And then he reappeared. It was his yellow headlight we saw now. He must have shot up the lake's shoreline and turned into the forest darkness, only to turn around again and shine his beacon out on the lake. "Thank you, Archie!" I thought with cold happiness.

We finally returned to Lutsel K'e at 10 p.m. I parked the Ski-Doo by the Arctic Institute office and bid Archie, Alice and Ellen goodnight. I headed over to my room in the Northwest Territories government house for transient workers, peeled off my Ski-Doo suit and slipped into a hot bath. I was still cold when I finally fell asleep at 11. For some reason I haven't driven a Ski-Doo since.

28

Boating Down the Athabasca River with Fred MacDonald Sr.

Traditional land-use mapping with the people of Fort McKay, Alberta

Fort McKay is the Aboriginal community at the epicentre of the Alberta Tar Sands. Today it is the home of many innovative joint ventures that provide labour and services to one of the largest ongoing construction and energy projects in the world. In 1949, however, its origins were far different, and its purpose directly linked to servicing an Aboriginal population of Cree, Métis, and Dene families whose traditional communities were stretched along the flowing waters of the Athabasca River. Fort McKay was an artificial community in that it sprang up to centralize government services to people who were being encouraged to move out of hunting and trapping and into welfare-state oversight and protection. This is not a process unique to Fort McKay, it has a Canadian history that extends from coast to coast to coast. Wherever it has occurred, there has been, predictably, a jarring contest between those who sought to embrace change and those who wanted to remain in the bush economy. Few have been successful in living in both worlds because their perspectives are so distinct and the skill sets necessary for success, so different.

Arguably Fred MacDonald Sr. was one of the few who straddled both worlds. In his long life he embraced small business, local Métis politics, and trapping as a necessary means to support his growing family and responsibilities. Even in relatively old age he had a knack for viewing his world from multiple perspectives. In 1994 when the Fort McKay Band Council approached the Arctic Institute of North

228

America to undertake traditional land-use mapping using a participatory approach, Fred was declared the best person to co-ordinate the project for the community. As a start, he thought it would be a good idea if he and I took a river-boat trip down the Athabasca from Fort McKay. I was on board.

I had no idea how far we were going. Fred said to come in mid-July and to bring warm clothes. "We'll be gone about three or four days." I arrived as planned and found Fred having coffee in his river-front house. About sixty, he had a strong frame and a friendly manner. He sported a kind of droopy, handlebar-style moustache. "Let's go down and check out the boat, Mike," he said, getting up from his kitchen table. We walked across the road to a newly painted pink and blue plywood skiff, about twenty-feet long, with a fifty-horse Mercury outboard on the stern. There were several red gas cans, two sets of oars, and a new Honda compact generator in the boat. "What's the generator for, Fred," I inquired. "It's for heating up my dialysis bags. I'll have to self-treat myself on the trip," he responded. "Don't worry, I do it all the time." Once again, my silly worries about bush and river travel paled in comparison with what my host faced. "We'll get going tomorrow, right after breakfast," said Fred. I spent the rest of the day picking up food and a few essentials like bug dope and film in Fort McMurray. Fred invited me to stay at his house overnight and he cooked a big supper of buffalo steaks, pickerel, and potatoes. We also had some rum.

We were on the river at 9. The motor started with one pull and soon Fred had us out in mid-stream, taking full advantage of the current and the mounting summer run-off flow. "First thing I want to show you is the colour of the Athabasca. Look how brown it is. Also, look at those large white foam bubbles floating by. When I was a boy, even at this time of year, the water was much clearer. And we never saw that foam crap. Something is changing the water quality." Fred next started to talk about bugs. "Sure they're sometimes a pain in the ass, and there are still lots of 'em. But there are far fewer than there used to be. And fewer types of bugs. We old folk notice this because we knew the river when things were different.

"To understand us, the people of Fort McKay, you need to know that we travel by river and creek and lake. The areas all along the water's edge are where we trap, and fish and hunt." I thought to myself, "They are a riparian people." Fred then launched into his observations about fish stocks. "Whitefish, grayling, pickerel, pike, trout, coneys, they are all in decline too. I think it's all related to water quality. There used to be eddies along this stretch of the river that were alive with tail flicks and rises this time of the year. Seen any so far? I haven't."

The skiff was flying along. "We're nearly at my trapline cabin, just around the next bend," observed Fred. A small clearing appeared on the eastern bank with a log cabin set back in the trees. A tall storehouse on poles was behind the cabin. "Here we are." Fred eased the bow of the skiff onto the shore and asked me to jump out with the bow line. I secured the rope around a big spruce stump in the meadow. Fred climbed out with his generator and a cardboard box full of dialysis bags. "Why don't you make us some sandwiches while I get this over with," he said as he rigged a plastic tube over a low-hanging branch and set the generator on the ground.

While we ate in the peace of the meadow, Fred reminisced as he underwent his dialysis procedure. "You know, in the 1930s and 1940s people lived all along this river. I'd say there was a community every ten miles or so. With the exception of essentials like tea, sugar and flour and mechanical gear like traps, guns and cast-iron stoves and axes, we were able to survive in pretty good style. And you know, 'there is still survival out there,' like our elder, Julian Powder, always says. I think we need to set aside pieces of bush land as a kind of bank account for future generations. We shouldn't be so sure there will never be another Depression. If everyone is dependent on store-bought food and cars and city living, who's going to survive if the world turns upside down? Not many, I'd guess." I agreed with him. After this discussion, Fred's dialysis session and lunch, we walked about the MacDonald cabin site. "It's still all functional, but I don't use it that much. Our family mostly comes here to picnic now. I was born here. This place means a lot to me."

We got back in the skiff and pushed into the current at about 2 p.m. "We'll go downstream to the old community of Lobstick for the night." I asked Fred about the derivation of Lobstick. "It means a tree close to the river with few or no limbs up top. In the old days a trapper would deliberately cut a lobstick to mark a trailhead or resting spot. Lobstick community got its name that way, I guess." We steered into the centre of the river and added the current's thrust to our speed. The skiff motored along past green thickets of aspen and dark clumps of spruce. We passed another craft, a jet boat full of oil people, roaring upstream. They waved as they passed. Fred observed that "if they ever hit a hidden sandbar going that fast, all of them will be pitched through the windshield." We entered a long, straight stretch of river, and up ahead I saw a tall aspen with no branches up top. "There it is," pointed Fred, "Lobstick."

We pulled into an eddy formed right offshore by an underwater reef. "This place probably exists because of the sheltering waters of this eddy; it is also a good place to string a fish net," commented Fred. I jumped out once again and tied us up. We both pulled the boat up higher so it would be safe for the night. We unloaded our gear and piled it on the sand beach. "Let's go into the rhubarb and see if we can find the cabins," said Fred. Off we stomped through tight stands of young aspen and cottonwood. Quite soon we came to some old, wooden grave markers. "I remember this graveyard, the cabins are up top of this hill. They used to overlook the river." Fred climbed up slowly in front of me. He was tiring quickly; this expedition would soon have to come to an end. Suddenly an old trapline cabin appeared in front of us. It was a bit bigger than usual. Fred said it was a local family's house. We walked around it and counted three good-sized windows. It had a big, old, rusty padlock, securely fastened on the front door. I looked up and saw that there was a hole in the roof where the chimney had recently fallen in. Curious, I climbed up onto a window ledge and gained the rooftop with my hands. I pulled up onto the old shakes and walked carefully to the hole. Looking in I could see one large room, with a bed to one side, and a homemade table and chairs by a cast iron stove. I lowered myself to the table top, ducked my head, and was soon inside.

The cabin was in pretty good shape. Children's drawings in crayon were pinned up by the stove. The plates and cutlery, pots and pans were all neatly in their places. The bed was unmade, and a rat had apparently burrowed down through the centre of the mattress. I looked into the exposed mattress ticking and coils and saw a brown leather wallet. I reached in and pulled it out. It contained Joe Poitrass' Treaty Card and twenty brand-new, one-dollar bills, all printed in 1951.

Suddenly feeling I had overstayed my welcome, I climbed back onto the table and pulled myself onto the roof again. I took the wallet and gave it to Fred, "God damn, god damn," he said. "Joe and I went to school together. He died last year, but his daughter still lives in Fort McKay. I'll give her the wallet." Fred went on to explain that Lobstick pretty well ceased to exist in the early 1950s, when its residents relocated to Fort McKay to be near the nurse, social worker, store, school, and RCMP. It was the same story I had heard so many times before in the North. During this period scores of self-sustaining bush and tundra communities were vacated for centralized services in a government town that also provided ready access to liquor, movies, television, cars and streets, organized gambling and a smoothly administered welfare economy. In no time at all the traditions of the bush economy were shaken to their core, and the seasonal round of hunting and trapping broke down.

Fred knew all of this by heart. I had nothing new to tell him. "It is sad to see homes like this forgotten and grown over. These were happy places to grow up in. We all visited one another up and down river, and had card games, dances and parties. You were always welcome when you arrived, by skiff, dog team and toboggan, or on snowshoes. It was more than survival; it was a way of life."

We hiked back down to the river and set up a camp. I cut wood and built a fire. Fred made dinner and I wrote in my journal. We played a game of cribbage and Fred sang me some Métis boat songs before bed. It was a full moon and a clear sky full of stars. Soon the northern lights were crackling overhead. Lobstick was happy to have visitors.

29

Camping on the Twin Sisters Plateau
Trying to reconcile Indigenous spirituality with oil and gas development

It all started when the British Columbia Ministry of Energy awarded Amoco an exploration and drilling tenure near the Twin Sisters, majestic peaks in the province's northeast – north of Fort St. John in the heart of Treaty 8 country. Hoping to find oil and gas lurking in the geologic folds beneath the mountains, the company and the province lacked knowledge of their spiritual significance to the East and West Moberly and the Saulteaux First Nations. In the Saulteaux tradition an ancient, wandering prophet knew he was in a special area when he saw the peaks in reality after seeing them in a dream. For the East and West Moberly people, the plateau around the Twin Sisters is a nursery for young game and a sanctuary for when times are tough. The First Nations would consider it sacrilege if the area were to be exploited for oil and gas. When Amoco's crews first turned up to exercise their exploration rights, they were confronted by an armed blockade of protesters. Seeking a joint solution to the impasse, the communities, the company and the government eventually asked the Arctic Institute of North America to mediate.

A series of preliminary meetings with all parties present were held in the local communities. These were useful, but ultimately dominated by government and industry PowerPoint presentations, mastery of obscure tenure-issuance jargon, and perceptions of foregone conclusions. Art Napoleon, a Saulteaux spokesman, suggested that to understand the First Nations' perspective of the Twin Sisters we should all spend a night, or two, on the mountain. Everyone

233

agreed even though the group included many levels of fitness. The oil group included a few geologists who regularly worked out and did field work that required them to hike and a couple of executives who looked badly out of shape. The government representatives were younger and urban, who were mainly concerned about bears and how to avoid them. The elders who wanted to come were pretty fit for their age, but not up to climbing a steep trail. They invited some middle-aged trappers and guides who were happy to carry big packs. We'd be a mixed group.

As organizers, Art and I had to figure out the best way to keep everyone together and spirits bright. We decided to take a helicopter to within three miles of our camp site on the plateau surrounding the Twin Sisters and pack in from there. The company agreed to pay for the helicopters, the communities promised game for the dinner and the government folks would come along for the ride "to observe." Noting their fear of bears, Art asked the two packers to bring their rifles – just in case. We planned to go on a Friday afternoon and to break camp on Sunday morning with a return helicopter ride.

Everything went according to the plan; there were a few surprises. The helicopter had to ferry our group of twelve up in three loads. The young government folk and the two packers went first with a view to setting up camp ahead of everyone else. The helicopter took off and five minutes later was approaching the landing meadow by a fire lookout. As it touched down a big black bear tumbled out of the fire warden's cabin and lit off into the woods. This really impressed the bear-o-phobes, who were reluctant to get out of the helicopter until the packers had loaded their rifles for the hike to camp. Rifles loaded, however, off they went.

The next helicopter load ferried the oil people to the lookout. They were all dressed in brand new Mountain Equipment Co-op hiking gear and carried new, frameless packs stuffed with dome tents, mummy-shaped sleeping bags, freeze-dried snacks, and second sets of nylon and silk shirts, socks and underwear. They sported brand new boots, too, which must have hurt their feet while they broke them in. They landed uneventfully, however, as the bear was by now long gone down the slope to the next valley.

The final flight took Art, me and two elders. The elders had never flown before and were quietly watchful as the machine picked up altitude and sped up the forested flank of the Twin Sisters. The two peaks loomed not that far above us as we set down on the meadow. One of the packers had returned with his rifle to walk with us to the campsite. The old people thought this was silly. Off we went into the bush. Before too long the big plateau meadow opened up. The elders remembered hunting here when there was much more game. Today we could see nothing but rolling grass, occasional scree slopes and the odd black and yellow spruce. We could easily see the tents arranged in a circle. Six of them screamed out their colours in the landscape: yellow, blue, red, green, brown and rust. There was also Art's old Jones Tent-and-Awning, canvas wall tent off to the side on higher ground. It was sort of a yellowed white with some black mould speckles. It would house the elders, Art and me. The packers had cut a pile of firewood and a cooking fire was burning down to usable coals. As we approached we could smell the lake trout and moose cooking in two big, cast-iron frying pans sitting on a welded-metal grill that had been thrown over the coals. The oil and the government people had taken out their interlocking aluminum mess kits and arranged them neatly on a plastic folding table one of them had brought. They were all now wearing fleece vests as the weather was turning cold.

The packers, who were running the kitchen, had big black pots of tea and coffee coming onto the boil. They had a grub box containing cheese, salt, flour, baking soda, lard, sugar, canned milk, coffee and tea, and chocolate. Both of them were also rolling homemades with plug-cut tobacco from leather pouches that they carried on their belts. Their cutlery was basic, wooden-handled knives, old forks and spoons, and chipped enamel plates and mugs. As soon as tea was ready, without asking, they served the elders first, then they moved on to everyone else. They both kept an eye on the trout and the moose and turned the meat as needed. I also noticed that they had some fry bread on the go in a third frying pan, plus a big pot of potatoes boiling away.

The elders and the packers dressed alike for the bush. They wore thick, wool pants, the kind that hold their warmth even when soaking, they were either salt-and-pepper or brown in colour, and carried the Trapper Nelson tag. The old men held their pants up with suspenders; the packers wore simple leather belts with plain silver buckles. All wore plaid-wool work shirts, either red or blue, made in China for decades of use. Similarly they all wore lace-up, work boots and loggers' socks. Interestingly, the old fellows had on wool slouch caps, the kind that my grandfather used to wear and rappers sometimes wear today. The packers both sported black Stetsons, worn forward and low on the forehead. All four of them had brought rain gear and a glance up and to the north showed they were going to need it.

Anticipating mountain weather, the packers quickly struck a big, canvas fly over the kitchen using poles that had been cut for this purpose many years before. They staked it down with twelve-inch, steel spikes driven home with a small sledge hammer. They also had some poles and trunk rounds rigged up for seating under the canvas when the rain hit.

Seeing this preparation, the oil and government people went over to check their plastic and nylon tents. Several of them had been pitched in natural hollows that would trap rain, but they all had waterproof floors. At least that is what the labels said. Flimsy rain flies were quickly hooked up to the tensioned fibreglass tent poles, and new Vibram soles pounded down on the yellow plastic tent pegs. All seemed in readiness for the approaching storm. The out-of-towners next put on their elaborate multi-pocketed nylon and polyurethane rain jackets over their fleeces and jeans. Some of these fancy jackets matched their owners' tents in colour. While this was happening the elders and packers were pulling on their Trapper Nelson 'Drybak' coats and turning up the collars. The packers also pulled fitted clear-plastic covers over their Stetsons. Dinner was nearly ready. We were all eating moose, trout, potatoes and fry bread with blackberry jam when the storm hit with a low pitched whine. Mountain rain fell in torrents. A cold driving wind bounded off the kitchen fly. The packers built up the fire and everyone huddled close to the flames. It was time for stories about prophets, dreamers, and sacred mountains. The elders worked their magic over hot coffees and tea explaining the mythic context of the place as the weather encircled us with no sign of giving up that night.

At about 9 p.m. the old people decided to wind down their story telling. "We have to save some for tomorrow," they said laughing. Art produced his guitar. He proceeded to sing a few of his recently recorded songs, some of which dealt with Treaty 8 and its early promise for the people of northeast B.C. He also played some classic campfire standards for everyone to sing and wrapped it up with Goodnight Irene. As the crew showed signs of heading off to bed he went over to the grub box for chunks of cheese and chocolate. "Anyone for some shirt tightener?" he asked. There were a few takers.

I had no idea where the packers were going to spend their night, as there wasn't room in Art's tent, and they didn't ask for any. I now saw them with short, sharp hatchets cutting all the low-hanging bows encircling two spruces on the verge of our camp. Both men were following the same procedure. The fallen bows were arranged underneath the large, overhanging limbs of each spruce to form a comfortable mattress. Next they each took a thick-wool blanket from their old frame packs, and a pre-cut square of heavy plastic sheeting. Using a couple of heavy-duty safety pins they quickly formed a sleeping roll from their blankets, then wrapped their rolls in the plastic. They next placed them on the spruce-bough beds, slipped in fully clothed, hat and all, and calmly smoked one last hand-made as darkness fell. A little wisp of smoke rose from each bedroll as they closed down their day, dry and warm in the falling rain.

After the mediation on the Twin Sisters Plateau ended, the B.C. Government prescribed cultural ground rules, with the sacred areas clearly defined by rivers and creeks in the watershed, wherein drilling was prohibited. This area corresponded exactly with the one defined by the Indigenous communities who participated in the process. The company respected the sacred area and drilled outside the margins. The verbal history of the mediation and the outcome is now well spread through and understood in many, but certainly not all, northeast B.C. communities.

30

"Would you consider becoming CEO of the Glenbow Museum?"

After 14 years at AINA, and the publication of Sami Potatoes, it's time for a change

At the conclusion of the Sami Co-Management Project I began to desire full-time work based in Calgary where I could be with my family more often, if not every day. They were all progressing according to their enthusiasms. Lynn had become a healthcare partner in her company's architecture practice, and was busy designing hospitals. Lance was about to graduate from high school as class valedictorian. A notable rugby player, he was poised to enter the University of Calgary's faculty of arts. Caitlin, now fourteen, was combining figure skating and soccer with academic success. One day the phone rang at my Arctic Institute of North America office, and a headhunter asked if I would be interested in the job of running the Glenbow Alberta Institute, Calgary's unique museum, library, archives and art gallery of the West. Like most people, I thought that the Glenbow was just a museum, and had to have founder Eric Harvie's eclectic, interdisciplinary vision explained in detail. Suitably informed, I entered the competition and happily was offered the position of president and CEO, starting January 1, 2000.

I was determined to continue my passion of working with Indigenous communities, and soon became involved with the Blackfoot repatriation process, begun by my predecessor at Glenbow, the globally-renowned, innovative museum thinker, Robert Janes. This process saw virtually all of Glenbow's sacred and ceremonial Blackfoot artifacts returned to the appropriate Blackfoot cultural organizations. In exchange, a new permanent Blackfoot Gallery called *Nitsitapiisinni: Our Way of Life* was designed by a combined Blackfoot and Glenbow team, telling the history of the Blackfoot people in their own idiom. It opened to the public in November 2001. A travelling Blackfoot exhibit was also prepared for a worldwide exhibition in 2002. I quickly became involved in marketing the exhibition in Britain, and went with it to Europe in 2003, and was present when it opened in Manchester to civic acclaim in January 2004. But I am getting ahead of myself. First I had to get to know the Blackfoot members of the *Nitsitapiisinni* team, and learn about their confederacy.

The Blackfoot Confederacy of the northern plains includes the Kainai, the Peigan (or Aapatohsipiikani), and the Siksika, all of whom had challenged the Glenbow in the mid-1990s to return the sacred and ceremonial Blackfoot materials in its ethnographic collections. Robert Janes, had successfully lobbied the Alberta government to enable the return of the artifacts, and just before I arrived it had occurred. As a result, relationships with the Blackfoot, and especially the *Mookakin* Society, who received the bulk of the three-hundred and eighty objects, were strong. Frank Weasel Head, a *Mookakin* leader, and Blackfoot medicine-bundle holder, was key to the ongoing relationship.

He suggested to Robert Janes that the Blackfoot would like to contribute their expertise to the creation of a new Blackfoot Gallery in Glenbow. This permanent exhibit would house the remaining secular artifacts in Glenbow's collection and feature a Blackfoot story-line created by a team of Blackfoot cultural leaders, and Glenbow's in-house curatorial and programming experts, especially Dr. Gerry Conaty and Beth Carter. The research was well under way in 2000, and my immediate challenge was raising about two million dollars to build the exhibit. The team brought both academic training and traditional knowledge to its task, and the process reminded me of co-management in the North. Every aspect of the design was talked through in minute detail, all decisions were reached by consensus and a written record of the team's progress was kept. Most of the time, science and tradition were in perfect alignment, but interestingly not so with the Blackfoot relationship with the horse.

The science side of the equine relationship was pretty clear. Columbus' second voyage to the Americas in 1494 introduced twenty-four stallions and ten mares to the New World. By the late Seventeenth Century, the advancing ranch-economy settlements created the basis of cowboy-horse culture and with it the horse culture of Aboriginal America. Cortez also played an important role in introducing the horse to Mexico in 1519. His expedition historian, Bernal Diaz del Castillo, recorded the pedigree of every single horse on the voyage (Chamberlin, 2006:187-188). Inevitably, the Spanish horse entered local Aboriginal cultures, probably by theft. By the end of the Seventeenth Century, the Apaches and Comanches were accomplished horsemen, astonishing the Spanish troops. The plains cultures quickly adapted the horse to warfare. The Blackfoot Confederacy acquired its first horses from the Nez Perce to their immediate south, probably in the early Eighteenth Century (Ibid 22). By 1877, when they signed Treaty 7 with the "Great White Mother," Queen Victoria, they were one of the foremost horse cultures in the world.

The Blackfoot team members didn't disagree with the above facts, they just argued that they were not the whole story. They had three stories about where horses came from, starting with a myth about a poor boy who was given an old mallard by a powerful water spirit that lived in a large lake northeast of the Sweetgrass Hills. By following specific instructions the boy returned to his people, but not with an old mallard. Overnight it turned into a strange, new animal, a big horse. The Blackfoot called it *ponokaomitai-ksi* or elk-dog in their language. Because the wolves had told them that animals with hoofs and horns were all right to eat, and animals with paws and claws were not, horses fell into the edible category. There was also the historic story of receiving big horses from the Nez Perce, after first seeing them in a disastrous battle with the Shoshone in what is today Idaho and Utah. Finally there was the oldest story of all about small horses emerging from the water in the days after the ice melted. In this creation story, the horses were too little for riding and not as useful as dogs for packing possessions on the hunts. Back then, small horses were eaten.

"Back then" was about eleven thousand years before the present, at the end of the last ice age, or Wisconsin Glacial Episode, and science doesn't accord the Blackfoot with that much cultural memory. The paleo-hunters of the Wisconsin geologic era might in some way have been proto-Blackfoot, perhaps. But they weren't Blackfoot in archaeological cultural terms. The impasse facing Glenbow's *Nitsitapiisinni* team was whether or not to include little horses in the exhibit.

After much discussion it was decided to include big horses in the gallery depicting Blackfoot life just before cultural contact with the whisky traders and the Northwest Mounted Police. Frank Weasel Head agreed to the big-horse focus, but still maintained that little-horse lore was important to understanding the origins of the dynamic Blackfoot origins horse culture. From his perspective horses were just coming back to where they had already been established a long time ago. Then, in mid-August 2000, a scheduled emptying of the St. Mary's Reservoir, just south of the Kainai Reservation, provided confirmation of this traditional memory.

Len Hills of the geology department at the U of C phoned me with some startling news. Len, an old AINA research colleague, wanted to report that an interesting late Pliocene animal trackway had been exposed to the drying winds of southern Alberta as a result of draining the reservoir to repair the dam. A student of his was working on the site for his master's thesis, and Len offered to give me a tour and explain some of the discoveries. Mammoth, sabre-toothed tiger, prehistoric beaver and other charismatic megafauna footprints were being revealed in the mud of an ancient lakebed, but the lakebed was drying fast and the winds were rapidly eroding the prints. We decided to go and see the site on the weekend.

I went down on Friday night with Lynn and my sister Kelly's young family. Her children Meredith and Henry, aged six and five, were eager to see the mammoth tracks that Uncle Mike was talking about. We arrived on a hot Saturday afternoon and immediately set up our tents beside the now-dry reservoir. We met up with Len after lunch to walk out onto the trackway. Almost immediately we were amongst dozens of mammoth tracks heading off in the direction of the Crowsnest Pass. Len pointed out one set of mother-and-child tracks, big and little, heading west side by side. Henry, who was riding high up on my shoulders, and scouting the horizon, reported that he couldn't see any mammoths. "I think we should go back to camp now," he said when Len pointed out sabre-tooth tiger tracks. Suddenly we came upon a herd of tiny hoof prints, looking as if the animals had been spooked into flight some eleven- to fourteen-thousand years ago, according to Len. "That is a herd of feral horses; the proper scientific term for them is eohippus, I think. A few days ago my grad student found a fire-cracked-rock cooking site at the ancient lake's edge. In it, perfectly preserved, was the backbone of an eohippus. It still had a broken projectile point in it, too. Imagine that, about twelve-thousand years ago someone had horse steaks right here."

Frank Weaselhead was right. The old people did have small horses long ago, even if they were only about twelve inches high at the shoulder. They ran this earth long before writing, science and museums existed. I pondered how the memory of those days had passed through the generations and centuries to the present. I wondered about the power of science in the face of oral tradition. Henry wondered how horse steak tasted, and what we were going to cook for dinner. "Will those mammoths walk by us tonight when we are in our tent?" he asked. I was careful not to say "no" categorically.

I said, "They might visit us in our dreams."

31

To Manchester with the *Nitsitapiisinni* Exhibition

"This way to the Blackfoot Indians"

Selling the travelling version of *Nitsitapiisinni: Our way of Life* didn't prove easy. To start with, at six-thousand square feet, it was twice as big as the temporary exhibition space in most large European museums. Jonathan King, a senior curator at the British Museum, told me that many English boards of trustees had stopped supporting touring shows because they took staff away from caring for existing collections; were very expensive to mount and organize; and because they don't make significant money.

I tried my hardest to get the Director of the British Museum, Neil MacGregor, to take the show, but without success. But then, the keeper of the Elgin Marbles, the British Museum wasn't an obvious supporter of our repatriation efforts with the Blackfoot. As it turned out we were only able to secure one booking in Great Britain, at the Manchester Museum of Science and Industry. It was to open on 29th January, 2004, with an informal canape reception attended by Mel Cappe, the Canadian High Commissioner, and the Lord Mayor of Manchester, Audrey Jones. The Glenbow fielded our curatorial installation team and three members of the Blackfoot Confederacy: Frank Weasel Head, Andy Blackduck and Sandra Crazy Bull who all promised to speak at the opening reception, Sandra would dance and all would be available to talk with the public during the first two weeks of the show. Their presence was seen as a major coup by the Manchester crowd, especially the museum's Acting Director Bob Scott.

I arrived in Manchester four days before the show opened and spent the time getting to know the museum and the city. From a museum person's perspective, Manchester is a world class opportunity to showcase the industrial revolution and all its achievements and disasters. The dark, satanic mills were largely gone, but their memory lives on in globally significant ways.

The permanent exhibit of the Museum of Science and Industry is rigorously focused on a series of "Manchester Firsts," whose sheer number and range still boggle the modern mind. First curated is the founding in 1821 of the Manchester Guardian newspaper, the mandate of which included social principles dictating high standards for national reporting and the arts. It printed socially unpopular views under the liberal and libertarian editorship of C.P. Scott. In 1825 St. Matthew's Church opened for civic worship. Here the followers of Robert Owen built a Hall of Science and gave lectures for the poor. In 1830 the Rocket won the first Rainhill Trials for steam locomotives, setting the stage for rail transport. In 1831 the first Special Board of Health was created to deal with a cholera outbreak and the squalid living conditions endured by workers. In 1832 the Liverpool and Manchester Railway began service as the first inter-city line in England. In 1833 the Manchester Statistical Society began the systematic collection of data in the interests of social reform. In 1835 Alexis de Tocqueville came to Manchester and wrote Journey to England, a chronicle of his astonishment at the social deprivation he saw. In 1842 Benjamin Disraeli called Manchester "a modern Athens," and his novel, Coningsby, was published in 1844. In 1842 Friedrich Engels came to Manchester to manage his father's factory. He wrote The Conditions of the Working Class in England based on this experience; it greatly influenced his colleague Karl Marx. In 1859 the Mutual Aid Self-Help Society laid the foundation for friendly societies, co-operatives and trade unions. In 1867 Manchester became the birthplace of Votes for Women, under the leadership of Emma and Richard Pankhurst. In 1867 the Manchester Council passed the first Local Improvement Act, which allowed council to close slum properties. In 1868 the Manchester Act influenced national legislation by creating the opportunity for by-laws and building regulations for workers' housing. In1868 the first Trades Union Congress met in Manchester, leading to the creation of the first Trade Union Acts in the 1870s. In 1870 the first School Board was established pursuant to the first Education Act, and in 1891 the first slum clearances began by order of the city council. The net effect of all these Mancunian firsts is overwhelming, and their curated presentation in the Museum of Science and Technology is a global statement of human innovation.

In so many ways Manchester set the course for a more civil and tolerant society, especially regarding labour rights and citizen-led organization, in the modern world. How appropriate that *Nitsitapi-isinni* should open here, of all possible cities in England. How interesting that Manchester was the only city that wanted the show. In its own small way this travelling exhibition broke new museum ground: it showed what repatriation of sacred and ceremonial objects could lead to; it gave a First Nation the ability to tell its own story in its own words to an international audience; and it showed that co-design with a civil-society museum could work. And, as it turned out, it also set the stage for international learning about the pivotal role of the Blackfoot in Manchester's earlier history.

The opening-night reception was very well attended, especially by the Manchester City Council members, including Mrs. Jones, the lord mayor. I spoke about the show's importance from a museological perspective, and went on for some time about my new appreciation for Manchester's role in civilizing industrial nations. I said that we were happy to be a part of Manchester's continuing tradition as a risk-taking and humane city. Frank and Andy spoke on behalf of the Blackfoot, building on this theme. Sandra danced with her young son for an appreciative audience. The lord mayor cut a ribbon and the exhibit opened to a large crowd of enthusiasts.

I walked over to the lord mayor and we exchanged obvious pleasantries based on our shared enthusiasm for Blackfoot culture. I gazed at her elaborate silver chain of office because it had what appeared to be Blackfoot trick riders on it. Lord Mayor Jones explained that

Manchester was only designated a royal city after Queen Victoria's visit in 1887 during her Golden Jubilee year. Recently bereaved by the death of her beloved Albert, she was in a deep depression that stubbornly refused to lift. Her trip to Manchester included attendance at the new Manchester Festival Hall for Buffalo Bill Cody's Wild West Show. One of the star attractions was the Blackfoot trick riders who participated in a mock buffalo round-up with real bison. Their riding skill and antics greatly amused the Queen, and she was seen and heard to laugh with joy. After the performance she met with the Blackfoot performers and congratulated them. They may even have talked about their Treaty 7, which had been signed in the then Northwest Territories in 1877. Meeting the famous "Great White Mother" must have been a signal event for those Blackfoot riders. After the Queen returned to London and Buckingham Palace she commissioned Manchester as a royal city, designated its mayor as a lord mayor, and ordered a unique chain of office which has been worn by all the lord mayors ever since. Manchester can therefore add to its great list of firsts the fact that it is connected to the Blackfoot Confederacy through the reign of the "Great White Mother."

Astounded by the lord mayor's quick recitation of civic history, I asked her if she would like to meet the Blackfoot. She said that she had made their history a special topic of interest for Mancunians and she would love to meet the delegation and ask them some questions. We walked over to Frank and Andy who were talking with a large crowd of opening-night guests. After quick introductions, Mayor Jones turned to Frank and said, "Tell me how your treaty is working out." "That is a long story, your worship," said Frank. For the next while he and Andy filled her in on the Blackfoot stance on the treaty which is sharply at odds with contemporary reality because there is a very large gulf between the Blackfoot oral record of what was promised by the Canadian negotiating party and what has been delivered. For her part, Lord Mayor Jones listened attentively.

The next day the Glenbow *Nitsitapiisinni* team breakfasted together and compared notes on the festivities. Frank, Andy and Sandra were amazed at the lord mayor's knowledge and interest about all things Blackfoot. After breakfast we went out onto the street in front of the hotel. We found ourselves standing under a large new directional sign that had just been bolted to a power pole near an intersection. It featured black lettering on a yellow background and a bold arrow pointing towards the Museum of Science and Industry. It read: "This way to the Blackfoot Indians." I took a photo of Frank, Andy and Sandra standing underneath it, all with big smiles.

32

Ray and Terry Come to Calgary

*"It looks as if a giant with a big pillow case of little
Monopoly houses had gone around sprinkling
them on the ground"*

After we opened *Nitsitapiisinni* in Manchester, I returned to Calgary and invited Ray and Terry Williams to visit our family and tour the great Canadian Prairies for the first time. I also wanted to show them Glenbow Museum's significant Mowachaht-Muchalaht collections, and to get their opinions on expanding our children's programming in the museum school.

I reached Ray and Terry at their Yuquot home via the Nootka Lighthouse Station on the Canada Coastguard radiotelephone and we had a wide-ranging discussion about dates and travel plans. I explained that their air fares would be covered by my Visa Air Miles account. Occasional trips to Gold River and Nanaimo were part of their lives, but other than the "Cook the Captain" expedition to Vancouver, and a subsequent trip to the New York Museum of Natural History, they had never left Vancouver Island. Nevertheless, they were definitely up for a Prairie experience.

At their end, the recently opened and well-advertised Nootka Island coastal hiking trail was keeping them very busy in the summer. Ray said that they were averaging forty visitors per day at Yuquot and they literally could not afford to leave home for fear of theft, fire and general tourist stupidity. As the last residents of their village, they were keeping eagle eyes on burial caves, the Spanish Government's stained glass windows in the Catholic church, and all of their personal survival gear – generators, outboard motors, and their freezer full of fish. "We can come in mid-September," said Ray. "By then tourism winds down because the kids are back in school or university, and we get our lives back."

So we planned a two-week trip for September. I explained that it would be starting to cool down then, but there would be no snow. I joked about Indian summer but Ray said he didn't get it. As it turned out, their trip to the Campbell River airport, the first leg of their journey, was anything but simple. First of all they lost a propeller in Muchalaht Inlet when a cotter pin broke. Luckily Ray had a spare and they had left early, so they had time to install it at sea. The lost prop was worth two-hundred dollars, and they would have to buy a new one for the journey home. There went most of their spending money for the vacation. They spent the night in Gold River with extended family and decided to hitchhike to Campbell River to save the bus fares. That decision nearly cost them their flight because it took them six hours to complete what would have been a three-hour bus trip. However they caught their flight and made it to Calgary.

I picked them up at the airport on Sunday afternoon. They were travelling light with just one medium backpack each. They were in good spirits and eager to get to our house and have a coffee in peace. The drive from the airport was notable. Ray said the Calgary sprawl "looked as if a giant with a big pillow case of little Monopoly houses had gone around sprinkling them on the ground." Terry said it was "the farthest from the ocean she had ever been in her life." When we arrived at our house, they both said it was "like home to be with old friends." We felt the same way. When we asked what they would like to do the next day, they said that they would like to go to the Glenbow to see where I worked.

I had given their introduction to the museum some thought, and offered to show them the warehouse collection first. That was where we had the totem poles in storage, two of which I was sure were from Yuquot although their written provenance was sketchy. First thing after breakfast we drove out to the southeast quadrant of the city where we found the warehouse, really nothing more than four bays in a strip-mall development. Inside the dark space were thousands of artifacts silently awaiting use in an exhibit, or for research, or what the museum trade calls 'de-acquisitioning,' the step before sale, trade or destruction for want of purpose, need, or because of poor quality. It was an eerie, soulless space.

Ray and Terry went straight towards the totem poles singling out the ones I thought were from Yuquot because of their carving style. They stood before them holding hands. Ray turned to Terry and said, "Let us sing to them." And they began a Mowachaht song that had never before been sung on the Prairies. After about ten minutes they were both in tears and the song came to its end. Ray turned and said, "We decided to sing to the poles because they have not heard their language in so many years." Terry added, "Wouldn't it be good to get them back to Yuquot? As soon as we get our cultural centre built, will you help us repatriate these poles?" I said that I would. After a moment of silence, we decided to go downtown to the museum.

The balance of the day was given over to my work meetings and phone calls. Ray and Terry were simply pleased to stay in my office, seated at the conference table, drinking tea and watching the ebb and flow of my work. At the end of the day Ray said, "We just like to watch what you do all day. It is so different from our lives." I asked them about our agenda for the rest of the week, and the coming weekend. "We have lots of options," I said. "We could drive out to Drumheller, to the (Royal) Tyrrell Museum and see the dinosaurs. Or we could go to the Majorville Medicine Wheel and see one of the largest medicine wheels on the Great Plains. Or we could go to the Rockies and have tea in an old railway hotel." Terry jumped right in, "We can have tea in a hotel in Nanaimo. Let's go to the dinosaurs and the medicine wheel. We don't have those things where we live." Ray nodded agreement.

For the rest of the working week, Ray and Terry focused on examining and verifying the cultural provenance of the Glenbow's Mowachaht and Muchalaht collections. They were paid as visiting curators, and added tremendous value to the written record of the artifacts. Saturday morning we were on the road by 9 a.m., cruising through the autumn Prairies. We talked about the upcoming harvest season and the different crops we were passing. Everything was new to them.

In Drumheller the Chamber of Commerce has erected a giant Tyrannosaurus Rex that features a hundred-and-six steps inside up to its toothy, gaping mouth. Here you can walk out on its tongue surrounded by its teeth and wave at the tiny people down in the parking lot. The previous year it had won the best Alberta attraction prize in a provincial-government sponsored contest. I knew this because Glenbow had come second with its celebrated, The Group of Seven in the West exhibit that toured widely from the National Gallery in Ottawa to Victoria. I stood on the pavement thinking of our loss to this bizarre reptile, and photographed Ray and Terry as they waved at me from between the huge plastic teeth far above. "Wow, that was the most fun we have had in a long time!" said Ray when they came back down. "I can't wait to show your pictures to our grandchildren!" said Terry. I shut away my silly anger as we returned to the car.

Ray and Terry spent hours studying the exhibits in the world-class Tyrrell museum. Terry commented that there are Mowachaht stories about giant lizards who lived long ago, and she felt quite at home in the various galleries depicting life-size dinosaurs. As we neared the end of the walk through time and left the age of the great lizards, the floor of the gallery depicted a beach seascape. Looking down there were human footprints in the sand. I said to Ray, "What are those?" "Tourists, Michael," he replied. On we marched to the exit, which is the museum gift shop. Interestingly neither Ray nor Terry was interested in a plastic T-Rex nor a souvenir T-shirt. It was getting late and we drove home to Calgary for dinner. I suggested an Italian restaurant in our neighbourhood. "You decide, Michael. We trust you. We enjoyed that Italian food we had with you when we went to the "Cook the Captain" opening at the Museum of Anthropology. Wow, that was about twenty-five years ago!" said Ray. "I think we will still like it today," said Terry.

We started out for the Majorville Medicine Wheel at 10 a.m. on Sunday. It was a two-and-a-half hour drive from Calgary, and we ate our sandwiches in the truck as we cut east on the Trans-Canada and then south on a secondary highway through endless fields of yellow genetically modified canola. Majorville is just an intersection between two gravel roads now; once it had a gas station and a one-room schoolhouse. Here we drove due east on another gravel road that eventually led to a southern turn-off onto a deeply rutted, dirt road through Crown grazing leases temporarily belonging to the giant XL Foods company. We were soon bumping over a landscape of rolling fescue grasses that had never felt the cut of a plough.

Here and there XL Herefords munched the tall grass as harriers cruised low with sharply outstretched wings over swale and sward seeking a Richardson ground squirrel cut off from its burrow. We actually saw a long-legged, brown wolf loping quickly over a low hill. Terry said that the grassy prairie, rolled like the open Pacific off Yuquot when a big westerly was blowing. Ray added, "That wolf back there was interesting, Michael. Back home they can change into a *kakowin* (orca) when they want to be in the ocean. Remember long ago I gave you that name? You remind us of a *kakowin* the way you like this prairie, but also love Yuquot and the sea."

There was my Blackfoot dream again. I realized that I had not told it to Ray and Terry, so I narrated it as we drove the last few miles of dirt to the medicine wheel. "Ahhhhhhhh," said Terry when I finished my story, "What an important dream." "Michael, the coast is calling you home," Ray asked.

Up ahead of us loomed the largest and highest hill in Wheatland County. It had rounded fescue-covered curves with no sharp features. It overlooked a wide bend of the Bow River, with three-hundred and sixty degrees of unobstructed views. On its crest was what appeared to be a pile of stones visible from quite some distance. I slowed down and looked at the landscape. It was the very end of summer and the tall grasses were just starting to brown up. No one had been here recently; there were no obvious signs like litter or burnt-out campfires surrounded by rings of rock. I parked the pick-up at the base of the hill where a trail led us up some two-hundred steps to the wheel. Ray and Terry walked with me as I explained what I knew about the place.

"The Blackfoot today know it is here and occasionally come to visit, mostly from the Siksika community. While the site has great Blackfoot significance, it has been partly excavated by archeologists who proved it has had continuous cultural use going back about five-thousand years. It has a pronounced rock cairn, some five-feet high in the centre, and twenty-eight rock ribs, or spokes, each extending out about thirty feet to an external rock circle. Interestingly, a buffalo has twenty-eight ribs. At the top of the hill the grass is worn low by people walking around the wheel's outer circumference. The natural inclination is to walk clockwise, with the sun. If you were an eagle flying high above the site looking down, you would see a wagon-wheel shape. Off to the northeast on the hill's edge is a secondary grouping of stones; a similar group occurs to the northwest. If you come to the wheel during the spring equinox, the sun rises precisely behind the northeast grouping and sets precisely behind the northwest one. I know because I have seen this happen. Many times when I have gone to the wheel a bald eagle has circled overhead." I stopped talking as we had reached the top.

Ray and Terry began to speak in Mowachaht, addressing the central cairn. After they had finished, I asked them what they had said. "We felt it was necessary to explain who we were, and where we came from. We said that we were not going to hurt anyone or anything here. We asked permission to be on this sacred territory so far from our home," said Ray. Terry was very silent. I thanked them for their words.

We spent our time quietly walking about the wheel. I looked south, down the gliding course of the Bow River. The sun glinted on the muddy waters and a few white pelicans were visible next to a small island in mid-stream. I thought of what I had been told by several Blackfoot elders, that the 'long ago' people came up here after first thunder in May, and waited for signs of the great bison herds returning. First, there would be dust clouds on the southern horizon. Next would be the sound of the herds' thunderous movement. Then there would be the smell of hundreds of thousands of animals. Finally, they came into view. The bison population that moved up the Bow Valley sometimes chose a path farther to the east, or they ran along the very eastern flank of the Foothills. It wasn't a given that they took the same route each year. The Majorville Medicine Wheel was an outpost to determine which route the migratory herds were taking. It was an important hunting location as well, as there are several buffalo jumps nearby where hunters organized drive corridors to frighten the herds over steep cliffs to their deaths. Today the deep coulees on either side of the hill are often full of white-tail deer and pronghorn antelopes. No doubt there was also good fishing in the Bow, a quarter of a mile below the hill's eastern slope. Whenever I went down to the river I marvelled at the effort to get so many boulders up to the top of the hill to create the wheel. There are literally tons of rocks up there, all far from their natural resting spots.

It was late in the afternoon as we began the walk down to the truck. Ray was eager to have a quick hike to the river. I agreed to go with him, but Terry wanted to sit on a bench-like rock and rest. She walked toward the rock and said a few Mowachaht words which translated, boiled down to: Hello bench-like rock, good for resting on. May I sit with you for a while? Ray and I went down the antelope trail and washed our dusty faces in the cool river water. "This is a beautiful place," he said as he picked up a small stone from the riverbed. We turned around to climb back up the exposed path to the medicine wheel. I could just see Terry's silhouette high above us. She seemed to be gazing down the river valley; the wind was blowing her hair about her face.

When we arrived at the top Terry was standing up, ready to leave. We walked over instinctively aware that something was upsetting her. "We need to go now," she said. "The voices are getting too loud and so is the drumming." Ray put his arm around her and gave her a hug. Then he walked over to the cairn and put his small stone on the pile. Terry was right; she had just lifted the "lid" that Frank Weasel Head talked about after he had interpreted my dream from a Blackfoot standpoint. Now the Mowachaht were experiencing Blackfoot spirituality from their point of view. While it wasn't threatening, it did establish its own clear limits. I looked above us; sure enough an eagle was circling in the updrafts. We got into the pick-up and began the long drive home through the fescue grasslands.

33

An Election in Alberta

"Would you consider running with us in 2008?"

My Glenbow Museum career was a great deal of fun as I was directly involved in programming temporary exhibitions and creating permanent galleries that Calgarians and others wanted to see. We began in 2000 when I started my CEO-ship, to poll Calgarians about their interests. It turned out that they wanted more Splendours of Egypt, and less The Western Saddle Tradition. Over some initial curatorial push-back, we obliged and paid visits started to boom. We even began to bank big profits – our Egypt show alone generated over a million dollars after all costs. As well, I was invited by the editorial page editor of the Calgary Herald, Doug Firby, to write regular op-eds "on anything you like, Mike." My colleague Colin Jackson, CEO of the adjacent arts complex, then the EPCO Centre now Arts Commons, and I began to organize the city's arts organizations forming an arts district with a volunteer board of fellow arts CEOs. This inevitably led to speaking invitations, especially by the many civic Rotary Clubs. The net effect was a growing public profile. Then I had an interesting unscheduled visit to my office right after the Calgary Stampede Parade ended on July 4th, 2007.

Alberta Liberal Leader Kevin Taft and popular Calgary Liberal MLA Dr. David Swann arrived at the Glenbow in their cowboy duds, sporting white Stetsons and big smiles. I invited them into my office for coffee. David casually shut the door behind him as we settled down around my meeting table. Kevin began, "Mike, we won't stay for long, but we want to ask you a question. Would you consider running with us in the 2008 provincial election? We've got some promising polling data, and we'd like you on our team!" I was overwhelmed at the suggestion. But I smiled right back and said, "Wow! How long can I have before you need a decision?" Kevin said, "You need to decide by mid-November – four months from now. But earlier is better." I promised to respond as quickly as possible, "all things considered." Then the two gentlemen finished their coffee and made their exit. Over the summer I discussed the idea thoroughly with Lynn, Lance and Caitlin plus many friends and slowly convinced myself it was the right thing to do.

It began to get a bit more serious when I received a phone call in early October, 2007, from the woman organizing the annual October Harvest Dinner for the provincial Liberal Party in northwest Calgary. She introduced herself, confirmed that I was indeed the Michael Robinson whose membership had recently been renewed, and then asked if I would step in as a guest speaker because their planned orator had just cancelled. When I asked why she thought I would be an interesting choice, she replied that she liked my guest editorials in the Herald "and some of our executive have heard you speak before and liked what you had to say." Succumbing to flattery on a Wednesday afternoon, I agreed to speak, then asked when the dinner was happening. "Friday night this week," she replied. "Just two days away!" I thought of it, but didn't jam out. After the caller hung up, I reached for the stack of file cards on my desk and started to jot down ideas: the sorry state of the Alberta Heritage Fund, the rapid approval of too many Tar Sands projects, the looming water shortage in the province, the chronic shortage of family doctors, the structural underfunding of the arts . . . there was lots to talk about.

Two days later I put on a blazer and tie and drove to the Dalhousie Community Centre. Lynn was due join me there later after a long day of meetings, so I walked in alone. The room was full of happy chatter and political humour. I guessed there might be two-hundred people present, and many were already seated at the folding tables that had been set up for the evening. The organizers escorted me to the head table. Someone offered me a glass of wine. My table companions bent forward to introduce themselves, and I struggled to remember the new names. My eyes kept focusing on the speech cards in front of me as I carefully went over the major themes in my head: the importance of community, the pressing need for environmental stewardship, the need to save petrodollars for the inevitable rainy day when the resources would run out, Alberta's duty to Canada as a "have province," the need to protect and improve our precious health-care system, and, overall, the need to change political parties after thirty-seven years of Conservative rule. Someone put a roast-beef meal in front of me and encouraged me to start eating before it got cold. I ate.

After about an hour of table talk and several glasses of wine it was time for the speech. I walked up to the lectern with my cards. I looked out at the audience and saw that Lynn had just arrived, too late for dinner. And that's how my political career began.

The audience laughed at my jokes, clapped for the key points and warmed up to my storytelling. At the end they were ready for something more, so I spontaneously gave it to them: I offered to stand as a candidate for the Liberals in the Foothills constituency where our family had lived for nearly thirty years. The audience stood up and gave me a standing ovation. I was hooked. After the speech people crowded round to shake my hand and to thank me for rising to the challenge. Lynn walked over and said, "Do you realize what you've just done?" I looked at her and smiled.

That night I could barely sleep. There was money to be raised, volunteers to recruit, a nomination form to fill out, and a campaign manager to find. It quickly became apparent that in Alberta, running as a Liberal, all of these tasks were virtually yours alone. After almost four decades of one-party rule, the Liberals were thin on the ground, and party organization was spare and basic. I rolled up my sleeves. To begin with I resigned my job as president and CEO of Glenbow, effective 31st December, 2007. Reasoning that I could get elected, it was time for a change after eight years of museum life. With a reduction in my workload downtown, but a stampede of new tasks in the constituency, I was quickly overwhelmed with political activity. Things improved after I hired Wade Prpich, a former MA student of mine, to be campaign manager. We worked well together and I won the Liberal nomination unopposed in December. We raised over thirty-thousand dollars to fight the campaign and recruited a hundred volunteers. The door-knocking began before the writ was dropped, and a stalwart sign crew led by Brian Stahl, a retired Calgary fire captain, had signs up on Day One of the official campaign.

Over the next two months, accompanied by a campaign volunteer, I knocked on eight-thousand doors out of a possible total of sixteen-thousand or so. As never before I met thousands of neighbours in Citadel, Hidden Valley, Edgemont, Sherwood, Hawkwood and Kincora. Media coverage ranged from euphoric to insulting, and we learned the strategic importance of name recognition and the electorate's personal experience of a candidate. Every day, seven days a week, for two months, we walked the neighbourhoods methodically trolling for votes. The competition certainly was evident in the growing sign war. Our principal opponent, the incumbent Conservative, who did not live in the constituency, was well represented with advertising on bus benches, billboards, lawn signs and the newspapers. His sign crew was an advertising company, who drove about in bright SUVs talking on cell phones. Occasionally we saw him striding about the neighbourhoods in his garish orange and blue campaign ski jacket. Somehow we never spoke during the campaign. He refused five invitations to debate without giving any reasons. In response I rented the Edgemont Community Hall, and held a one-candidate debate for about two-hundred supporters.

As the election day drew near, the team thought we were closing the traditional gap in Foothills of about two-thousand votes between Liberals and Conservatives. We had a fresh phone list of over four-thousand supporters and growing rapport at the doors. By now my doorstep spiel was honed and refined, and focused on the Heritage Fund, environmental planning in the Tar Sands, and improving access to family doctors. I could intuitively read constituents better, and I had a growing sense that more and more of them wanted the change I represented. I also knew that I was running the race of my life, something that I had been in training for since high school, possibly leading to the chance to make real change in Alberta. Somehow I felt that I was running to protect the land and waters of the place Lynn and I had adopted as our home in 1978, some thirty years before.

March 3rd, 2008, dawned bright and cold. On that day Alberta experienced the lowest turnout on record, some thirty-nine per cent of registered voters. This also qualified as the lowest voter turnout in any province in Canada since Confederation in 1867. In Foothills forty per cent of registered voters cast ballots: 251 for the New Democratic Party, 411 for the Green Party, 972 for the Wildrose Party, 4,909 for the Liberals, and 6088 for the Conservatives. I'd gathered nearly forty per cent of the votes; the incumbent tallied forty-eight per cent. If only I had convinced one-thousand, one-hundred and eighty more citizens to cast their ballots for the Liberals.

I remember that day well. It offered, once again, a new beginning; one tempered with hard lessons learned about how people perceive the truth in political terms and how hard you have to work to generate political change in Alberta. I took the rest of March off to consider my future, and to think about how my past influenced my present. I also realized that I was becoming a good loser in the sense that it was okay to lose for the right reasons. As long as I was being loyal to my values, I was winning. The whole experience was a part of the synthesis I was living in my career. It was increasingly apparent that NGOs were the ideal place for me to work and that there could also be new options in politics. I was fifty-seven and ready for change.

34

Making the Bill Reid Gallery of Northwest Coast Art Sustainable

Starting a new public art gallery in the heart of one of Canada's most expensive cities

Because of my Blackfoot dream what follows was probably inevitable. After my political career ended in March of 2008, I took a month off to recuperate, began to write the stories that form this book, and inevitably began to reactivate my consulting practice of advising NGOs and their boards on sustainability, program development and CEO recruitment. This practice ranged geographically from Haida Gwaii to Toronto, and by September of 2008 it was in full fling when I received a telephone call from Herb Auerbach, one of the founders of the Bill Reid Foundation (BRF), which in May had opened the Bill Reid Gallery of Northwest Coast Art (BRG) at 639 Hornby Street, a block north of the Vancouver Art Gallery. He said that he had heard about my work from some mutual Haida friends, and he wanted to speak with me about the new BRG.

I arranged to fly out to Vancouver, and we met at the BRG and lunched at Hy's Steak House, next door. The new gallery featured a superb collection of Reid's work, acquired and now owned by the BRF, and was slowly building a rapport with young Indigenous artists who were continuing Reid's work of revitalizing Northwest coast art forms for a growing B.C. and national market. The BRG was attempting all of this with a temporary CEO, George MacDonald, the well-known ex-CEO of the Canadian Museum of Civilization, who was leaving at year-end. A true NGO, the BRG had no government support for its operations and was attempting to operate in the black with shop profits, attendance revenue and a reliance on philanthropy. While I wasn't told this initially, there was also a growing reliance on debt, specifically a one-million-dollar bank loan at prime plus four per cent.

It quickly transpired that Auerbach and the BRG board were seeking me as a potential new CEO, rather than as a consultant providing advice. Long story short, after a week of negotiations, I accepted an offer of employment for four days per week, starting January 1st, 2009. I was free to continue consulting, at least one day per week, which I desired, and ultimately it meant a move back to Vancouver after thirty years in Calgary. Lynn would join me as her firm had a Vancouver office, but first she had to wind down her Calgary practice. In the interim I negotiated bedroom accommodation in my sister Kelly's basement in Burnaby, about a forty-five-minute, one-way commute to the BRG in the heart of Vancouver.

After signing my contract and reporting for work on January 1st, 2009, MacDonald invited me to lunch at Vancouver's delightful Sylvia Hotel on English Bay. The event, a kind gesture, was a symbolic passing of the reins of office, except for one comment: "I wish you all the best, Mike. You have about one chance in a million of making the BRG sustainable." Ouch.

All my values and life experience jumped to attention. Reaching back to law school, and case-briefing technique, I borrowed the "Facts, Issues, Resolution" model. Then I burrowed down in the BRG's books and historical files to learn the facts about: the lease agreement with the landlord; the loan agreement with the bank; the staffing complement and their roles and responsibilities; the existing pattern of gallery monthly revenues; shows being prepared for exhibition; the method(s) of curatorial decision making; the cash contributions to date of all donors; the prospect list for new donors; the government (non-operations) grants applied for; and the media profile of the gallery. Suitably apprised of the situation, the issues became apparent.

Chief among the issues was the looming monthly cash shortfall, and the impossibility of maintaining the existing levels of staff and operations expenditures with a bank loan as the main external source of cash flow. At its financial peak in the past decade, Glenbow (with a twelve-million- dollar annual budget) raised no more than fifty per cent of its annual revenues from the gift shop, paid attendance, functions and events. Corporate contributions, an innovative contribution agreement with the provincial government, and foundation grants were essential for successful operations. The BRG was assuming total annual revenue projections of five-hundred thousand dollars with even higher assumptions of core revenues, and they simply were not being met. Suitably briefed of this reality I initiated the layoff of the associate director, and moved to hire an on-site, full-time business manager with accounting credentials. Consulting curatorial expenditures ended. Volunteer curatorial help was sought, and no new bank loans were negotiated. To their everlasting credit, many board members increased or maintained their annual donations, and board member Toni Cavelti made a superb gift of signed Bill Reid gold castings which I sold in the BRG civic network to generate operations revenue. So inspired, we made payroll, lease and loan obligations in the fiscal year, 2009.

Driving home one day to my basement suite, I thought of how Glenbow had survived its first years in the 1960s, before the oil boom, when cash was short. Former Premier, Peter Lougheed, a dedicated Glenbow supporter and friend of the founder, Eric Harvie, had suggested that Glenbow donate its collections to the Government of Alberta, in return for a contract to provide public access, care and curatorial services by the NGO staff of the museum. The contract was adopted and, broadly speaking, the government undertook to provide about one third of Glenbow's annual operating revenue. This had saved the institution. Perhaps the same approach would work at the BRG, I reasoned.

So began a one-year, drawn-out negotiation with the B.C. Government to achieve the same level of support for the BRG using exactly the same model. The negotiation was back-stopped by a superb evaluation of the BRG's collection undertaken by Dr. Martine Reid, Bill Reid's widow. With a firm evaluation of the asset value, over ten-million dollars, and the presence of competent NGO staff running the gallery, there was hope of success. A year's worth of negotiations ended with the government's best offer: a one-time payment of one-million dollars. The BRG's board quickly declined it and all hands went back to work. It was a difficult time, but it greatly focused the BRG's programming efforts.

Acknowledging the importance of new exhibitions, both in the galleries and in development, Martine Reid joined the BRG as chief curator. She was followed by Kwiaahwah Jones, a young Haida curator, who brought a network of aspiring and established Northwest Coast artists to the gallery. Jim Hart, one of the strongest mentees of Bill Reid's final decade of life, brought a team of Haida carvers to the BRG to complete a monumental masterpiece piece called The Dance Screen (The Scream Too), in full public view. Beau Dick, a Kwakwaka'wakw master carver from Alert Bay, was invited into the BRG orbit by Jones, and contributed The Box of Treasures: Gifts from the Supernatural. Tsimshian artist Morgan Green then brought her unique hollow-form jewelry to the BRG and she was followed by weaver Meghann O'Brien, working in the traditions of Raven's Tail and Naaxiin textiles. Overall, the infusion of new talent and the core collection's strength continued to increase paid attendance, and to give Vancouverites, and others, a reason to return to the BRG for new experiences. And then an idea emerged to enhance the gallery's sustainability.

Bill Reid Foundation board chair David Gillanders also had a distinguished volunteer association with Simon Fraser University (SFU), and believed that SFU might respond positively to the offer of the BRG collection asset as a gift to the university, again using the Glenbow example. As it turned out, Gillanders was right, and SFU President Andrew Petter enabled negotiations to start with enthusiasm for a potentially good outcome. I negotiated the fine points of the deal with Dr. Pat Hibbitts, SFU's vice-president of finance and administration in 2011. Once it was in place, the BRG NGO contracted to provide care, maintenance and provision of public access to the SFU Bill Reid Collection at the BRG's 639 Hornby address. In return, about one third of the gallery's operating costs were provided by the university, based exactly on the Glenbow model. In theory, now borne out by practice over the intervening nine years of operations, the BRG's paid admissions and shop profits contribute about a third of the revenues, along with another third from grant writing, philanthropy and corporate donations. The net result is sustainability. Thinking back to my lunch with George MacDonald at the Sylvia Hotel in 2009, luckily we found, "the one chance in a million." Suitably resolved, I decided to resign my CEO-ship at the end of 2014 after six years at the BRG. It was time for new leadership to move on beyond start-up problems.

You can absolutely sense the joy and happiness that synthesis creates when you walk into a work place where it prevails. I'll never forget seeing Fanny Chow, the BRG's business manager, smile broadly the first time we made our pay-day cheques without drawing on the bank loan; when Paula Fairweather and Meredith Leyland-Areskoug saw their marketing wizardry draw large crowds to our openings; and when our dazzling young Haida curator, Kwiaahwah Jones welcomed the amazing Beau Dick to the BRG as a presenting artist. While the business model had to support the gallery's mission, and breaking even, or better, was a must, the emotional power of success was radiated by the staff. As Jim Boulding occasionally said some thirty-five years before, "You know, I don't know what psychic energy is, but I sure as hell know when it is present!" Watching it form and take root at the BRG was a joy.

Telling the BRG story as the final chapter of this book closes the circle of life my experience begun by my father when he took me to Yuquot in 1978. Little did either of us realize that early cross-cultural encounters would lead to a values thesis that a corporate setting failed to satisfy, but found deep fulfilment in multiple NGO situations. More than ever I think my life has taught me to articulate a values thesis; to try and apply it broadly – even in antithetical settings; and, most importantly, to seek a workable synthesis in the evolving process. The BRG is an example of how a love of great art is not enough to ensure a gallery's success and perpetuity. That love has to be tempered with a corporate vision that enhances its ability to break-even and to stay alive. When enough money flows into the aesthetic coffers, much good can accumulate to inspire others and new ideas. Ultimately I think this whole process has taught me to shy away from simple solutions, to recognize that life is a struggle, and to understand that from that struggle comes joy and happiness when synthesis is achieved.

35

Saying Goodbye to Dad

"Nice view, eh"

In the late autumn of 2005 my Dad was moved into the Purdy Pavilion extended care facility at the University of British Columbia Hospital, right across the street from where he used to teach medicine. In a room he shared with three others, he had a window facing a classroom block in a bland concrete tower. His view featured one leafless tree to the right, and the scene was framed by dingy white curtains. Most of the time it was raining and grey. Dad was in the final days of his life, battling Lewy Body disease, a condition in which a form of non-metastatic plaque grows in and around the brain, interfering with and finally cancelling out the thought processes. Visits were hard. Sometimes he'd recognize me and say something wonderful like, "Nice view, eh," pointing towards the window. Other times he'd look up trying so hard to organize just one thought, and failing. Our family knew he was not far from death and everyone assumed he'd never make it out of his room again. For some reason I thought differently.

I drove down to the hospital one November day and explained to the head nurse that Dad was going for an afternoon drive with me. After some resistance she agreed to my plan. We dressed him in his sweatshirt and sweatpants, pulled on his Velcro runners, added his fleece vest, and I wheeled him out to the waiting car. "Am I going home?" he asked hopefully as we pulled away. "Nope, Dad. We are going to Spanish Banks to the little stream to see if the salmon are returning."

We headed down Chancellor Boulevard, the road he had driven to work virtually every day of his working life, through the forests of the University Endowment Lands. At Blanca Street we turned north and down to Spanish Banks past his parents' old house on Tolmie Street. "That's a nice house," he managed as I asked him if he remembered it. We reached Marine Drive and turned west, parallel to the beach. "Oh, we're at the beach," he said. A little farther on we came to the stream that had been cleaned up and re-seeded with chum salmon by a group of high school students, led by my god-daughter Viveca Ellis. We pulled into the parking lot, and I looked over at Dad. "Remember when you used to take me on those long car trips all over B.C. to talk about the diagnostic centre and your work?" I asked. Dad looked blank. "Remember the first trip you took me on to Friendly Cove where we bought that beautiful basket with the eagle designs on its sides?" Again nothing.

Hoping to prod his memory I said, "Let's get out and see if we can see any spawning salmon." I went to his door and opened it carefully. I had to almost lift him out as his limbs were very unsteady. I held him close by his arm and we walked over to the little stream's edge. I was looking seaward as he suddenly said, quite clearly, "Look, there's one." He was right. Almost at our feet, a bruised and battered chum was finning in the gentle current. Perhaps it had already spawned; perhaps it was awaiting a mate. "Life is a struggle," Dad said.

We both looked down at the old salmon. I was trying hard not to cry. I thought about all the conversations we had had together on those early trips around the province. I thought about how they had led me to places like Kunga House, Kelly Lake, Fort Good Hope, Fort McPherson, Kittygazuit, Lovozero, Jona, Moscow, and the Majorville medicine wheel. I thought about the centrality of Yuquot in my life, and the importance of friends like Ray and Terry Williams. I thought of Lynn, of Lance and Caitlin. And I thought about Dad and his final struggle. I reached out and gave him a hug, and said for the first time in my life, "I love you, Dad." He looked back at me through sparkling blue eyes.

Afterword

Wherein all the Characters have a Final Discussion with the Author about the Book

"God, Robinson, you sure can bullshit!" said Jim Boulding. I looked around me and realized all of the characters in the book were in the room. They were sitting on chairs and having Russian tea in the Lovozero's *Dom Kultura*. Tat'yana of Jona was serving cakes and the Komi ladies were helping the Gwich'in women in the kitchen. "Jim, don't forget that West Coast Survival was based on my youthful memories. I wasn't fully formed as a writer or observer when those things we did were locked in my memory." I said. "Well, I don't think you gave me enough credit for saving you from a career in some plastic, arsehole university. That stint you did as executive director at the Arctic Institute of North America was long enough!" "Clam up, Boulding and let some others speak," interjected Myrna.

Gerry Andrews rose and addressed the audience: "I want to congratulate you, Michael, for getting us all together. It was great fun to work on the Monkman Project in the final phase of my life, but it is even better to see all the cast here today. I'd like to invite everyone to my room before dinner for a taste of the old red sock." Lloyd said he would come, and Leif asked if it was normal in Canada to "eat a sock?" Dorthea said that she would explain the "nuance of the surveyor general's comments later."

Ray walked to the centre of the room. "Michael, I would like to speak to all of these people who travelled such a long way to attend this meeting." "Go right ahead, Ray," I said. "I wondered about coming such a long way with Terry to talk about Michael's book, but we decided it was important. He put us all in there for a reason. Harry Dick, Maurus, Molly, Terry and I talked about it at Yuquot. We decided he put us in the book because we love our home so much. And when we read about you other guys, it seemed the same for all of us. We all really love the land and waters where we live." Frank Weasel Head stood up and smiled at Ray. "I am really glad to see you. Mike told me about you and Terry when we discussed his dream. He really feels a part of your territories, and is especially connected to the killer whales who swim in your waters." "That is why we call him *Kakowin* back home" said Ray. "When he took us to that medicine wheel we saw a brown wolf running in the tall grasses. We Mowachaht know that a wolf can turn into a killer whale and jump into the sea. We think Michael is like that wolf; he loves your territory as much as ours. And he is at home in both places."

James Ross stood up and pushed his ball cap back on his thick head of hair. "We Gwich'in are glad that we didn't get referred away from this hall today! I am proud to be here with all you guys. Every one of you who cares about the land needs to work hard to convince the world to slow down. We need to preserve what we have left before it is too late. And judging by the health of the American stock market, we think that our elders sure made a good decision about saving Husky Lake and all those whitefish for the Gwich'in!"

"I'm glad you put in the story about our camping trip to the dried up reservoir, Uncle Mike," said Henry McKenzie, who had just graduated with his BA from McGill. "Meredith and I still think about those mammoth tracks you showed us, and those tiny horses too." Over in the corner I noticed Frank smile as he raised the teacup to his mouth. Meredith added, "We both think those camping trips we did with you and Auntie Lynn and Mom were very important in opening our eyes to the natural world."

Captain Andreeva, still in his full dress uniform jumped to his feet smartly as Meredith sat down. With a golden smile to the room, he said, "On behalf of the North Atlantic Submarine Command I want to thank Professor Robinson for his kind description of our lunch in the captain's mess. It was a great pleasure to have him as our guest. As you can see, I am still wearing the fine *na pamyat* watch he gave me that day. When I read the book I was struck by his obvious love of Mother Russia, especially our old pensioners who have lived through so much history. Perhaps he is so attuned to them because of his lovely wife Lynn, whose mother was a Russian, a Kalmyk I believe. But whatever the reason, the stories he put in the book make Russians like me realize that we are all alike as humans in our need for countryside, for homeland and for national identity. After this meeting is over, I would be pleased to give you all tours of the *Novosibirsk* in Murmansk harbour.

Ollie, John and Ed all said they would like to visit Captain Andreeva's submarine. "Have you ever broken through the fixed ice at the North Pole, captain?" inquired Ollie. "Yes, in fact last year we surfaced once at the North Pole in open water after we placed a small Russian flag directly beneath on the seabed. "Was that to claim our North Pole for Russian sovereignty?" asked Ed. "You don't have to answer that question, captain," said Mr. Gorbachev. "I would just like to say on this occasion that the Russian Sami have not ceased to impress me with their entrepreneurial zeal and enterprise. I wish especially to recognize Nina Afanas'eva and her Russian Sami Association for the contribution they made to Mr. Robinson's book. They have made a Canadian book international and as such have shown that the process of what we Russians call "stewardship of the land" is applicable everywhere. It is entirely appropriate that Canada and Russia should appear together in this book because our shared North binds us together like sisters and brothers."

Well, we are sister and brother, said Caitlin and Lance, and we missed our Dad when he went on all these trips to meet you guys! But we loved going to Kittygazuit and Yuquot and Gwaii Haanas with Mom and Dad in the summertime. And we liked going out to Auntie Joan's in Bragg Creek to play in her tipi! We also liked going to the Medicine Wheel to camp overnight with Elmer and the Callious. It seems like we've been to a lot of your homes for dinner! We just haven't been to the Kola Peninsula yet!

At this point Fred MacDonald asked if there was going to be dancing, or if the whole gathering was just about talking and drinking tea? The faux Cossack singer quickly picked his accordion from its case and stood up to face his audience. Vice-Premier Kalaida walked over to the oldest Komi woman and bowed before her and asked her to dance. As the accordion notes of a Komi love ballad filled the air, Fred took up his violin and Andrei added his clarinet to form a trio. Nina walked over to me and said, "Mikhail Geoffreyovich, it is time to dance!"

Selected Bibliography

Bown, Stephen R. *Madness, Betrayal and the Lash: The Epic Voyage of Captain George Vancouver.* Vancouver: Douglas and McIntyre, 2008.

Chamberlin, J. Edward. Horse: *How the Horse Has Shaped Civilizations.* Toronto: Knopf Canada, 2006.

Haig-Brown, Roderick. *The Whale People.* London: Collins, 1962.

Robinson, Michael.P. and Karim-Aly Kassam. *Sami Potatoes: Living with Reindeer and Perestroika.* Calgary: Bayeux Arts, Inc., 1998, and Moscow (Russian Edition): Gorbachev Foundation, 2000.

Robinson, Michael P. *Sea Otter Chiefs.* Calgary: Bayeux Arts, Inc., 1996.

Fort McKay First Nations/ AINA. *There is Still Survival Out There.* Calgary: The Arctic Institute of North America, 1994 and 1996 (Second Edition).

Robinson, Michael P. and David Hocking. *The Monkman Pass and Trail: A Brief History.* Calgary: Petro-Canada, 1982.

Ryan, Joan. *Doing Things the Right Way: Dene Traditional Justice in Lac la Martre, NWT*: University of Calgary Press/ AINA, 1995.

Walbran, John T. *British Columbia Coast Names 1592-1906: Their Origin and History.* Vancouver: Douglas and McIntyre, 1991.